COMMUNISM IN MEXICO

A Study in Political Frustration

Communism
in MEXICO

A STUDY IN POLITICAL FRUSTRATION

by Karl M. Schmitt

AUSTIN UNIVERSITY OF TEXAS PRESS

Library of Congress Catalog Card No. 64–22390
Copyright © 1965 by Karl M. Schmitt
All Rights Reserved

Manufactured in the United States of America
Printed by University of Texas Printing Division, Austin
Bound by Universal Bookbindery, Inc., San Antonio

PREFACE

From the early years of the Mexican Revolution the United States government and many of its people have expressed alarm that our southern neighbor had gone or was going Bolshevik, or, in later terminology, Communist. During the 1920's these fears had some basis, however superficial, in the attraction of Marxism for certain revolutionary leaders and in the freedom permitted to radicals of all types to organize and propagandize throughout the country. What U.S. critics failed to understand properly was the pride that Mexico's leaders had in the revolution that they were creating, and their determination to exclude foreign influences and pressures. A Communist uprising in 1929 was ruthlessly put down, relations with the Soviet Union were broken in 1930, and the Communist movement suppressed and persecuted for about five years.

With the inauguration of President Lázaro Cárdenas in 1934 persecution ceased and in time the government sought the collaboration of the Communists. The movement attained its greatest successes in the 1930's. U.S. alarm reached new heights. Writers talked of Red Mexico, labeled Cárdenas a Communist, especially when he expropriated the oil industry in 1938, and expressed fears for the security of the United States. Many of the specific charges laid to the regime were accurate enough. The government's benevolent attitude led to an increase in Communist Party strength, permitted Communists to penetrate government and labor organizations, and enabled Communists to entrench themselves in the teachers' union.

What was not then and frequently still is not taken into account is that Cárdenas attempted reconciliation with all groups. He restored peace between the government and the Catholic Church after years of bitter strife, recompensed the oil interests after the expropriation, and left some property to the expropriated hacienda owners whose lands were taken for distribution to the peasantry. Furthermore, Cárdenas never accepted the Communists in a government coalition, refused to let them incorporate into the government political party, and did not permit them to form a large bloc in the Congress. In other words, he carefully excluded them from positions of political power despite their other infiltrations. To demonstrate, we have only to remind ourselves how easily Communist power was broken in labor in the matter of a few months in the late 1940's, and how easily the official Party could shift to the right after 1940 with a minimum of political unrest. True enough, Communists have remained strong in one faction of the teachers' union, but they have long been a minority and dare not use their position for political agitation. The one group that tried it in the late 1950's was crushed.

Despite the weakening of the Communist movement in Mexico during the past fifteen years, a considerable number of newspaper and periodical writers in the United States have continually raised the problem of Communist influence in Mexico. The rise of an anti-Communist movement in the country, with its attendant press releases and publications, has seemingly led to the belief that Communism is on the ascendant. In fact the very existence and growing popularity of such a movement attests the opposite. At one time it was impossible to aspire to a political career in Mexico if one was anti-Communist, because such a position seemed contrary to Mexico's basic political orientation of complete tolerance of political beliefs. Today this is no longer true. Leading politicians are openly anti-Communist, and the government is actively hostile to Communism. Many Communist leaders are in prison, others are restrained by fear of government suppression, and those at liberty are constantly quarreling among themselves.

My interest in Mexican Communism began in the years 1955 to

1958 when I served as a political officer in the Department of State. I read the Communist press daily and soon immersed myself in Party documents. When I left Washington to begin teaching at The University of Texas my interest continued, and during the past several years I have collected materials for this book. The cutoff date for the body of the work is June 1962, but a Postscript updates it for major changes and developments through the summer of 1964. I am deeply indebted to Dr. Nettie Lee Benson, curator of the famous García Collection of The University of Texas Library. I also owe much to Dr. Rollie E. Poppino, of the University of California at Davis, and to Dr. David D. Burks, of the University of Indiana, both of whom were former colleagues in the Department of State. My thanks also go to Mr. David Garza, who assisted me in the final preparations. Finally I must acknowledge the contribution of my family, who granted me the hours of peace and quiet to write the manuscript and tolerated my many absences in quest of materials.

I alone am responsible for all statements of fact and interpretation contained herein.

Karl M. Schmitt
Austin, Texas

CONTENTS

COMMUNISM IN MEXICO
A Study in Political Frustration

I. The History of the Mexican Communist Movement

Almost unique among its counterparts in other areas, the Mexican Communist movement includes not one but three political parties in addition to the usual array of party wings, front groups, and infiltrated organizations. This political splinterization has resulted from Mexico's particular development in the twentieth century, notably the Revolution of 1910, as well as from more recent personal conflicts and animosities among the Communist leaders themselves.

The Founding of the Mexican Communist Party

The orthodox Mexican Communist Party (Partido Comunista Mexicano—PCM), founded in 1919, was among the first to be organized in Latin America following the successful Bolshevik Revolution in Russia. Its foreign ties were evident from its inception, and its close association with the mother country of Communism has persisted through the years. But in terms of Mexican history it came a few years too late to be effective in the country's drive for economic development and social reform. Mexico's Revolution had already occurred and was in the process of some consolidation by the time the Communists appeared on the scene.

In common with other political parties of the time, the PCM had its native antecedents in the Mexican labor movement, whose founders and leaders were deeply influenced by anarcho-syndicalism. One of the principal tenets of these labor anarchists was abstention from legal political competition in favor of revolutionary action. The point need not be labored that consistency in this policy cannot be found. The early House of the World Worker (Casa del Obrero Mundial) signed its pact to support Carranza in 1915 and the Casa's offspring, the Regional Confederation of Mexican Workers (Confederación Regional de Obreros Mexicanos—CROM) organized several parties for legal political action. The fact remains, however, that for many years anarchism was strongly rooted in Mexican trade unionism.

The first major move by Mexican labor to involve itself in politics came with the founding in February 1917 of the Worker Socialist Party (Partido Socialista Obrero—PSO) by labor leader Luis Morones and his followers. With a program to improve the lot of the worker by means of political action as well as by labor union agitation, the PSO participated in the congressional election campaign of 1917. Its utter failure led to the Party's collapse, but Morones founded the CROM in May 1918 and at the union's annual convention in the spring of 1919 pushed through a resolution to found another worker's political party. As a result the moribund PSO met with other socialist groups, parties, and factions in a National Socialist Congress in Mexico City later in the year.[1]

In the meantime various socialist-minded foreigners were making their way into Mexico for one reason or another during the years 1917 to 1919. Linn A. Gale hurried down from the United States to avoid the draft of World War I. He soon joined the small Mexican Socialist Party, founded a magazine, *Gale's*, which became that Party's official organ, and became a leading figure in directing the organization.[2] Other U.S. citizens, some draft dodgers, some adventurers, also became involved in Mexican socialism. These included Charles Francis Phillips (alias Frank Seaman), Roberto Haberman, and Michael Gold (alias Irwin Granich). Carleton Beals circulated among this group, but appears to have remained outside the political arena.[3]

More important by far than the Americans to Mexican socialism

---

[1] Vicente Fuentes Díaz, *Los Partidos Políticos en México*, II, 21–22.

[2] Robert J. Alexander, *Communism in Latin America*, p. 319.

[3] Carleton Beals, *Glass Houses: Ten Years of Free Lancing*, pp. 31–52.

was the Indian nationalist Manabendra Nath Roy. Born in Bengal about 1886, Roy became attracted early in life to politics in behalf of Indian independence. Involved in German intrigues to supply money and weapons for an Indian uprising during World War I, Roy came to the United States, where German agents planned to supply Indian nationalists with munitions. He attended Stanford University for a short while, met there a girl whom he later married in a New York jail, and finally fled with her to Mexico in 1917 when U.S. authorities began rounding up Indian nationalists after the United States entered the war against Germany. In Mexico Roy renewed his contacts with the Germans, who supplied him handsomely with funds. He in turn dispensed some of it to Revolutionary comrades, and the remainder he used to live fashionably in Mexico City. Shortly after his arrival he made contact with the U.S. expatriates and in collaboration with them he began to write articles for Mexican publications defending Mexico in its quarrels with the United States. Roy also published, in Spanish, a book and some pamphlets on India. In these writings of 1918 and early 1919 there is no hint of Marxist influence, but as his bonds with U.S. and Mexican socialists grew stronger he inevitably adopted some of their views. In the summer of 1919, as the various Mexican leftist groups talked of forming a new socialist party, Roy began to finance a small paper, *El Socialista,* run by Francisco Cervantes López, leader of the Red Marxist Group (Grupo Marxista Rojo). Roy also joined the Mexican Socialist Party and with the funds at his disposal began to vie with Gale for predominance in the Party.[4]

By the late summer of 1919 all the persons and elements were present in Mexico for the founding of a Communist party. Marxian socialist thought had penetrated several organized factions and parties, news of the Bolshevik Revolution in Russia and its successes had been heard and discussed, and various Mexican governments had demonstrated their tolerance of "revolutionary" political organizations. Under these circumstances the Mexican socialists held a Congress in Mexico City from August 25 to September 4, 1919, financed and greatly influenced by Roy. Almost immediately upon opening, a dis-

[4] Gene D. Overstreet and Marshall Windmiller, *Communism in India,* pp. 20–24.

pute arose over the seating of Luis Morones, to whom Gale objected because of Morones' friendly relations with Samuel Gompers and the American Federation of Labor. Roy, as chairman, broke a tie vote and Morones was seated. Gale, with his group, eventually withdrew from the Congress and the Mexican Socialist Party, and formed his own organization, which he labeled the Communist Party of Mexico. Just before, or perhaps during the Congress, Roy had been introduced to Michael Borodin by Charles Phillips. Borodin, under the guise of a Russian commercial representative, had arrived in Mexico in the summer of 1919 as an agent of the Comintern. He promised Roy aid in the struggle for Indian independence if Roy would found a Communist party in Mexico and have himself named as Mexican delegate to the Third International Congress. Roy therefore tried to convince the Socialist Congress to join the Comintern, but Morones and his followers objected strenuously. Roy then gathered the extreme left socialists around himself and with Borodin's blessings formed the Mexican Communist Party (PCM).

The Party dates its founding officially from September 25, 1919, but operations did not begin until November. Roy named four other members to comprise the Party's political bureau, including José C. Valadés, the Party's leading theorist for several years, and an American, M. Paley, who had been organizing miners around Pachuca. Meeting in Roy's commodious residence for lack of an office, the group named Roy and Phillips as delegates to the Second Comintern Congress of 1920. Phillips left by way of Cuba, and Roy and his wife went directly to Spain in November on Mexican diplomatic passports. Leaving behind several quarreling groups of radicals, two of whom called themselves Communists, Roy arrived in Russia where he performed brilliantly at the Communist Congress, especially in his report on colonial areas. He never returned to Mexico, nor did he show any further interest in the country's Communist movement, immersed as he became once again in Indian affairs. Nevertheless he continued to travel on his Mexican passport as late as 1925. Gale's Communist Party also elected a delegation for the Soviet Congress, but lacked money for its passage. In this difficult position it sent credentials to a Japanese, Keikichi Ishimoto, who had been in Mexico during 1918 and had written later from New York of his plan to go to Moscow. Gale also sent him a detailed report, extremely critical of Roy, on the Mexican Communist movement. It is uncertain that Ishimoto ever reached Moscow, but if he did, his report obviously failed of its purpose. Gale's movement thrived for a short while in Mexico with support from Carranza. With Carranza's overthrow early in 1920, Gale was deported by the new government. Upon his return to the United States he was arrested as a draft dodger and by 1921 had recanted his radicalism. His movement in Mexico eventually disappeared.[5]

The First Ten Years, 1919–1929

The PCM, the officially recognized Communist organization in Mexico, made little progress politically during its early years. At the end of 1919 a small youth wing was formed, but barely managed to exist until mid-1921, when it was strengthened by the adhesion, among others, of Rafael Carillo, later to become secretary general, and Jesús Bernal, a longtime stalwart and militant, who later became a member of the dissident Communist Mexican Worker-Peasant Party (Partido Obrero-Campesino Mexicano—POCM). During 1921 youth cells were formed in labor organizations, and finally a new body, the Federation of Communist Youths (Federación de Jóvenes Comunistas), was established. In its Declaration of Principles the Federation announced as its purpose the destruction of the present capitalist bourgeoise state by means of the dictatorship of the proletariat exercised by soviets to attain the final Communist society. Petitions to be telegraphed to President Harding were soon circulated

---

[5] *Ibid.*, pp. 24–27; Beals, *Glass Houses*, pp. 48–52; Fuentes Díaz, *Los Partidos Políticos*, II, 35–36; Alexander, *Communism in Latin America*, pp. 319–320; Ricardo Treviño, *El Espionaje Comunista y la Evolución Doctrinaria del Movimiento Obrero en México*, pp. 19–20; Rodrigo García Treviño, *La Ingerencia Rusa en México*, pp. 28–30; Rosendo Salazar and José G. Escobedo, *Las Pugnas de la Gleba, 1907–1922*, II, 63–65. These accounts vary on some details, but I have relied for the most part on Overstreet and Windmiller since their account is based on Roy's *Memoirs*; I have relied secondly on Beals, who knew Roy intimately, and thirdly on Salazar and Escobedo, who were participants in some of the events discussed.

among the laboring class demanding that the United States raise its blockade against the Soviet Union. Public meetings were organized and parades marched past the U.S. legation and consulates for the same purpose.[6]

The Political Bureau itself struggled along with difficulty during 1920. In January it began publishing a semimonthly organ, *Vida Nueva,* and sometime during the year it began holding its meetings at the headquarters of a small bakers' union. The meetings often included Genaro Gómez, leader of the bakers; Manuel Díaz Ramírez; and Rafael Carrillo. Apparently from this group was formed the Party's Central Committee, because in February 1921 the first plenum of the Central Committee was held. At that time a collective directorate was established, composed of a three-man secretariat including José Allen, José C. Valadés, and Manuel Díaz Ramírez, with the latter named secretary general. Díaz Ramírez was sent to Moscow to attend the Third Comintern Congress in June 1921 as the Party's official delegate, the first Mexican representative in Moscow. Upon his return the Bureau made preparations for holding the Party's first congress. It met from December 25 to 31 with its primary resolution calling upon workers not to participate in the political upheavals of the time since this would weaken the forces of the proletariat for the coming socialist revolution.[7]

During 1921 several important Mexican revolutionary leaders joined or associated themselves briefly with the Communists, e.g., General Mújica, governor of Michoacán, and General Felipe Carrillo Puerto, governor of Yucatán. The latter headed the Socialist Party of Yucatán which he had founded earlier. As a member of the Latin American Bureau of the Third International, Carrillo Puerto intended to link his party with the Comintern at the Congress at Izamal in August 1921. Plutarco Elías Calles, then Secretary of Government in General Alvaro Obregón's Administration, frustrated this plan by sending a group of CROM leaders to pressure other Yucatán leaders to frustrate Carrillo Puerto's design. They were successful, and after

[6] Fuentes Díaz, *Los Partidos Políticos*, II, 36–38; Treviño, *El Espionaje Comunista*, p. 21.

[7] García Treviño, *La Ingerencia Rusa*, pp. 31, 45–54; Fuentes Díaz, *Los Partidos Políticos*, II, 38.

1921 until the mid-1930's no serious threats arose that important political sectors of the Revolution would join the Communists.[8]

During the first two years of its existence the Party made its greatest effort to influence Mexican society through trade union organizations first by infiltrating existing bodies and then by establishing unions under its own control. In September of 1920, scarcely a year from its founding, the PCM organized the Communist Federation of the Mexican Proletariat (Federación Comunista del Proletariado Mexicano) under the direction of Sen Katayama, a Japanese trade union leader and Comintern agent. Its three-point program consisted of opposition to political action by labor, to government jobs for union leaders, and to the affiliation of Mexican labor to the A.F. of L. Within a few months the Federation claimed eighteen affiliates, fifteen of which were in the Federal District. These comprised the most radical unions in Mexico such as the textile workers, the bakers, the brewery workers, the streetcar workers, and the employees of the Ericcson Telephone Company. There was a great turnover among these affiliates and the Federation never achieved any real importance in the Mexican labor movement. This Federation and others that the Communists formed later "remained largely propaganda groups directed by foreigners, and to a considerable extent supported by foreign funds."[9]

The desire among many labor leaders to establish a single Mexican labor confederation, and widespread dissatisfaction with the moderate and opportunistic trade unionism of Luis Morones and his CROM, led to the calling of a trade union congress in February 1921. The Mexican Labor Party; CROM; the Pan American Federation of Labor; the Communist Federation; both Communist parties; the Federation of Communist Youths; and the Latin American Bureau of the Red International of Labor Unions (RILU) all sent delegates. Over strong opposition from the moderates, the Communists succeeded in allying the newly organized General Confederation of Laborers (Con-

[8] Alexander, *Communism in Latin America*, p. 321; Fuentes Díaz, *Los Partidos Políticos*, II, 29–30; Chester M. Wright, "Mexico, the Hopeful: A Survey of Her Political and Industrial Situation As She Takes Her First Steps in Reconstruction," *American Federationist*, XXVII, No. 12 (December 1920), 1088.

[9] Marjorie Ruth Clark, *Organized Labor in Mexico*, pp. 79–80.

federación General de Trabajadores—CGT) with the PCM and
RILU. The Communist victory was short-lived, however, because at
the CGT's first congress in September 1921 the Communists were defeated and affiliation with the Comintern broken. Thereupon the Communists withdrew from the CGT. This defeat apparently demoralized
the Communist movement for the next two or three years. Katayama
and Louis Fraina, a U.S. Communist who accompanied him, changed
the Party line to sponsor political campaigns within the constitutional
system, and Fraina provided the PCM with funds to participate in the
1922 elections. Many Party members with anarchist backgrounds objected to the new line, spent the money on other things, and showed
Fraina a few posters as evidence of their campaigning. Apparently he
was taken in.[10]

Following the Katayama-Fraina interlude, the Party fell under the
control of artists and intellectuals. Early in 1922 the great trio of
Mexican art (Diego Rivera, David Alfaro Siqueiros, and José Cle-
mento Orozco) and some others formed the Revolutionary Union of
Technical and Plastic Workers (Sindicato Revolucionario de Obreros
Técnicos y Plásticos). Most of the members, with the notable exception of Orozco, joined the PCM and their magazine *El Machete* soon
became the official organ of the Party. Its editors were Rivera, Siqueiros, and Xavier Guerrero. In 1923 these three were elected to the
Party's Executive Committee and, although Díaz Ramírez remained
secretary general, they soon dominated it since the working class
members were no match for these intellectuals. Rivera also organized
and dominated the Communist Union of Painters and Sculptors, and
Carlos Gutiérrez Cruz organized the League of Revolutionary Writers.
In that same year Bertram D. Wolfe, then a U.S. Communist, arrived
in Mexico, ostensibly to work as a teacher. He soon involved himself
deeply in PCM affairs. He found the Party now thoroughly engaged
in politics but according to his views backing the wrong candidate,
Adolfo de la Huerta. De la Huerta was paying the Party a subsidy,

[10] Treviño, *El Espionaje Comunista*, pp. 21–23; Fuentes Díaz, *Los Partidos
Políticos*, II, 37; Clark, *Organized Labor*, pp. 81–83; Salazar and Escobedo,
Las Pugnas, II, 115–116; Alexander, *Communism in Latin America*, p. 321.
For background on Katayama see the introduction by Louis C. Fraina to Kata-
yama's book, *The Labor Movement in Japan*.

and the PCM had in turn agreed to support him in a revolt if necessary. Wolfe protested to the Executive Committee that Calles, not de
la Huerta, offered the best opportunities for continuing the revolution.
Wolfe's success is attested by the fact that the PCM supported the
Calles-Obregón organization when de la Huerta revolted in late 1923,
and in Veracruz the Party actually raised troops to aid the government. After Calles' victory the government offered the PCM a subsidy,
which it accepted over Wolfe's protest and retained for some years.[11]

The year 1924 marked a further advance in the development of
Mexican Communism. For one thing Mexico and the Soviet Union
established diplomatic relations with the exchange of ministers. The
Soviet Legation almost immediately sought out labor leaders and
intellectuals. It financed trips for them to the USSR and paid the cost
of publication of their impressions of their travels. From these groups
was formed the Society of Friends of the USSR (Sociedad de Amigos
de la URSS—SAURSS). The year 1924 also witnessed a thorough
shake-up in the Party's leadership. In April, probably under Wolfe's
direction, every member of the Executive Committee save Díaz Ramírez was replaced. Rafael Carrillo from the youth organization was
named secretary general and Wolfe himself became a member of the
Committee and the Party's delegate to the Fifth Comintern Congress
to be held that year. Attending the Party meetings at which these
changes were made was Jay Lovestone, secretary general of the U.S.
Communist Party, who insisted that the anarchist tendencies of the
PCM be further curbed and that organization and discipline be
tightened. At the Third Congress of the PCM, held a year later in June
1925, Wolfe reported that some real progress had been made in the
matters of organization, finances, and discipline. The Party program
pointed out that the Anti-Imperialist League had been recently
formed, that plans were afoot to organize a national peasants' league
out of existing state leagues, and that the work of penetration into the
CROM and CGT was continuing. Party leaders criticized President
Calles as the left arm of U.S. imperialism and the policeman of
Yankee bankers and oil magnates. The congress finally renewed the

[11] Bertram D. Wolfe, "Art and Revolution in Mexico," *The Nation*, CXIX,
No. 3086 (August 27, 1924), 207–208; Alexander, *Communism in Latin America*, pp. 322–323.

Party's Executive Committee but made few changes, retaining Carrillo and Wolfe, the former as secretary general. Despite the attacks
on the government, the subsidy continued and the Party retained its
one seat in the Senate won in the 1924 elections. Wolfe, however, was
expelled by the Mexican government as a pernicious alien in July,
a month after the Third Congress. For the next three years the Party
prospered, though on a small scale. During 1927 the official Comintern report noted that the PCM had doubled its membership to 1,000,
with 600 workers, 50 peasants, and the remainder artists and intellectuals. The Party continued to enjoy a subsidy and the tolerance
of the government if not its support. This situation lasted until a mis-
reading of Mexican political turmoil and international economic collapse in 1928 and 1929 brought disaster to the Party.[12]

In the meantime the Communist movement undertook once more a
campaign to gain influence among the working class, rural as well as
urban. The PCM continued its efforts to get the CROM to join the
Red International of Labor Unions, and in Moscow the Mexican labor
attaché, a CROM leader, was invited to attend a meeting of the RILU
Executive Bureau. The attaché in turn invited the International to
send an observer to the next CROM convention. These auspicious be-
ginnings were cut short by the rigid sectarianism and short-sighted-
ness of the first secretary of the Soviet Legation, who as a dinner
speaker at a CROM banquet berated his hosts for not holding membership in the RILU. Relations between CROM and the International
immediately cooled and the invitation to send an observer was can-
celed. As a result the PCM was thrown back on its old tactics of infiltrating among rank-and-file labor union members. During 1926 and
1927 the Communists sought to take over control of the textile mill
workers, but except in one factory in Jalapa, the CROM beat them
off. Hernán Laborde, secretary general in the 1930's, became one of
the leaders of the railroad workers' union and participated in an unsuccessful strike in 1926. Siqueiros led a miners' union in Jalisco
in 1927 and 1928, while the Party in the Federal District set up a
joint committee with a food handlers' union to found a Mexican affiliate for the Latin American Trade Union Confederation (Con-

[12] Treviño, *El Espionaje Comunista*, pp. 26–27; García Treviño, *La Ingerencia Rusa*, p. 55; Alexander, *Communism in Latin America*, p. 323.

federación Sindical Latino Americana—CSLA), the Latin American branch of the Red International of Labor Unions. A new labor organization was thus founded in 1928 but it soon collapsed.

Political events in Mexico, however, seemed for a short time to offer the Communists some hope of government support in labor. CROM was rapidly losing favor in government circles and beginning to disintegrate. Its leader, Luis Morones, had bid for the Presidency in 1928 but had been passed over in favor of Alvaro Obregón. As relations between government leaders and labor leaders cooled, long-felt antagonisms against Morones among state politicians began to be expressed openly, with several defections. Moreover, when Emilio Portes Gil assumed the office of chief executive as Provisional President following the assassination of President-Elect Obregón, Communist prospects looked bright indeed. As governor of Tamaulipas, Portes Gil had made friendly overtures to the Communists and continued to sympathize with them after his election to the Presidency. In response to his friendly attitude, the PCM made a second attempt within a year to found a labor confederation. Their efforts resulted at the end of January 1929 in the founding of the Mexican Unitary Trade Union Confederation (Confederación Sindical Unitaria Mexicana—CSUM). The new confederation endorsed political action but said it would not take part in election campaigns. The CSUM won over some CROM affiliates but hardly was it organized when Portes Gil's attitude began to change. CROM was rapidly weakening, and the government had no further need for the Communists. The CSUM never developed into an important labor organization and virtually disappeared in the disaster of 1929.[13]

Peasant organization proceeded more slowly and with greater difficulty than did the urban labor movement. Zapata had welded the peasants of Morelos and surrounding areas into a powerful fighting force for a brief moment, but permanent sustained efforts during peacetime presented totally different problems in view of the isolation and dispersal of the peasantry. The first important and successful peasant organization began in 1923 in Veracruz state with the League of Agrarian Communities of the State of Veracruz (Liga de Comuni-

[13] Alexander, *Communism in Latin America*, pp. 325–328; Clark, *Organized Labor*, pp. 134–135 and 196; Treviño, *El Espionaje Comunista*, p. 30.

dades Agrarias del Estado de Veracruz). It was the most radical
league of its kind, under the leadership of Ursulo Galván and with the
encouragement of Adalberto Tejeda, twice governor of Veracruz,
who held Communist sympathies. In 1926 Galván, with the aid of
Tejeda, now a member of Calles' Cabinet, forged the National Peasant
League (Liga Nacional Campesina) with more than fifteen state affiliates. Galván, primarily a politician, served in the state and federal
legislatures. Without question he aided the peasants, but he also used
them to advance himself and his immediate followers. He became
moderately wealthy and one of the largest landholders in Veracruz
while leader of the League.

Galván joined both the Veracruz League in 1924 and the National
Peasant League in 1926 to the Communist Peasant International. He
and Manuel Díaz Ramírez, former PCM secretary general, held seats
on the Presidium of the International. Early in 1929 Galván affiliated the Peasant League with the CSUM and adopted a program calling for the abolition of the present government and the substitution
of peasants and workers' soviets for the federal legislature and cabinet. Shortly thereafter the League participated in the creation of the
Worker and Peasant Bloc (Bloque Obrero y Campesino) to support
Pedro V. Rodríguez Triana, an old Flores-Magón follower, for the
Presidency in the elections scheduled for that year. Galván was made
president and Diego Rivera vice president of the Bloc. Rivera did
not actually play much of a role in the Bloc because during the early
months of 1929 he was painting murals in the National Palace. Like
the CSUM, the Bloc achieved little prominence in Mexican labor
and political circles and was destroyed in the upheavals of 1929.[14]

Revolt, Suppression, and Persecution, 1929–1934

Although the year 1929 began auspiciously for the Mexican Communist movement with the consolidation of numerous peasant and
urban workers' organizations in a national labor confederation, with
sympathetic overtures from the government, and with the continuing
slow but steady growth of the Party, the year drew to a close by in-

[14] Clark, *Organized Labor*, pp. 154–157; Alexander, *Communism in Latin
America*, pp. 324–327.

augurating the most disastrous phase of the movement to that date. The catalyst was the economic recession that hit the United States late in 1929 and Europe as early as 1928. The Comintern interpreted these economic difficulties as the last phase in the general crisis of capitalism and alerted its subsidiaries the world over. In Mexico a political crisis brewing in early 1929 broke out in March as a full-scale revolt of army elements under Generals Aguirre and Escobar. The PCM interpreted this tumult as the final phase in the internal struggles and contradictions of the Mexican bourgeoisie, and their opportunity to seize power. Their tactics called for support of Calles (the real power behind Portes Gil) to suppress the Escobar rebellion, and then for an attack on Calles to overturn the government. Splits over this decision occurred within both the PCM and the National Peasant League. Guadalupe Rodríguez, leader of the Peasant League in Durango and member of the Executive Committee of the National Peasant League, supported the plan and lost his life in the attempt to seize power. Galván refused to fight and went over to Calles. In September he was expelled from the Peasant International, and he, Rivera, and Siqueiros, among others, were expelled from the PCM and CSUM. The National Peasant League began to split apart, many of its leaders joining non-Communist leftist state politicians. Galván died in 1930, and Rivera joined the international Trotskyite movement for some years. Official suppression of the Communist movement followed the revolt. Party offices were closed, *El Machete* was forced to cease publication and its presses destroyed, and Party members, Communist youth and trade union leaders, and officials of the Anti-Imperialist League were arrested and imprisoned. The Mexican government expelled two Soviet agents who were accused of participation, and in 1930 broke diplomatic relations with the USSR. During 1932 more Communists were arrested for spreading propaganda among soldiers, and Communist-led strikes were broken by troops. Most of those who escaped arrest went into hiding until Cárdenas ended the persecution in 1934.[15]

[15] Fuentes Díaz, *Los Partidos Políticos*, II, 39–40; Clark, *Organized Labor*, pp. 264–265; Alexander, *Communism in Latin America*, p. 329; Treviño, *El Espionaje Comunista*, p. 31.

Revival and Furthest Advance, 1934–1940

One of the first acts of Lázaro Cárdenas after his inauguration as President in 1934 was to stop the attack on the Communists and to free the Communist leaders imprisoned on the Islas Marías. The PCM, however, did not know how to respond to these friendly overtures, and to the end of the Cárdenas Administration was never able to get its policy line straight. The Party quietly accepted the official tolerance of the new Administration, but when the struggle for power between Calles and Cárdenas broke out into the open during 1935 the Party hesitated to support their benefactor. Professing to see little difference in the two leaders, the Communists adopted the slogan "Neither with Cárdenas nor with Calles; with the Cardenista masses." By the end of the year, however, the PCM was seeking, in line with Comintern policy, to form a "popular front" with the official Party, which was now completely dominated by Cárdenas, and it began to praise the Revolution of 1910 as part of the "national liberation movement." The Communists made it clear on the other hand that they would continue to criticize the Administration for any concessions to the imperialists, and they did so until the early months of 1937. During this phase the Party line continued to sponsor the "popular front," with the purpose of turning the Administration into a "workers and peasants' government" that would eventually inaugurate the socialist society.

Just as the Party had difficulty with its political line under Cárdenas, so too it hesitated over its trade union policy. The end of the persecution coincided with the Comintern's abandonment of its policy of isolationism in favor of cooperation with non-Communist organizations. The Communists of Mexico were somewhat reluctant to adopt the new approach in view of their previous failures. Furthermore, by 1934–1935, the labor picture in Mexico had altered appreciably from that of the 1920's. The CROM was a shadow of its former self and Luis Morones had fallen from his eminence as the country's labor czar. A host of independent unions and confederations had emerged, and the star of a young and vigorous new leader, Vicente Lombardo Toledano, was rising rapidly. Lombardo had been Morones' right-hand man but had split with him in 1932 to form the General Confederation of Workers and Peasants of Mexico (Confederación General de Obreros y Campesinos de México—CGOCM). Cárdenas' labor policy was to reunite these scattered organizations into a single confederation, and Lombardo Toledano appeared to be the chosen instrument. The Communists' first important cooperation with Cárdenas occurred in the labor movement in June 1935 when the revived CSUM signed a pact of solidarity with non-Communist unions including the railway, miners, and electrical workers' organizations, and the CGOCM of Lombardo Toledano. The signers mutually agreed not to raid each other, not to cooperate with capitalists, and to work toward the formation of a single national trade union central. By the fall of that year the signers had established a National Committee of Proletarian Defense (Comité Nacional de Defensa Proletaria), and when Lombardo returned from a trip to the Soviet Union in November, he and Hernán Laborde, PCM secretary general, publicly embraced. Lombardo and his traveling companion, Víctor Manuel Villaseñor, delivered a series of six lectures to overflow audiences on their experiences. Both revealed themselves ardent Marxists and partisans of Stalin and the Soviet experiment.[16]

In February 1936 the National Committee of Proletarian Defense, under the leadership of Lombardo Toledano, sponsored a national labor congress at which the proposed central labor confederation was established. The Confederation of Mexican Workers (Confederación de Trabajadores Mexicanos—CTM), as the new organization was called, chose Lombardo as its first secretary general. His forces and those of the Communists quarreled over the important post of secretary of organization. Lombardo's aide, Fidel Velázquez, won the office, and the position of secretary of education went to Miguel A. Velasco, the only Communist to be elected to the Executive Committee. The Communists soon evidenced dissatisfaction with their role in the new confederation. Relations with Lombardo Toledano remained strained throughout 1936, and early in 1937 the Com-

[16] Vicente Lombardo Toledano and Víctor Manuel Villaseñor, *Un Viaje al Mundo del Porvenir.* See also Fuentes Díaz, *Los Partidos Políticos,* II, 40–41; Treviño, *El Espionaje Comunista,* p. 33; Alexander, *Communism in Latin America,* pp. 330–332.

munists finally withdrew and formed their own central. At the meeting of the CTM National Council in April, Lombardo bitterly denounced the Communist maneuver as contrary to the Comintern's own popular-front policy. The CTM, he declared, was a "united front of the proletariat," and could not therefore support a single ideology. He also refuted the Communist assertions that they had created the CTM and that the Cárdenas Administration remained "progressive" only because of Communist vigilance. The quarrel was next carried to the United States Communist Party because of both the stature that the latter had attained in the 1930's and the important role that it had played in the PCM's early years. Lombardo and the PCM both sent reports to Earl Browder, and Browder took the unprecedented step of publishing Lombardo's version in the New York *Daily Worker.* The PCM sent other messages and eventually a delegation to New York. After long conferences with Browder, the Mexican Communists agreed to end the labor split and requested Browder to explain the decision to the Party. He agreed and attended the PCM Central Committee meeting of June 26–30, 1937. While in Mexico, Browder also had long talks with President Cárdenas and Lombardo Toledano.

The events of the spring of 1937 marked another important turn in the development of Mexican Communism. Not only was the breach within the CTM healed, but the PCM adopted a policy of uncritical support for Cárdenas, while Lombardo Toledano took a major step toward his final commitment to the Communist cause. After 1937 he supported the official line in international affairs on every major issue, including all the tortuous turns of World War II and the immediate pre- and postwar years. In addition he received a government subsidy for many years for the Workers' University (Universidad Obrera—UO), which he founded in 1936, and for *El Popular,* the official CTM organ in the 1930's. For the Communist Party these years marked the zenith of its prestige and influence in Mexico. Secretary General Laborde openly embraced the Cárdenas regime as a highly advanced popular-front government, and extravagantly praised its agrarian reforms, assistance to labor unions, economic nationalism, and support for the Loyalist regime in the Spanish Civil War. The PCM also endorsed Cárdenas' reform of the official government party to give representation to labor, peasant, and other groups in addition to its geographical organization. Beyond this the PCM advocated the transformation of that party into a "people's front" of Mexico that would include the PCM. In this Cárdenas disappointed the Communists, as he did too in granting asylum to Trotsky and in refusing to re-establish diplomatic relations with the Soviet Union.

Not only did the alliance with Cárdenas give the Communists unprecedented opportunities to recruit in labor unions and peasant organizations, but it also increased the Party's prestige, and opened government agencies to Communist infiltration. The PCM grew particularly strong in the Departments of Education and Communications. In time, if one desired a good teaching job the best avenue was through affiliation with a Communist cell in the Education office. So firmly established were the Communists in education that in mid-February 1938 the Political Bureau (the old Executive Committee) sponsored the First Communist Pedagogical Congress and published some of the proceedings. The Communists, however, did not exploit these openings to their fullest advantage. The Party grew rapidly, attaining perhaps a maximum strength of 30,000 in 1939, but the new members were never properly indoctrinated nor fully incorporated into the Party. Thousands entered for opportunistic reasons and little effort was ever expended to commit them to Communist principles. When internal troubles plagued the PCM beginning in 1939, and when official support was withdrawn a few years later, the inflated membership quickly declined.[17]

Discord, Disunity, and Decline of the Communist Movement, 1940–1962

WEAKNESSES IN THE MEXICAN COMMUNIST PARTY

The first rumblings of discontent in the Mexican Communist Party occurred with the signing of the Hitler-Stalin pact in the late summer of 1939. Many Party members could not stomach this alliance with

[17] *Hacia una Educación al Servicio del Pueblo. Resoluciones y principales estudios presentados en la Conferencia Pedagógica del Partido Comunista.* See also Alexander, *Communism in Latin America*, pp. 330–334, 338; Treviño, *El Espionaje Comunista*, pp. 34–35; Fuentes Díaz, *Los Partidos Políticos*, II, 42.

the very incarnation of fascism they had been taught to despise. Expulsions followed refusal to accept the Party line. Then in early March 1940 Secretary General Hernán Laborde and his second-in-command, Valentín Campa, a top railway labor leader, were expelled without explanation from the Party's Executive Committee and an Extraordinary Party Congress met in mid-March. Attending the Congress were James Ford, a leading member of the U.S. Communist Party, Dmitri Manuilsky and Leon Haikiss, members of the Comintern, and Victorio Codovilla, one of the Comintern's principal agents in Latin America. The main speaker attacked Laborde and Campa for corruption and for the acceptance of subsidies from the government. Others criticized them for "right opportunist deviation" because of their uncritical support of the Cárdenas Administration and their designation of the government party as a true popular-front organization. The official explanation does not ring true, but no adequate alternative has ever been substantiated with conclusive evidence. It appears that the answer may lie in part in Laborde's and Campa's opposition to the known desire of Stalin to rid himself of Trotsky. Two months after the Congress, PCM Leader David Alfaro Siqueiros led the first and unsuccessful attack, and several months later the Party assisted the foreigner Jacques Mornard in his hatchet murder of the old Bolshevik. Whatever the reasons, the Congress not only confirmed the expulsion of Laborde and Campa from the Executive Committee, but expelled them and some of their followers from the Party. Successive purges followed through the 1940's of other militants who remained friendly to the old leaders. At that same 1940 Congress a young peasant leader, Dionisio Encina from the Laguna region, was elected secretary general. Encina had risen to prominence by leading a peasant strike in 1936 in the Laguna area against the landlords. Cárdenas settled the strife by expropriating the land and turning it into a collective. Communist influence in the Laguna declined somewhat with the establishment of peace and the organization, under government auspices, of the National Peasant Confederation (Confederación Nacional Campesina—CNC) (not to be confused with the National Peasant League), but the area has continued to be an important concentration of Communist strength to the present.

Under the leadership of Dionisio Encina from 1940 to 1960 the

PCM experienced a long and steady decline, partly because of internal weaknesses and partly because of external obstacles. Since 1940, despite the renewal of diplomatic relations with the Soviet Union in 1942, Mexico's political leaders have swung to the right. They have veered from the rapid and radical programs of change of the Cárdenas years to a policy of consolidation of social gains and their slow but steady expansion, and of placing primary emphasis on economic development. This switch has not augured well for the Communist movement, which chafed at the slowness of reforms even under Cárdenas. Furthermore, the new leaders of Mexico have had far less sympathy and tolerance for Communism than did the Cárdenas government. Beginning in the late 1940's the government began to purge Communists, including Lombardo Toledano, from leadership positions in the CTM and other important labor unions, a process that was virtually complete by the mid-1950's. Beginning in 1954, and especially since 1957, the government has adopted a hostile attitude not only toward Communist agitation but also toward Communist propaganda and organizational efforts.

Within the PCM Encina did not offer the dynamic and imaginative leadership necessary to hold the gains made by his predecessors. His narrow dogmatism, his suspicion and distrust of subordinates, his jealousy of his leadership position, and his inability to organize and indoctrinate at the grass-roots level contributed heavily to the decline of membership from a high of 30,000 to a low of 2,000 or 3,000 when he was finally deposed at the Thirteenth Party Congress in May 1960.

Without hesitation or questioning, Encina followed all the tortuous shifts of the Party line as laid down by the Kremlin in international affairs and domestic theory. When the Germans invaded Russia in June 1941, Party policy abruptly changed to its former anti-Fascist line, and taking a cue from Earl Browder of the United States, adopted the thesis in 1943 that trade union and political conflicts should be placed in abeyance at least until the common military victory be achieved over the Fascist enemies, Germany and Italy. The new line was "national unity" and support for the United Nations. That same year, 1943, witnessed one of the many purges that Encina carried out, with the result that whole cells of workers in the streetcar, railway, and textile unions either left the Party or ceased to function. With the end of Browderism in 1945, the Party reverted once more to its attacks on U.S. imperialism and to the call for the adoption of socialism in Mexico. By that time, however, membership was down to 13,000, according to PCM figures.[18]

GROWTH OF GOVERNMENT HOSTILITY TO COMMUNISM IN LABOR ORGANIZATIONS

If the Communists suffered some decline in labor influence during the war, they suffered disaster in the early postwar years. Lombardo Toledano, who in 1938 had become head of the new international popular-front Confederation of Latin American Workers (Confederación de Trabajadores de América Latina—CTAL), turned his post of CTM secretary general to his protégé Fidel Velázquez in 1940. As head of the CTAL, during the war he subordinated worker interests throughout the Hemisphere to the drive for military victory. He established friendly relations with all Western Hemisphere governments, whether democratic or dictatorial, conferred frequently with U.S. political and labor leaders, and urged all labor organizations to maintain industrial peace and concentrate on production for the war effort. In May 1945, however, he quickly changed his policy in the international field when Jacques Duclos, the French Communist, launched his attack on Browderism. U.S. imperialists and their allies once more became the enemy; but for the Mexican elections of 1946 Lombardo Toledano, in a CTM meeting, made the motion of adherence to conservative Miguel Alemán, the choice of the government party leaders for the Presidency. Alemán was duly elected with labor support but showed little sympathy for labor agitation. Strikes in vital enterprises were forcefully suppressed and no concessions appeared likely to accrue to Lombardo. In these circumstances he proposed to Mexican leftists of all hues the founding of a new party. He pushed a resolution supporting such a party through the CTM Congress of March 1947 and specified that CTM officials join the new party. In the next few months a number of top leaders in the CTM, including Secretary General Fidel Velásquez, became convinced that to split

[18] *Materiales del Comité del D.F. para su Discusión en el XIII Congreso del Partido Comunista Mexicano*, pp. 17–22; Alexander, *Communism in Latin America*, pp. 335–342; Fuentes Díaz, *Los Partidos Políticos*, II, 41.

the CTM from the government party, now called the Institutional Revolutionary Party (Partido Revolucionario Institucional—PRI), would be suicidal. Therefore, late in 1947, after Lombardo had publicly announced his intention to launch a new political organization, the Thirty-second National Council of the CTM reversed the decision of the March Congress and expelled three officers from the directive board for announcing their adherence to Lombardo's party. Velázquez and other leaders tried to dissuade Lombardo from his plans and when he insisted in following through with them, they expelled him from the CTM, in January 1948. Within a short time the CTM withdrew from Lombardo's CTAL, and in 1949 the Communist leaders were expelled from the railroad, miners, and petroleum workers' unions. By 1950 all that was left to the Communists were their own small and ineffectual organizations.

FOUNDING OF THE COMMUNIST-FRONT PEOPLE'S PARTY

Despite his discouragement by the CTM leaders, Lombardo Toledano proceeded with his plans for a new party. During 1947 he held a series of conferences and round-table discussions with Mexican Marxists of various persuasions. Impressed apparently by the limited appeal that an openly Marxist party would have on the Mexican electorate, Lombardo finally organized in June 1948 what he innocuously called the People's Party (Partido Popular—PP). Presented as a nationalist political organization whose purpose was to fulfill the as yet unachieved goals of the Mexican Revolution, the PP attracted a sufficient following to be registered as a bona fide political party, but it has never been able to offer serious opposition to the official party, the PRI. At the People's Party's Second National Assembly in November 1955, Lombardo introduced some minor changes in the formal structure of the Party, announced the leadership's intention to guide it toward a more Marxist orientation, and demoted his second-in-command. Only the last move constituted a development of any significance because it led first to a serious internal struggle within the Party and finally to a purge of the disaffected elements and to a withdrawal of some of their sympathizers.[19] Although the shift

[19] Alexander, *Communism in Latin America*, pp. 343–346.

toward Marxism meant no vital change in the Party's nature or organization, the Third National Congress in October 1960 took up the
theme again. In several ways Lombardo's actions prefigured those of
Fidel Castro of Cuba in 1961. The PP leader announced that the
Party would be restructured and reoriented toward Marxism-Leninism, that it would adopt the principle of democratic centralism in its
operations, and that the name would be changed to the Socialist
People's Party (Partido Popular Socialista—PPS). Except for the
new name, the so-called changes did little more than announce publicly what had been the Party orientation from the beginning. Since
1948 the party of Lombardo Toledano has overshadowed the orthodox Mexican Communist Party, frequently to the latter's discomfiture,
within the Mexican Communist movement. The PPS attained its
maximum strength in 1952, when Lombardo Toledano ran for President. Party strength leveled off until 1955, and then slowly began to
decline as enthusiasm waned and internal struggles took their toll.
Lombardo attempted to recoup his political losses by masterminding
the violent student strikes in the spring and summer of 1956. In October the government crushed the agitation, broke Lombardo's hold
in several student and youth organizations, and weakened it in others.
Lombardo's *campesino* leader, Jacinto López, has led numerous ex-
peditions of landless peasants in seizing both private and *ejido* lands
since 1957. Although the squatters have been dislodged, López has
been instrumental in publicizing the land problem, and perhaps
influenced the vast land distribution program of the Administration
of President Adolfo López Mateos.

Lombardo's next attempt to gain influence in urban areas occurred
in 1958 when he participated in the plans for railway agitation. Unlike the student disturbances of 1956, which the PPS directed almost
unchallenged, the railway agitations owed their direction to members
of the PCM and POCM as well as to Lombardo Toledano. When
agitation for higher wages led to violence and government countermeasures, Lombardo disavowed his support and denounced the ex-
tremism of his onetime collaborators. Lombardo and his Party escaped the severities meted out by the government to the PCM and
POCM, but he not only failed to increase his political influence but
suffered a setback as well. During the past several years the PPS has

been comparatively free of government harassment, and has been given wide latitude in its propaganda and recruitment activities. Nonetheless, it has never recovered from the losses it suffered in the late 1950's.

FOUNDING OF THE COMMUNIST-SPLINTER MEXICAN WORKER-PEASANT PARTY

The third Communist party, the Mexican Worker-Peasant Party (Partido Obrero-Campesino Mexicano—POCM), originated in 1950 from an amalgam of political factions composed of excommunicated members of the Mexican Communist Party. From the beginning it was indistinguishable from the orthodox party except in size and personnel. The ultimate aim of its leaders has been the unification of Mexican Marxists into a single powerful political party, but their more immediate goal was reunification of all POCM members with the PCM. For a decade even PCM-POCM unity appeared to be a forlorn hope because of the fear and hostility of the PCM secretary general Dionisio Encina toward those whom he had purged. With Encina's overthrow in 1960 and the more friendly attitude of the new PCM leaders, the way seemed open at last to unite the two parties. This hope did not materialize although some important POCM leaders entered the PCM.

COOPERATION AND COMPETITION AMONG THE THREE COMMUNIST PARTIES

Relationships among and between the three Communist parties have varied from open and cordial cooperation to bitter and vindictive conflict. Basically the parties are in agreement in their long-term goals of establishing socialist and communist regimes on the model of the Soviet Union. On numerous occasions all three have praised the government of the Soviet Union as a model of democracy and well-being. On the other hand, a basic split exists as to the tactics advocated to reach these ends. The POCM has consistently recommended a "direct action" approach through infiltration of the labor unions. POCM leaders, with their principal support, small as it is, in the railroad union, have advocated winning control over the masses, and from that vantage point taking over political control. The PCM has been more cautious, but has not hesitated at times to incite to strikes, demonstrations, and riots. It is unsparing in its criticism of the PRI and the government, but for many years has disavowed the use of force to gain power. Lombardo Toledano and the PPS have been still more prudent. Not only does the Party disavow violence, but it does not hurl unqualified criticisms against the President or the Administration. Specific policies and specific officials of the government have been vigorously attacked, but on the other hand the PPS has been quick to praise those government activities which are in accord with PPS policy. In fact, the PPS often attempts to take credit for government measures which coincide with its own program. On occasion, the PPS will advocate outright cooperation with the PRI. Beyond these tactical differences, personal amibitions and personality traits divide the three parties. Lombardo Toledano and the other intellectuals who predominate in the leadership posts of the PPS tend to regard the lower-class leaders in the PCM and POCM with considerable disdain, while the latter in turn are suspicious of Lombardo and distrust his upper-class mannerisms. At the same time, old-line POCM and PCM leaders have thoroughly disliked and distrusted each other. Referring to these divisions both within and among parties, a feature writer in the leftist newspaper *El Popular* lamented in the spring of 1960 that "as never before the movement of the left . . . [is] today . . . completely divided and in totally opposed camps, with the consequent satisfaction of the sectors of the right, within and outside official circles." This commentator further remarked that the disorientation of the left was not new, but that it had by then reached a climax.[20] By mid-1962 the situation had not changed.

The results of this complex situation have been that the three parties (1) on international matters follow unswervingly the Soviet line; (2) on domestic issues concur at times, violently disagree at others; (3) feud bitterly for control of "front" groups but at the same time superficially cooperate in carrying out their programs; and (4) occasionally coordinate their efforts during election campaigns.

In recent years party relationships have followed the pattern outlined above. All three supported the Soviet suppression of the Hun-

[20] Lino León Orozco, "¡El Camino está a la Izquierda! Pero ¿Donde está la izquierda?" *El Popular*, April 16, 1960.

garian revolt in 1956; all three give unqualified support to the Castro regime in Cuba; and all three ceaselessly condemn U.S. influence in Mexico. All three have verbally supported the "peace" movement at home and abroad, but with control of the "peace" partisans firmly in the hands of PCM members since the mid-1950's, the PPS ardor has noticeably cooled toward the local movement. In August 1958 all three concurred in a manifesto calling upon the government to free several labor union strike leaders,[21] but PPS-PCM disagreement flared up with regard to the settlement of the teachers' strike in Section IX of the National Teachers' Union.[22] All three parties also supported the railroad strike in February 1959. Although Lombardo tried to convince his Communist colleagues that they should not try to extend their victory further, the leaders of the railway union, supported by Campa of the POCM and Encina of the PCM, made additional demands on the government in March. When the government routed the strikers and overthrew the railway union's leaders, Lombardo stingingly rebuked his fellow Communists for fruitless provocation which had wiped out past gains.[23] On the other hand, he has joined them in continuous demands that the government release the strikers.

For electoral purposes the PPS, PCM, and POCM formed a coalition for the presidential campaign of Lombardo in 1952. The alliance proved to be fragile and ephemeral. Following the election, Lombardo supported President-Elect Adolfo Ruiz Cortines in the face of an armed threat by the major opposition party. The PCM, rallying to the opposition candidate, bitingly condemned Lombardo for "selling out to the victors" and attacked the POCM as Trotskyites.[24] Despite the bitterness of the 1952 aftermath, local electoral coalitions have been formed from time to time. Attempts to re-establish the coalition

[21] "Manifiesto del PP, el PCM y el POCM a los trabajadores," *La Voz de México*, August 10, 1958.

[22] The PCM has consistently supported the dissident faction in Section IX of the teachers' union, but the PPS has been apprehensive over their intemperate demands. Cf. the statement of PPS leader Candido Jaramillo in *El Popular*, August 17, 1958.

[23] Vicente Lombardo Toledano, *La Situación Política de México con Motivo del Conflicto Ferrocarrilero*.

[24] *Noviembre*, August 7, 1952. The POCM denied the charge.

for the 1958 presidential elections failed to materialize. Aware of its weaknesses, the PPS favored supporting the PRI candidate, Adolfo López Mateos, as the single candidate of the "left." The PCM and POCM, however, interpreted such a move as a capitulation to the ruling party, and entered into an uneasy alliance behind the PCM candidate, the senile Miguel Mendoza López, who described himself as a Catholic and a socialist. On the other hand, in the state of Guerrero, the PPS and the POCM supported a joint slate of candidates for federal senators and deputies.[25]

Other forms of cooperation have been exchanges of greetings on the occasion of party congresses, mutual attendance at social functions, as for example the commemoration of the Russian October Revolution, the use of each other's news organs for announcements or advertisements, and joint travel to the Soviet Union to participate in international or Soviet celebrations.

The PPS and PCM have been most insistent in their propaganda for the need of some kind of a formalized unity of action. The PCM has called for a "National Democratic and Anti-Imperialist Front," and the PPS for a "National Patriotic Front." Though substantially the same in program and concept, neither has ever materialized, because neither party will join any permanent coalition which it cannot lead. Of the three parties, only the POCM is willing to subordinate not only its interests but its very existence for the sake of unity. Its program formally advocates union with like-minded parties.

CÁRDENAS AND THE NATIONAL LIBERATION MOVEMENT

With the failure of PCM-POCM unification efforts under the most favorable conditions that appeared in over a decade, and with the coolness of the PPS toward POCM unity proposals in 1960–1961, Mexican Communists and Marxists have placed their hopes for unity in a new organization, the National Liberation Movement (Movimiento de Liberación Nacional—MLN). This movement grew out of the Latin American "peace" conference of March 1961 in which

[25] Alberto Lumbreras, "Lo Positivo y Negativo en la Campaña," *Guión*, III, No. 25 (June 1958), 31–35.

former President Lázaro Cárdenas played a leading role.[26] For some years those Marxists and leftists in Mexico who for one reason or another could not accept membership either in Lombardo's PPS or in the openly Communist PCM and POCM, have rallied around Cárdenas as their spokesman in behalf of faster social reform, economic nationalism, and nonalignment in international affairs. Cárdenas for many years gave little public encouragement to this loosely associated group. After his retirement from the Presidency in 1940, he removed himself from the public eye, although he remained a power in the PRI by virtue of his following among Mexican labor leaders, political leaders, and bureaucrats. He emerged from time to time to speak his mind in behalf of world peace, independence from U.S. control, and improved living levels for the lower classes. In 1949 and 1950 he lent his name and prestige to the founding of the Communist-controlled World Peace Council and to the Mexican "peace" movement, and in 1956 he accepted a Stalin Peace Prize. However, he played no active role in the various "peace" campaigns, national or international, and in his acceptance speech of the Stalin Peace Prize carefully avoided identifying himself with the Soviet Bloc or the local Communists. In 1954 he condemned U.S. intervention in Guatemala and in 1959 he visited Cuba and gave his blessing to Castro's reforms, which he identified with Mexico's Revolution. Since 1957 he has again taken up the cause of the Mexican *campesino* and since 1959 has spoken frequently in behalf of the labor and political leaders imprisoned for their participation in the railroad strike of that year. Despite these activities, many of which imply criticism of the Mexican government and the PRI, Cárdenas has refused to lead a new political movement. In the spring of 1961 he renounced his PRI membership, but it is doubtful that his action had any real political significance.

Cárdenas' renewed political interests, particularly since 1959, and his initiative in promoting the 1961 hemisphere "peace" conference, gave new hope to Mexican Marxists, including the Communists, that a strong leader with national prestige was at hand to unify the far left

[26] Mexican newspapers gave the conference very little coverage. For the fullest account of proceedings see *El Popular*, March 4, 5, 6, and 8, 1961.

of Mexican politics. For a few months in 1961 that hope seemed to be well grounded. Cárdenas struck out bitterly at what was termed the "conspiracy of silence"—the paucity, at the instigation of the government, of newspaper and radio coverage of the "peace" conference. In April he denounced the U.S.-supported invasion of Cuba and threatened to go personally to assist Castro. Although, allegedly on government orders, he did not travel to Cuba, he did lead a student protest demonstration against U.S. intervention. In Yucatán in May he publicly renounced his PRI membership and called upon the *campesinos* to seize by force their just rights and needs. But that was as far as he went. When Castro announced that Cárdenas had been invited as a guest of honor, together with the Soviet cosmonaut Yuri Gagarin, for the anniversary celebration of the July 26 movement, he declined, and in early October at the twenty-fifth anniversary celebration of the establishment of the Laguna cooperatives he described himself as an enemy of violence and a follower of discipline and honest work. Late in the year he seemed to accept that discipline of which he spoke by accepting, along with other past Presidents of Mexico, a government appointment personally made by President López Mateos. The appointments were made primarily to remove powerful political figures such as Cárdenas and Miguel Alemán from the area of strife that was rapidly building between pro- and anti-Communist forces in the country. Some leftists accused Cárdenas of selling out to the government.[27]

The MLN, together with the "peace" movement, has been composed of various types of Marxists. PCM influence appeared to be growing but was being seriously challenged by more moderate and flexible leaders who had no clear party commitments. On June 16 Lombardo Toledano announced a PPS decision not to participate in the national "peace" congress opening that day, and to withdraw entirely from the MLN and the local "peace" movement. Various explanations were offered, but after the verbiage is cleared away, the primary reason lies in the fact that the PPS could not dominate the movement. Following a PPS policy of long standing, Lombardo with-

[27] *New York Times*, June 10, 1962, p. 27. The firmness with which the López Mateos Administration handled Cárdenas since early 1961 led to much speculation that his power has declined appreciably. I am inclined to agree.

drew his people because he could not lead, but announced simultaneously his adherence to the international movement, in this case the World Congress of Disarmament and Peace. He also proposed the founding of a new and broader Mexican "peace" organization.[28]

In mid-1962, then, the Communist movement in Mexico was badly fragmented, its one hope for unity of recent years shattered apparently beyond repair. It had no leader of national stature capable of welding the many quarreling groups into a single political force capable of challenging the party in power. Most importantly it had nothing to offer the Mexican masses that the López Mateos Administration was not providing and even if it had, its incompetence in grass-roots organization would stifle its proposals.

[28] *Excelsior,* June 17, 1962, pp. 1 and 9; June 20, 1962, p. 5; June 21, 1962, p. 5. At the end of the month a further rift appeared in the MLN when the Executive Committee ordered its agent in Baja California not to support Alfonso Garzón for municipal president of Mexicali. Garzón was a protégé of Braulio Maldonaldo, former governor of Baja California, who has belonged to the left wing of the PRI and is a leading member of the MLN.

II. Orthodoxy and Schism in Mexican Communism

The Mexican Communist Party (Partido Comunista Mexicano—PCM)

For the first twenty years of its existence the Mexican Communist movement had few serious internal troubles. Some members were purged, others drifted away of their own accord, but none of these considered establishing a rival Communist organization. Ironically the Mexican Communist Party (Partido Comunista Mexicano—PCM) began to suffer severe internal strains at the very time it enjoyed its greatest influence and prestige, that is, during the administration of President Lázaro Cárdenas (1934–1940). These difficulties led, as we have already seen, to the overthrow of the top leadership in 1940 and the institution of a series of purges that substantially weakened the Party. From these discontented elements there arose in 1948 a Communist-front party, the People's Party (since 1960 called Partido Popular Socialista—PPS),[1] which we shall discuss later in this chapter, and in 1950 the Mexican Worker-Peasant Party (Partido Obrero-Campesino Mexicano—POCM), that swears allegiance to the international Communist movement as openly as does the PCM. Although the POCM has always desired to merge with the PCM, many of the orthodox Communists have long condemned the POCM as schismatical if not heretical. The PCM has insisted that

[1] Hereafter consistently referred to as the PPS.

merger take place individually so that "undesirables" could be eliminated, while the POCM has wanted an institutional merger of the
parties en masse. Despite much personal hostility among the leaders,
the two parties have worked together from time to time on specific
projects, but when the inevitable quarrel occurs, mutual recriminations are hurled back and forth. The PCM has frequently accused the
POCM of Trotskyism, right or left deviation, as the case may be, and
opportunism. The theoretical arguments were never the source of
the discord. What the PCM leaders have most feared is their displace-
ment by POCM leaders in their own party if an institutional merger
took place.

LEADERS AND FOLLOWERS

The PCM reached its greatest numerical strength and greatest political influence in the 1930's, with the rank and file numbering perhaps 30,000. The intraparty feud that ended in 1940 with the replacement of Hernán Laborde by Dionisio Encina as secretary general
weakened the Party and reduced its membership. Ruthless purges of
real and potential opponents were carried out by Encina for about
eight years.[2] These troubles, together with the swing to the right in
Mexican governmental circles, resulted in heavy losses to the PCM,
losses from which it has never recovered. In recent years Party officials have made exaggerated claims for Party membership—15,000
in 1954 and 65,000 in January 1957—and occasionally have announced plans to seek the entry on the ballot of their candidates for
political office. (For legal recognition the Mexican Electoral Law
currently requires a political party to have 75,000 registered members.) The PCM has not been able to gain this registration since the
1940's, when requirements were lower and the government more lax
in enforcement. At the opening of the decade of the 1950's the Party
numbered some 5,000 members. Renewed intraparty disputes beginning in 1956 slowly eroded even this reduced membership.[3] A

[2] Dionisio Encina, *Liberemos a México del Yugo Imperialista*, p. 46.
[3] United States Department of State, *World Strength of the Communist
Party Organizations*, Intelligence Report No. 4489R–9, January 1957, p. 73.
Intelligence Report No. 4489R–12, January 1960, p. 87, still estimated Party
strength at about 5,000. Although Encina gave no figures, he admitted great
numerical weakness in 1954. Cf. Encina, *Liberemos a México*, p. 47.

report of the U.S. Central Intelligence Agency to a Senate committee in November 1959 estimated PCM strength at 2,500,[4] but continued dissension and government harassment have probably lowered it still further.

Over the years the leadership of the PCM has revealed itself the least effective of the three Communist parties in terms of persuading Mexican interest groups or the populace at large to support its general program or specific aspects thereof. Many of the leaders are of lower-middle- and lower-class origin with little education. Dionisio Encina, secretary general from 1940 to May 1960, inept, insecure, and incompetent, distrusted every member who showed leadership capabilities. Many of these potential leaders he demoted, purged, or attacked following his own rise to power. Narrow and dogmatic, slavishly dependent on his Soviet masters, and ineffective in oratory, Encina relied on his more talented wife, Paula Medrano de Encina, for direction and guidance. Intellectuals have not been well represented in the leadership ranks except for a few artists and public school teachers who have risen to prominence.

The bulk of the membership, similar to the leadership, comes from the urban and rural lower middle and lower class. Few of the members are women. Intellectuals and professionals are also something of a rarity in the PCM. Left-wing and Communist-sympathizing intellectuals are more likely to be attracted to the PPS of Lombardo Toledano, himself an intellectual. A number of well-known artists, including such giants as Diego Rivera (now deceased) and David Alfaro Siqueiros (imprisoned in August 1959) and lesser but well-known painters such as José Chávez Morado and Xavier Guerrero, have long been Party members but seldom participated in Party policy making. Their contributions have been financial to a Party chronically short of funds and prestigious to a Party suffering from widespread ridicule and opprobrium. In addition to a number of public school teachers, a few medical doctors are also known Party members.

---

[4] Testimony of General C. P. Cabell, deputy director of the Central Intelligence Agency on November 5, 1959 before the Subcommittee To Investigate the Administration of the Internal Security Act (published by the Subcommittee as *Communist Threat to the United States through the Caribbean* [see p. 161]).

Membership is concentrated primarily in the Federal District and in the Laguna area comprising parts of the states of Durango and Coahuila. Smaller bands are scattered elsewhere in other central and northern districts and in the states of Sonora, Nuevo León, Tamaulipas, Michoacán, Baja California, Norte, and Veracruz. There has been in recent years little or no Party activity in the southern states and on the Yucatán Peninsula.[5]

Following the series of purges of the 1940's, the PCM regained much of its earlier unity and coherence. In his report to the Twelfth Party Congress of 1954, Encina claimed that "the greatest success [of the Party], without any doubt, has been the consolidation of its internal unity."[6] This internal unity of which Encina boasted lasted, at most, for two more years. Storm signals appeared as early as 1957, first within the Party organization in the Federal District and then reaching into the highest levels of the Party. By the summer of that year disgruntled younger members in the Federal District were able to force the calling of a special conference of the Federal District organization of the Party. At the conference, the dissidents, without much difficulty, wrested control from supporters of Encina. The revolt became public news in early October 1957 when the new Federal District Committee published in a twenty-two-page pamphlet a scathing indictment of the current national leadership.[7] No new Party problems were revealed, but the unique character of this document lay in its accusation that the main responsibility for Party failures rested with the Central Committee and the Political Committee, and that the highest leadership of the Party resisted the acceptance of just criticism. It may be argued that the conflict was in part an internal power struggle, and the fact that a number of aspiring and ambitious

[5] In his 1954 report Encina listed the Laguna area and the Federal District first among the areas of PCM activity. He also listed Yucatán, Tamaulipas, and Nuevo León. There has, however, been little evidence of activity in Yucatán in recent years. Cf. Encina, *Liberemos a México*, p. 47.

[6] Encina, *Liberemos a México*, p. 46.

[7] *Resolución de la Conferencia del Partido Comunista en el Distrito Federal 11–23 de Agosto, 2–19 de Septiembre.* The introduction of this document outlined the complaints of the dissidents. They pointed out that after thirty-eight years of existence the Party was still weak in organization, membership, and ideology, and that its political influence did not correspond even remotely with that which a true party of the vanguard of the working class should have.

younger men made up the dissidents supports this contention. On the other hand, several members of Encina's inner clique joined the revolt, indicating deeper problems and issues than mere desire for power. J. Encarnación Pérez Gaitán, long considered Encina's right-hand man, wavered at first, tried to adopt the role of compromiser, and finally joined the dissidents, becoming the secretary general of the now rebellious Federal District Committee. At a plenum of the Central Committee, October 22 to November 2, 1957, Encina and his associates in the leadership positions were again severely criticized.[8] Encina, however, was able to retain control of the Political Committee, the governing inner core of the Party, and by appeals to the rank and file throughout the country, he was able to purge rebellious members on the Central Committee and in the state and regional organizations except in the Federal District. As a result, Encina was able to postpone the call for a Party congress which the Federal District organization insisted upon to consider their accusations.[9] The split within the Party remained an open sore for many months and probably contributed in part to the Party's poor showing in the electoral campaign of 1957–1958.[10] Early in 1959 Encina and several companions attended the Twenty-first Congress of the CPSU in Moscow, and rendered a full report on the journey at the Central Committee Plenum, July 23 to August 7. Both activities clearly demonstrate his continued control over the Party to that time.

A related conflict swirled around the Party's official organ *La Voz de México* and the Party's print shop. Both had long come under intensive criticism, the one for lack of imagination and uninteresting reporting, the other for inefficient operation. Party leaders supervising those activities countercharged that nonprofessionals were forced

[8] *La Voz de México*, November 10, 1957, printed the resolution of the Plenum of the Central Committee.

[9] *La Voz de México*, August 10, 1958.

[10] Abelardo García Treviño, "Próximas Purgas Rojas en México," *El Universal*, January 22, 1958, p. 2. García maintained that this group of ambitious young men were determined to overthrow Encina and his faction. They accused Encina of following a national-Communist or Titoist line (for which there is no evidence whatsoever) and his followers of various crimes. Juan José Meraz, secretary of finance, was accused of pilfering funds and of attempting to seduce a young Communist woman.

upon them by the Political Committee and that nowhere in the country was there support for the newspaper. As the upshot of the conflict, the Political Committee early in November 1958 fired Manuel Terrazas, José Montejano, and Gerardo Unzueta, director, administrator, and editor-in-chief respectively. Terrazas had been director of *La Voz de México* for over ten years, and had become disgruntled at criticism leveled against him without reciprocal attempts by other leaders to assist him solve his problems. As a result he joined the dissidents. The Federal District Committee came to his immediate support in a special conference held November 9, 1958.[11]

The turning point in the struggle for power within the PCM occurred in September 1959 with the arrest of the secretary general and several other members of both factions on charges of "social dissolution" for their participation in the railroad strike the preceding March. The removal of Encina demoralized his faction and encouraged the opposition. At the October Plenum of the Central Committee, the dissidents were clearly in command. Jesús Lazcano, an Encina supporter, was dismissed as director of the Party book shop on charges of misappropriation of funds; except for Terrazas, the former staff of *La Voz de México* who were opponents of Encina were reinstated; and a merger with the POCM, long opposed by Encina, was advocated. This Plenum also abolished the office of secretary general, appointed a new three-man committee to govern the Party, and determined to hold the next congress in the Federal District, where dissident strength was greatest, rather than in Torreón, where Encina support was strongest.

The anti-Encina faction, now in undisputed control, rapidly pushed forward to hold the long-delayed Thirteenth Party Congress. Early in 1960 the Central Committee ruled that the Congress should be composed of delegates, each representing twenty-five bona fide members. In April the Party organization in the Federal District convened to elect a new executive committee and name delegates to the Congress scheduled for the next month. The anti-Encina forces dominated both slates.

Seventy-six delegates, representing 1,900 members, assembled on

[11] *El Universal*, January 3, 1959, p. 2, and *Materiales del Comité del D.F. para su Discusión en el XIII Congreso del Partido Comunista Mexicano.*

May 26 to open the Congress. Although the Federal District forces comprised only 20 per cent of the total (15 delegates representing 325 members) the anti-Encina forces were able to dominate the presidium of the Congress. Only two members of the presidium were apparently Encina supporters, Arturo Orona, director of the Party's labor wing, and J. Encarnación Valdez Ochoa, a companion of Encina on his 1959 trip to Moscow. Several former members of the POCM, including Consuelo Uranga and Eduardo Montes, were elected delegates from the Federal District, but did not serve on the presidium. In the election of the new Central Committee the anti-Encina group attempted to be conciliatory. Although it assured itself of a majority in that body, it did support the election of several Encina men, but not Encina himself. Manuel Terrazas and Arnoldo Martínez Verdugo emerged as the dominant personalities within the Party, with the famous artist David Alfaro Siqueiros serving as a front man to give the Party some prestige.[12] At the Congress the old leadership again received severe criticism for its incompetence, opportunism, and suppression of criticism.[13] Thirteen members, mostly intellectuals, led by José Revueltas, were expelled, but various members of the POCM, including that Party's longtime leader, Valentín Campa, were formally admitted into the PCM.[14]

The new leadership has not resolved the Party's problems. Membership has not increased, indoctrination programs for rank and file have not improved, and unity has not been attained. The new leaders are no more democratic in party affairs than were the old. To compound the troubles of the PCM, no single national leader has emerged to succeed the deposed Encina. In addition there is some division between those who favor the policies of the USSR against others who favor those of Red China. In many areas there is great distrust between leaders and followers, while state leaders are virtually independent of Mexico City. The Central Committee of December 1961

[12] Siqueiros held a press conference on June 14, 1960 to explain the accomplishments of the Congress. Cf. "Actividades comunistas en Iberoamérica," *Estudios Sobre el Comunismo*, Año IX, No. 32 (April–June 1961), 97.

[13] "The Party Enters upon a New Stage," *World Marxist Review: Problems of Peace and Socialism*, III, No. 9 (September 1960), 50–52.

[14] *La Voz de México*, July 26, 1961.

dissolved the Federal District Committee and ordered its reorganization because of its insubordination, dismissed an alternate of the Central Committee for criticizing the new leaders, and called for the meeting of an Extraordinary Congress to achieve unity in the Party.[15] By the end of June 1962 the Congress had not met nor had the difficulties been solved.

The Communist Youth of Mexico (Juventud Comunista de México—JCM), the youth wing of the PCM, was revived in 1948 following a resolution passed at the Tenth Party Congress of that year.[16] It was expected that able young people recruited through JCM activities could be attracted into the Party to furnish the PCM with a steady stream of needed cadre leaders. The JCM has not flourished, however. In 1954 J. Encarnación Pérez, one of the top leaders of the Party, reported that the JCM had been established in a few states, but not nationally. He said that the Party as a whole had underestimated the amount of aid and assistance the youth organization constantly needed to become an effective adjunct. For this reason, he explained, a brief chapter had been added to the Party statutes obliging every member and Party organization to work for the JCM.[17]

To the present the JCM has not been materially strengthened. A National Congress for its reorganization, held March 23 to 25, 1957, elected a seventeen-member national committee charged with overseeing the enforcement of the general policies and resolutions of the organization. The national committee in turn elected a seven-member national executive committee responsible for carrying out the JCM's daily operations. Manuel González Salazar was re-elected secretary general, the highest position in the organization. Resolutions of this reorganization congress spoke of the need to unify worker, farmer, and student youth, of the solidarity of Mexican youths with the Cuban Popular Socialist Youths (Communist), and of the intention to send a Mexican delegation to the Sixth World Youth Festival scheduled

[15] *Ibid.*, January 18, 1962.

[16] The Juventud Comunista was organized in 1919 almost simultaneously with the formal organization of the Party itself. Cf. *Noviembre*, September 16, 1948.

[17] J. Encarnación Pérez, *Sobre Las Modificaciones a Los Estatutos*, p. 20.

for that summer. The Congress has had little noticeable effect on JCM recruitment and growth. Membership remains at most at about 500, of whom the most active are in Mexico City and in the Laguna district in northern Mexico where the Party has contact with perhaps several thousand *campesinos* on communal lands.

The most successful JCM activity for the past few years has been the sponsorship by its Laguna branch of annual youth festivals, the first of which was held in 1954. These have consisted on several occasions of a judicious combination of sports and oratory and have attracted some attention throughout the country, drawing several hundred youths yearly.[18] The Sixth Festival in 1959, however, was something of a disappointment to the Communists since interest was lower than usual and some of the events were rained out.

The JCM has also attempted to enhance its importance by joining and attempting to lead the student disturbances of the past few years in Mexico City and Guadalajara. Its plans were frustrated by the youth followers of Vicente Lombardo Toledano, who managed to monopolize leadership positions. Early in March 1956 the PCM openly endorsed the student strike at the National Polytechnical Institute, insisting that all student demands, including the ouster of the school's director, be met by the government. JCM leader Manuel González Salazar attempted to participate in the leadership of the strike and rioting that continued into the summer and fall of 1956, but was effectively overshadowed by Nicandro Mendoza, a loyal adherent of Lombardo. JCM elements also appear to have participated in the student riots in Guadalajara in May 1957, but again not in leading roles. The dominant youth leader in the state university in Guadalajara, J. Guadalupe Zuno Arce, shunted them aside.[19] The JCM was further frustrated in its drive for recognition when the election of its slate of candidates for officers of the student federation at the University of Morelia was nullified by the school authorities.[20] The group also joined the anti-government agitation surrounding the labor difficulties in 1958–1959. One of its most bitter, though fruitless, attacks occurred in March 1960. JCM leaders protested Army

[18] *La Voz de México*, June 10, 1957.
[19] See Chapter III, "The Confederation of Mexican Youths."
[20] *La Voz de México*, August 10, 1957.

occupation of the National School for Teachers, denounced the arrest of the railroad strike leaders and their own party leaders, and attacked the press of Mexico City as being sold out to the government. But to no avail. Members of the JCM also distributed leaflets attacking not only the press but the President of the country, and carried signs reading "Executive Power or . . . dictatorship?"[21]

The propaganda of the JCM is disseminated through the PCM newspaper *La Voz de México*. The youth organization has long planned to publish its own journal, *Nueva Vida*, but it is not known whether this publication has ever appeared. Much JCM propaganda is identical with that of the Party but is usually slanted toward students and youth groups.

ORGANIZATION

The Twelfth National Ordinary Congress of the Mexican Communist Party, held in September of 1954 in Mexico City, adopted the basic statutes which, theoretically at least, govern Party members and organs. These statutes have been modified in some details by the Thirteenth Congress (1960). However, a comparative study of Party statutes and Party activities reveals strikingly the gulf between theory and practice.

By the terms of the statutes, the Mexican Communist Party adheres to the principles of democratic centralism. These principles include: (1) the election of all directive boards from below, (2) the obligations of the directive boards to report periodically to their respective party meetings, (3) strict party discipline and the subordination of the minority to the majority, (4) unconditional acceptance by lower party boards of decisions made by higher boards.[22] Party policy may be discussed and criticized at all levels, but once a final decision has been reached at the national level, it must be unconditionally accepted and practiced by all members.[23]

The base organization of the Party is the cell, which may be established according to territory, such as a town or neighborhood, or according to place of work, such as a factory, mine, school, or hos-

[21] *El Popular*, April 1, 1960.
[22] *Estatutos del Partido Comunista Mexicano*, Article 13, p. 7.
[23] *Ibid.*, Articles 23, 24, and 25, pp. 8–9.

pital. A cell may be organized with a minimum of three Party members, but in all cases the establishment of a new cell must be approved by the next highest Party echelon. A meeting of all cell members, called a General Assembly, should be held every two weeks, with special sessions called when necessary. Between meetings the work of the cell is carried on by a secretariat of three members elected for one year. A cell of less than ten members elects only a single secretary. When a cell expands to more than twenty members but less than fifty, it is broken up into groups of ten, with a leader appointed for each group by the General Assembly. The secretariat then acts as the coordinator for the whole. Presumably, all cells that increase to more than fifty members are divided into two cells. When a cell in a place of work increases to more than fifty members it may be broken into several cells organized according to departments or other subdivisions of the business or, in a large factory, by labor shifts. Although each such cell will have its own general assembly and secretariat, all the cells within the business enterprise may, "under the vigilance of the Central Committee," designate a committee to coordinate their activities.[24]

The principal tasks of the cell are to apply the Party political line, to know the problems of the masses within its radius of action, and to direct the struggle for their solution. To carry out these tasks the cell members are expected to perform the necessary propaganda and organizational work among the masses, to participate in the political economic and cultural life of the workers, and to pay their dues to support the cause.[25]

For the purpose of infiltrating and influencing various organizations such as labor unions, youth and women's clubs, and cultural societies, the Party makes use of the "fraction," composed of two or more members working under the direction of a regular Party organization. The fraction, headed by a secretary, attempts to carry out the Party program within the infiltrated organization, and in doing so may meet and discuss plans with non-Party members.[26]

Coordinating and supervising the work of the cells in a given area

[24] *Ibid.*, Articles 44, 48, 49, and 50, pp. 15 and 17.
[25] *Ibid.*, Articles 45 and 46, pp. 15–17.
[26] *Ibid.*, Articles 51, 52, 53, and 54, pp. 17–18.

is the Party's municipal, or district (comprising several municipalities), organization. The highest Party organ on this level is the
Municipal (or District) Conference which meets ordinarily once a
year to hear, discuss, and approve the report of the outgoing Municipal (or District) Committee and to elect a new Committee. The
Conference also names a three-member Audit Committee.[27]

In addition to its exercise of jurisdiction over the cells, the Municipal (or District) Committee studies the general problems of the
masses within its area and organizes studies of Marxism-Leninism
and of the Party political line. This Committee, meeting in ordinary
session twice a month, elects a secretary general and a secretariat of
three to five members from its ranks to carry on the Party's daily
work. The Audit Committee supervises the income and expenditure
of funds by the Municipal Committee and reports to the cells and the
State Committee every two weeks, and to the Municipal (or District)
Conference at its annual meeting.[28]

Next in rank above the municipal organization of the Party is the
state or regional organization (comprising several states or parts
of several states). The highest Party organ in this echelon is the State
(or Regional) Convention which meets ordinarily every two years to
discuss Party problems, hear the reports of the outgoing State (or
Regional) Committee, and to elect a new Committee. When necessary the Convention also elects delegates to the Party Congress. The
Convention also names a Finance Committee of three members. The
State (or Regional) Committee, whose size is determined by the
Central Committee, meets every two weeks to direct Party affairs in
the intervals between conventions. It names a secretary general and a
secretariat of from three to five members to carry out the Party's
daily tasks. The State (or Regional) Committee, besides reporting
to the Convention, reports monthly to the Central Committee and to
the Party Congress when it convenes. The Audit Committee acts as
watchdog over income and expenditures of the State (or Regional)
Committee, reporting bimonthly to the latter's dependent organs and
to the Central Committee, and to the Convention when it meets.[29]

[27] *Ibid.*, Articles 39 and 40, p. 14.
[28] *Ibid.*, Articles 41, 42, and 43, pp. 14–15.
[29] *Ibid.*, Articles 36, 37, and 38, pp. 12–14.

At the national level the highest Party organ is the Party Congress, which meets ordinarily every four years. To be a valid meeting, a given Congress must represent at least 60 per cent of the membership, the method of representation to be determined by the Central Committee. The tasks of the Congress are to discuss and approve the report of the Central Committee, to modify the statutes and program when necessary, to lay down the Party's tactical line, and to elect the Central Committee. Decisions taken at one Congress may be modified only by a subsequent Congress.[30]

The Central Committee, composed of proprietary members and alternates, the number of which is set at each Congress, meets every six months. As the highest directive body between congresses, it is responsible for directing all Party activities, for seeing to the faithful fulfillment of the Party program and statutes, and for managing the Party's finances. From among its members the Central Committee elects a Political Committee, a secretary general, and a secretariat, and establishes the various commissions considered necessary for the fulfillment of the Party's work. The Central Committee also names a Central Control Committee of five members to handle problems of discipline and a Financial Control Committee of three members to handle Party funds and to render financial reports. The Central Committee also controls the Party fees, names Party candidates to federal electoral posts, and approves candidates for lesser posts when presented by lower Party organs. When the Central Committee considers it necessary, it may call a national convention to discuss specific important problems of Party policy. Such a convention is made up of members of the Central Committee and of delegates elected by the state and regional committees according to the method designated by the Central Committee.[31]

In practice, the Party has been organized only superficially along the lines laid down in the Party statutes. It has never been organized on a nationwide basis, nor on a statewide or regional basis anywhere except in the Federal District. In those states (thirteen in 1954)[32]

[30] *Ibid.*, Articles 27 and 28, pp. 9–10.
[31] *Ibid.*, Articles 20, 31, 32, 33, 34, and 35, pp. 10–12.
[32] Encina, *Liberemos a México*, p. 47. Encina also reported that the Party in

where a state committee had been established, the Party was usually confined to the capital city and a few other municipalities, with scattered cells elsewhere. For example, the Federal District Committee exercised control in 1954 not only over the capital and environs but also over some cells in the state of Mexico. The Coahuila State Committee governed only the Laguna region comprising parts of the states of Coahuila and Durango. The Tamaulipas Committee ruled Tampico, Nuevo Laredo, and Matamoros within the state as well as parts of neighboring San Luis Potosí. The Nuevo León Committee exercised jurisdiction only around Monterrey, and the Chiapas Committee only in the Soconusco area.[33] Conferences and conventions have not met regularly,[34] and power has not resided in fact where the statutes designate. Throughout the organization the executive bodies from the cell to the national level have dominated the so-called "superior organisms" such as the General Assembly or the Party Congress. Furthermore, the higher the level, the more strictly has control been exercised. The greatest freedom of discussion and action has been on the cell level, the least freedom on the national level.

Power has ordinarily resided in the small inner core of leaders who comprise the Political Committee, about which the statutes say almost nothing. Each member of the Political Committee, except for the secretary general, has had charge of a national committee responsible for one of the major activities of the Party: organization, women's affairs, finances, trade union activities, education, youth, rural workers' affairs, etc. The Central Committee, while not as powerful as the Political Committee, must not be discounted, consisting as it has of members of the latter and representatives from some of the states.

The top-level organization of the Party abandoned statutory regulations following the overturn of the entrenched Party leadership by the October 1959 meeting of the Central Committee. The Central Committee, except for some drastic changes in personnel, has been

---

Veracruz and Guanajuato was being reorganized and that "organizing committees" were at work in Yucatán, Zacatecas, and Chihuahua.

[33] Pérez, *Sobre Las Modificaciones a Los Estatutos*, p. 15.

[34] The Twelfth National Congress met in 1954, the Thirteenth in 1960.

left intact with twenty-six members and five alternates. The Political Committee, temporarily replaced by a three-man secretariat in October 1959, was restored by the Thirteenth Congress, in May 1960. The office of secretary general was also abolished, with the result that the Party now presents an appearance of having adopted the principle of collective leadership.[35]

Similar situations exist on state and municipal levels where the committees dominate party activities, but organization is weakened on these levels by a high turnover in personnel. Then, when party activity lags or when factionalism appears in a given state, the Central Committee assigns one of its members to work with the State Committee until the difficulties are overcome.[36] There is no evidence that the state organization (or the national) has elected secretariats as the statutes direct. The secretary general spoke of the necessity of creating a national secretariat in 1954, but apparently no action has been taken. The daily work of the state committees apparently is divided among their members, each of whom is chairman of a committee on the state level for one of the Party's major activities. The State Committee of Coahuila, reflecting its relatively prosperous status in 1957, had, in addition, furnished a president as top officer as well as a secretary general and seven secretaries.[37]

On the cell level, the term *General Assembly* does not seem to be used by the Party, despite its use in the statutes. Furthermore, many of the articles concerning the division and control of large cells must be inoperative, since there is no evidence that cells of this size exist. For the most part, cells amount to between five and ten members, several of whom are often inactive.[38] The small size of Communist cells, particularly those in business enterprises, accounts in part for the weakness of Communist influence in strikes or labor agitation. At best the Communists support rather than lead labor unrest. Cells appear best organized in the Federal District, and although there is

[35] "Leaders and Followers," in the first part of this chapter, has a fuller discussion of these changes.

[36] Encina, *Liberemos a México*, p. 54; *La Voz de México*, July 18, 1957.

[37] *La Voz de México*, June 18, 1957.

[38] The secretary general referred to this problem in his report to the Twelfth National Congress. Cf. Encina, *Liberemos a México*, pp. 55–56.

evidence of cells in other parts of the country, it appears that in some towns the only active cell members are the members of the Municipal Committees.

Certain Communist militants work alone outside any Party organization because they believe that, for one reason or another, they cannot afford to be identified with the PCM. These *aislados* (isolated members) are known only to top Party leaders.

PRINCIPLES, PROGRAMS, AND PROPAGANDA

In line with Party goals, PCM propaganda is not designed primarily to bring the Party to political power in Mexico, but rather to enhance the prestige of international Communism (the Sino-Soviet Bloc) in Mexico and to improve relations of all types between the Bloc and Mexico. Concurrently it aims at diminishing U.S. influence in Mexico and at undermining the amicable relations that exist between that country and the United States. It attempts to develop unity of action with non-Communist groups and organizations on issues that have broad popular support, such as opposition to Western-allied dictators, inflation, and war. And it also calls for rapid industrialization of the country, nationalization of natural resources, and unity in the field of organized labor on both the national and international levels.[39] Since 1958 PCM propaganda has become more militant and daring than it formerly was. This development, coupled with its more vigorous agitation in 1959, undoubtedly led to more stringent government regulation and suppression of Party activities and personnel. It seems as though the Party was seeking martyrs.[40]

For purposes of analysis, Communist propaganda may be divided into two general categories: that directed to specific target groups, and that designed to cut across the various groups. By and large, PCM propaganda concerns itself primarily with Mexican interests but occasionally becomes involved in non-Mexican international issues. In the latter case it attempts where possible to tie the inter-

[39] This program is not unique with the Communist Party of Mexico. See Subcommittee To Investigate the Administration of the Internal Security Act, *Communist Threat*, p. 142.

[40] Cf. the call in *La Voz de México*, May 1, 1960 for mass demonstration in behalf of the arrested railroad strikers.

national situation to Mexican developments of a similar nature. Some issues are transitory, some are of years' duration. On most occasions the Party organ, *La Voz de México,* broadly swipes at its enemies and defends its protégés. Frequently, however, it runs campaigns over a period of weeks or even months in behalf of a long-term Communist goal, using specific events as they arise as ammunition for its propaganda weapons. The evils and dangers of U.S. influence in Mexico constitute a major theme of Mexican Communism.[41] Having long accused the United States of designs on Latin American, and specifically Mexican, resources, *La Voz de México* in 1956 took advantage of the then bitter dispute over American shrimp boats' fishing within nine miles of the Mexican coast, an area claimed by Mexico as her territorial waters. The paper carried headlines that the United States was "ransacking" Mexican natural resources. Simultaneously attacks were levied against U.S.-owned business in Mexico such as Woolworth and Sears, Roebuck; U.S. farm employers of Mexican braceros; alleged U.S. cotton "dumping"; U.S. exploitation of non-renewable natural resources; and the "stranglehold" of the United States on Mexico's foreign trade.[42] North Americans in general were denounced for their racial prejudices, and the Autherine Lucy case, then much in the news, was cited on several occasions to highlight this charge. On less frequent occasions *La Voz* took scattered shots at the Mexican government and Mexican capitalists for cooperating with the oppressors. Another campaign was launched against the Mexican government's continuing drive for increased productivity in all sectors of the economy; articles strongly critical of the introduction of new methods and machinery in agriculture and industry charged that the Mexican government had been inspired by Yankee imperialists to carry out the program. Focusing attention on reports that unemployment had resulted from greater productivity per worker, the articles reached the conclusion that this constituted an-

[41] For one example, see the report of PCM's Political Committee in *La Voz de México,* March 7, 1956.

[42] *El Popular,* April 19, 1956 reported that on the previous day the PCM had distributed pamphlets in support of student agitation on the grounds that they were fighting to defend the national culture against Yankee imperialist penetration as exemplified in President Truman's Point IV program.

other example of capitalists conniving to exploit labor. Since mid-1959 the PCM has kept up a continuous barrage of propaganda directed toward the Mexican government for the release of agitators imprisoned in connection with the railway strike in the spring of that year.[43]

Attacks on the United States, or on sectors of its people, business groups, or government officials have not abated over the years. If anything they have become more shrill with the continued ineffectiveness and frustration of the Party's leadership. In February 1960 *La Voz de México* hailed the Latin American tour of President López Mateos as an opportunity to unify the Latin American struggle for freedom from the imperialist oppression of U.S. monopolists.[44] PCM propaganda has also called for the dissolution of the Joint Mexican-United States Defense Commission, a World War II creation, and of the Organization of American States. The former has been labeled a "means for the military submission of Mexico to the designs of the American warmongers" and the latter "an arm for the subjection by the United States of all the countries of Latin America." [45] Since 1961 the Party has bitterly attacked the Alliance for Progress as a plan to buy the government elites of Latin America and thereby perpetuate the colonial status of the area.

One of the most important Communist propaganda themes supports Soviet attempts to increase trade and cultural and political ties between Latin America and the Bloc. On some occasions Communist writers encourage the strengthening of ties with all countries, including the Bloc nations, while at other times they single out the Soviet Union, Red China, or the satellites for specific purposes. An editorial in *La Voz* on July 16, 1956 urged closer economic and cultural bonds with the USSR claiming their present weak status resulted from the objections of U.S. "imperialists" and those Mexicans allied with them. Several articles early in September 1956 eulogized Czechoslovakia and Red China, urging closer economic ties with the

---

[43] XX, "Actividades Comunistas en Iberoamérica," *Estudios sobre el Comunismo*, Año X, No. 35 (January–March, 1962), 77.

[44] *La Voz de México*, February 20, 1960.

[45] *Plataforma Electoral del Partido Comunista Mexicano* in *Problemas de México*, I, No. 4 (July 15, 1958), 310.

latter. This theme, repeated in November of that year, included a demand for the establishment of diplomatic relations with Red China.[46] The Party line has remained unchanged in this respect too. *La Voz de México* has continued to demand closer ties between Mexico and the Bloc in cultural, diplomatic, and economic matters.[47]

Another major theme of Communist propaganda has been the desirability of world peace. PCM writers have demanded world disarmament, the abolition of atomic weapons, the cessation of nuclear bomb tests. For Mexico, the Communists urge neutrality should a hot war develop.[48] Throughout, the PCM has parroted the Soviet peace line, and has attempted to capitalize on the basically pacifist sentiments of the Mexican populace. The Party has demanded that the United States cease its nuclear tests and has called for disarmament on Soviet terms. Superficially, it appears to have enjoyed some success in that one of its major specific goals has been to prevent the formation of any sort of military pact, alliance, or agreement between the United States and Mexico. The PCM has frequently taken credit for the failure of all such attempts and the cessation of talks leading thereto. Such an interpretation is unwarranted since neither the populace nor the government supports the Soviet "peace" program nor the local Communist attempts to gain signatures for their various "peace" petitions. The PCM was unable, moreover, to prevent the extension in the late 1950's of a multimillion-dollar credit from the United States to Mexico for the purchase of U.S. military equipment or the building of a satellite-tracking station at Guaymas.

U.S. "warmongering" and the U.S. military establishment are favorite targets of PCM propaganda. In June of 1956 *La Voz* featured photos of the atom spies, the Rosenbergs, calling them the "innocent victims of the . . . hatred and sinister madness of the [U.S.] military caste."[49] In September *La Voz* construed the visit of General Maxwell Taylor as an attempt to extend U.S. colonialism, and urged

---

[46] *La Voz de México*, November 22, 1956.

[47] *Ibid.*, February 20, 1960.

[48] *Ibid.*, November 22, 1956. The paper demanded, with regard to the Hungarian and Egyptian crises then current, that no soldiers leave Mexico to further "imperialist policies." Cf., *ibid.*, January 3, 1959.

[49] *Ibid.*, June 19, 1956.

all Mexicans to reject U.S. military aid or a pact. The following year the PCM protested a $10 million U.S. loan for military supplies. The *La Voz* writer accused the Ruiz Cortines Administration of intent to subordinate Mexican sovereignty to imperialistic American war-mongering, and called on all patriotic Mexicans to protest.[50]

On non-Mexican issues the PCM simply repeats Soviet propaganda. Reactions in *La Voz de México* on developments in Hungary and Egypt in 1956 are illustrative of this policy. The outbreak of the revolt in Hungary caught the PCM by surprise, and for several weeks events in that country were met with complete silence until Moscow's attitude could be determined. As the Soviet drift became clear by mid-November the Party finally gave unqualified support to Soviet suppression of the revolt, denouncing the rebels as fascists and agents of Yankee imperialism. On November 22, *La Voz*, in response to mounting virulent condemnation of the USSR's actions in Hungary, bannered: "STOP THE REACTIONARY AND ANTI-COMMUNIST HYSTERIA!" The supporting article called upon "progressive" Mexicans to fight for the dissemination of the "truth" about the situation in Hungary. Hoping to distract attention from the Hungarian revolt, *La Voz* played up the resurgence of "imperialism" with the attack of Israel, Britain, and France on Egypt, calling for the withdrawal of troops from Egypt and the retention of Suez by the Nasser Government.[51] On November 29, Diego Rivera defended Soviet intervention in Hungary as just and necessary, blaming the Catholic Church and the United States for the outbreak. The later execution of the Hungarian rebel leader Imre Nagy was called "an act of justice of the Hungarian people."[52]

Within the Latin American area the PCM was severely critical of the rightist dictatorships of Batista of Cuba and Trujillo of the Dominican Republic, and also of Stroessner in Paraguay and Somoza in Nicaragua. However, it adopted an equivocal position toward Perón of Argentina, usually determined by Perón's shifting attitude toward the Argentine Communists and his relations with the United States. For the frankly leftist but equally dictatorial regimes of

[50] *Ibid.*, July 25, 1956.
[51] *Ibid.*, November 22, 1956.
[52] *Ibid.*, July 26, 1958.

Jacobo Arbenz (1950–1954) and Fidel Castro of Cuba (1959–present), the PCM has had nothing but praise. As a result it greeted the overthrow of Batista in January 1959 as a "great triumph of the Cuban people,"[53] but bitterly condemned U.S. intervention in the overthrow of the Arbenz regime,[54] and the attempt against Castro in April, 1961.[55]

Domestic political issues loom large in Communist propaganda at all times, but particularly with the approach of national elections. Preparing for the presidential and congressional elections of July 1958, the PCM Central Committee as early as mid-1957 began to call for the repeal of that section of the federal electoral law which provides that a minimum of 75,000 members is necessary for a party to enter candidates on the ballot. The Central Committee also called for the mobilization of "Progressive and democratic forces" in a "Democratic Front for National Liberation" to participate in the campaigning, and claimed that it could not support Lombardo Toledano's plea for a broad coalition to accept the PRI candidate.[56] By February 1958 the PCM had nominated its own candidate[57] and drawn up its own electoral campaign program. Broad in scope, it demanded benefits for most sectors of society, including the military, but not large commercial and industrial sectors. However, even to these latter groups an indirect appeal was made by the promise of protection of the Mexican economy from foreign competition.

The PCM electoral program well summed up the principal domestic propaganda themes of the Party as repeatedly stressed in *La Voz*.[58] These themes may be paraphrased as follows: The primary cause of the sufferings of the Mexican people is the penetration and intervention of U.S. capitalist monopolies in the basic areas of the Mexican economy, and the submission and surrender to those mo-

[53] *Ibid.*, January 3, 1959.

[54] Encina, *Lib* . . . p. 47.

[55] *El Popular*, April 30, 1961.

[56] Dionisio Encina, *Posición del Partido Comunista Mexicano Frente á La Sucesión Presidencial* in *Problemas de México*, I, No. 4 (July 15, 1958), 273.

[57] *¡Una Política Y Un Candidato Que Sí Responden a Los Intereses del Pueblo!* in *Problemas de México*, I, No. 4 (July 15, 1958), 291–298.

[58] *Plataforma Electoral* in *Problemas de México*, I, No. 4 (July 15, 1958), 299–320.

nopolies by the procapitalist bourgeoisie in and out of the government. Imperialist enterprises control the vital sectors of the country's economy and impede its free and full development. The Mexican government pursues such a policy because it is made up fundamentally of elements of the reactionary bourgeoisie: great landholders, capitalists, and wealthy politicians.

The PCM claims: workers' salaries are insufficient to buy necessities, and great masses of unemployed are facing hunger and misery.[59] Prices are extraordinarily high and rising daily.[60] The rights of workers, rural and urban, are often violated. The right to organize and the right to strike are restricted; bourgeois intervention in the present unions severely limits the worker in the struggle for his rights. More than two million rural heads of families have no land. Those with land frequently lack credit and water, and are often forced to sell cheap to middlemen or to the Ejido Bank. The Indian masses, abandoned, illiterate, and diseased, live in unimagined misery, discriminated against socially, economically, and politically. Women and youths do not receive equal pay for equal work. Poor youths cannot get an education. Schools are lacking throughout the country, and higher learning is closed to the sons of rural and urban workers.

The right to vote is openly trampled on, the Party says. The freedoms of expression, thought, and assembly are reduced to a minimum and often nullified by the accusation of "social dissolution," by the arbitrary acts of public officials, and by the lack of proper means of expression by the workers.

The PCM proposes a number of moves to resolve these problems. To defend the economic and political independence of the nation, the Party insists on prohibiting the investment of foreign capital in the basic sectors of the economy and in all sectors where it would compete with national capital. The Party also advocates a special progressive tax on profits of foreign capital, proposes limits to foreign exploitation of national resources, and favors the concomitant de-

[59] *La Voz de México*, October 4, 1956 announced this topic as one of a series of talks to be given on October 6, 1956.

[60] This theme was attacked by J. E. Pérez in *La Voz de México*, January 3, 1959.

velopment of state enterprises. It would limit the amount of profit taken from the country, demand a high percentage of reinvestment, and immediately nationalize all public services, sulfur deposits, and other strategic resources. The Party also calls for the diversification of foreign commerce by opening trade without restrictions with all countries, especially with the Sino-Soviet camp, to break Mexico's dependence on the United States.

To democratize the political regime, the PCM would amend the electoral law to remove qualifications on political parties. It also calls for the establishment of a parliamentary regime or a division of powers, and respect for municipal freedom and civil rights. It demands the abolition of the crime of "social dissolution" and alliances between unions and political parties. In behalf of the urban working classes the PCM stands for an increase in salaries and pensions by at least 50 per cent, a forty-hour week, and the extension of unionization and social security to all workers. The Party insists that politicians keep out of union affairs and that they respect the right to strike. The Communists also demand that employers split with the State the cost of unemployment benefits, stop productivity campaigns, and give equal pay for equal work. These rights and privileges should be extended to public employees as well as to employees in private enterprise. Landless rural workers are entitled to land of their own at the cost of the large landholdings still in existence. Such lands should be in the form of cooperatives (*ejidos*) or collectives, as the farmers desire. They are entitled to easy credit terms, the cancellation of old debts, and guaranteed prices. They should also have the right to organize, free of government control.[61] The Party program ends with an extensive list of items in behalf of the general welfare. These include rent freezing, lower transport fares, increased budget allotment for education and less money for the military, abolition of compulsory military service but higher pay for military rank and file. In the field of education the PCM sponsors the nationalization of all primary and secondary schools, more scholarships for students

[61] The Communists proposed this identical program for the *campesinos* at the National Agrarian Congress of 1959. Cf. "Los comunistas defienden los intereses de los trabajadores del campo," *Problemas de la Paz y del Socialismo*, Año III, No. 3 (March 1960), 109.

of the lower classes, and more schools to combat adult illiteracy.[62]

PCM publications have not failed to support the Soviet position on every major international event, and within Mexico have attempted to apply Soviet historical, social, and economic interpretations to domestic events. The lack of propagandistic success bears a direct relationship to the failure of the Party not only in recruiting new members but in retaining the old. The blunt sectarianism, the lack of finesse or subtlety, the narrowness of view of Party positions, have eliminated all but a hard core of dedicated Communists, despite the fact that on many issues Communist and non-Communist Mexicans have much in common. Communist demands for world peace, disarmament, outlawing of atomic armaments, a ban on further nuclear test explosions, and peaceful coexistence accord with some of the deepest aspirations of the Mexican people and government officials. Campaigns in behalf of youth and students, women, labor, the *campesinos*, teachers, and the underprivileged in general should find a sympathetic audience from those who support revolutionary ideals. And the strident nationalism of the Communists ought to win them adherents from all walks of life. They do not, in large part because of the unrealistic, distorted, and exaggerated interpretation given to events by Party spokesmen. Their unqualified praise for the Soviet Union and all its works, their unrestrained criticism of the United States, their violent attacks on all political opponents in Mexico, their insistence on leading any reformist coalition or movement that they sponsor, and their uncompromising position on all issues have denied them the support of much of Mexico's dissatisfied and restless "left."

ACTIVITIES

The primary activities of the Mexican Communist Party consist of the holding of Party congresses, conferences, and meetings, electoral campaigning in state and federal political contests, agitation in

[62] There has been virtually no shift, except in details, in PCM propaganda and program from the time of Encina's *Report to the Plenum of the Central Committee* of the PCM in October 1949, through the report of the Political Committee, *El Partido Comunista y la Devaluación del Peso*, in 1954, through the *Plataforma Electoral* of 1958 (*Problemas de México*, I, No. 4 [July 1958], 299–320), to the resolutions of the Central Committee Plenum of December 1961.

behalf of announced goals, and publication of articles, speeches, and news reports, in part for the training and indoctrination of members and in part for propaganda purposes. Lesser activities include recruitment and organization of new members, training programs, and money raising.

It may be assumed that fund raising in the PCM as in every political party occupies a considerable amount of time in the thought and action of Party leaders. Obviously, the Party is not wealthy, but it does seem generally to have enough money on hand to carry out its essential publication activities. Party officials are also known to travel extensively through central and northern Mexico on Party business, either electoral or organizational. Many have also traveled to Bloc countries, but there is some evidence that these trips have been financed in part by the Soviet Union or Soviet-sponsored organizations.[63] Except for these "necessities," money appears to be chronically short. In a report to the plenum of the Central Committee in the fall of 1949, Encina complained of weak Party finances and at the Twelfth Congress in 1954 he again reported that the financial work of the Party was still deficient despite some recent improvements. He qualified this pessimistic situation by pointing out that the Party's "Economic Campaign" of 1952 to raise 200,000 pesos for the regularizing of the Party newspaper had been a complete success. He said that it was the first time the Party had fulfilled a program of this type 100 per cent.[64] During the past years Party finances have suffered drastic setbacks, as have all Party activities. When the police ousted the Party from its offices in 1958, it was reported that the rent had not been paid in six months,[65] and since the spring of 1959 the Party newspaper has appeared irregularly because of financial difficulties.

Party statutes devote a section of five articles to finances. They

[63] *La Voz de México*, July 20, 1957 reported that the World Festival Fund, heavily subscribed to by officially sponsored member groups in the USSR and satellite countries, assumed much of the financial burden of sending Mexican delegates to the Sixth World Festival of Youth and Students held in Moscow that summer.

[64] Encina, *Liberemos a México*, pp. 46–50.

[65] *El Universal*, August 24, 1958, p. 1.

state that Party funds are made up of dues from members, income from the masses, gifts from sympathizers, and income which other activities may provide. Membership dues are set up on a monthly quota system ranging from 25 centavos for a member earning up to 100 pesos, to 20 pesos for those earning 901 to 1,000 pesos. Members earning over 1,000 pesos monthly have their quotas fixed by the cell to which they belong. Farmers pay, either monthly or at harvest time, the minimum quota, which, however, may be increased by the state or regional organization. Housewives and nonworking women also pay the minimum. Income from dues is divided four ways, among the cell, the Municipal Committee, the State Committee, and the Central Committee. The first two receive 20 per cent each, the last two 30 per cent each. The distribution of other income is determined by the Central Committee.[66]

There is little specific information available on the actual sources of PCM income but it is unlikely that much is collected by dues; probably not more than a few pesos trickle in by this means. The Party seemingly derives some income from social functions and raffles which are held from time to time, usually for specific purposes. In addition to limited aid received from the Soviet Union or Bloc organizations, the Party receives the bulk of its funds from wealthy members or patrons such as Xavier Guerrero and D. A. Siqueiros.[67] Probably, the Party also receives financial assistance through its labor wing, the UCSE, since such farm organizations are the recipients of considerable government subsidies and loans.[68]

Recruitment, integration, and training of new members are of continuing concern to Party leaders and members,[69] but there is little

[66] *Estatutos del Partido Comunista Mexicano*, pp. 20–21.

[67] Encina, *Liberemos a México*, p. 50, reported that the fundamental defect in Party finances continued to be lack of support by the members and the necessity of relying on sporadic gifts of friends of the Party and some organizations, especially those of the *campesino*, and on special campaigns. See also the extensive financial report rendered in 1962 by Camilo Chávez, *Urge un Cambio Radical en la Situación Económica del Partido*.

[68] See Chapter IV on organized labor (UCSE) and Chapter V on international Communism.

[69] Encina, *Liberemos a México*, pp. 48–49, said: "Recruitment is the fundamental task in the strengthening of the Party." He also complained that one of

evidence of well-planned, sustained programs. Annual recruitment plans, generally so overly ambitious as to prove impossible and therefore discouraging, have been announced for several years by the PCM high command. Implementation has never matched plans and proposals, with the result that not only has there been no growth in recent years but, on the contrary, decline. Sporadic attempts to screen and integrate new members have been made without much success, and occasional indoctrination programs have been attempted at several levels of Party leaders and members, apparently without measurable results. The first course of studies in a Party school were underway at least by 1954, but there is no evidence of a regular program. A series of training lectures were held for cadres of the Federal District in 1956, following the Twentieth Congress of the CPSU, to study the results of that Congress.[70] The lectures were later published in *La Voz de México* for the benefit of provincial leaders and the rank and file. A few examples may be noted:

1) J. E. Valdez, "The Principle of Collective Leadership: The Role of the Masses and of Personality in History," *La Voz de México*, June 16–22, 1956.

2) A. Martínez Verdugo, "Mexico and the Breakdown of the Imperialist Colonial System," *La Voz de México*, July 2–5, 1956.

3) Anon., "On the Suppression of the Cult of the Personality and Its Consequences," *La Voz de México*, July 7, 1956.

The Party also convened, in November 1956, the First Women's National Conference of the Mexican Communist Party. Presided over by Paula Medrano de Encina, wife of the Party's secretary general, the Conference enjoyed no more success than that called by Lombardo Toledano the previous June. It formulated a five-point program

---

the greatest difficulties in the Party was the low political level not only of the rank and file but of the cadres themselves, and a "dangerous underestimation of the study of theory and politics."

[70] A Party regional conference in Jalisco heard a report on a planned recruitment program aimed at workers, peasants, and youth, and voted to convene statewide meetings of sugar workers and women's groups in order to recruit. The conference also discussed the Twentieth Congress of the Communist Party of the Soviet Union and the means by which the PCM might apply the themes of the Congress. Cf. *La Voz de México*, September 12, 1956.

calling for the improvement in the status of Mexican women,[71] but there is no evidence that it resulted in successful recruitment of women into the Party or that it was followed up by a campaign or succeeding conference to implement its goals. Unquestionably a number of Party leaders have acquired some training and indoctrination by visits and trips to the Bloc countries. The worth of this Soviet program is difficult to evaluate, but apparently little of what was learned has trickled down to the rank-and-file members.

The ineffectiveness of these various programs is attested by the leaders' repeated complaints of weaknesses in the Party, attributable in large part to their failures in these activities. In 1949 Encina reported to the Party's Central Committee that cadre indoctrination was weak and that state leaders (cadres) were not carrying out the Central Committee program; that the Party was neither growing nor leading the struggle of the masses; that Party finances were deteriorating and the Party newspaper failing; and that women and youth groups had not been organized within the Party. Encina's 1954 report to the Twelfth Party Congress began in a more optimistic vein, noting some improvements on each of the above points. Nowhere, however, did he give the impression that the Party was flourishing. Party finances were still termed "deficient," the number of women Communists "very small," and the cadres little interested in the Party's doctrinal publication, *Teoría*.[72] Two years later in an autocritical document published in January 1956, the Federal District Committee, the most important of the subnational sections of the Party, complained that many of its cells were inactive; that the Party was stagnant; that some of the Federal District leaders held a defeatist attitude; and that activity, aggressiveness, and enthusiasm of the Party were almost completely paralyzed. A year later, with conditions unchanged, the Federal District organization revolted against the Party's national leadership, and eventually ousted Encina and his followers.

[71] *La Voz de México*, November 10, 1956.
[72] Encina, *Liberemos a México*, pp. 50–52. See also Chávez, *Urge un Cambio Radical*, p. 11, and Edelmiro Maldonado L., *Informe al V Pleno del Comité Central sobre el Tercer Punto del Orden del Día (–13 Dic.—61)*, p. 8.

Communist agitation for a number of years has been carried out
only sporadically, in part because of the ineffectiveness of Party
leadership and in part because of increased government vigilance and
pressure. Although the Party took credit for mobilizing public opinion against U.S. assistance to the Castillo Armas rebels in Guatemala
in June 1954, it had to admit its utter failure to arouse the people
against the last devaluation of the peso.[73] A simple explanation is that
the Communists were not needed in the first instance to anger Mexicans at what they believed to be unwarranted intervention by the
United States in a neighboring country, and the Communists went un-
heeded in the second instance because of basic popular loyalty to the
regime. Communist-inspired or Communist-led labor strikes have
been rare for about ten years. Even with relation to student disturbances since 1956, and the strikes of 1958–1959, PCM activity must
be characterized as one of participation rather than of leadership. At
the present time it is in no position to mobilize more than one or two
hundred people in serious protests and street demonstrations. Typical
of Communist agitation was the protest meeting called by the PCM
Municipal Committee of Torreón in the summer of 1956 to demand
elimination of speculation in the town market before the old market
was torn down and replaced by a new one under public ownership.[74]
There is no evidence that the authorities were moved to action. Agitators also spread through the crowds at Acapulco in February 1959
on the occasion of the visit of President Eisenhower with President
López Mateos. They tried to distribute pamphlets denouncing the
visit as a U.S. attempt to enslave Mexico. The pamphlets also repeated long-standing Communist slogans condemning any sort of
U.S.-Mexican military agreement or the intrusion of U.S. capital into
Mexican oil development. The agitators had no effect on the meeting
of the presidents. The vast majority of the people at Acapulco, in holi-
day mood, loudly welcomed the visiting U.S. President; few of the
celebrants even saw the pamphlets or were aware of anti-U.S. sentiment among them.

Electoral campaigns afford the Communists better opportunities to
place their ideas and program before the populace than do their agi-

[73] *Ibid.*, p. 49.
[74] *La Voz de México*, September 19, 1956.

tation tactics. Election time, particularly a presidential year, focuses Mexican attention for many months on political issues and organizations. The Communists attempt to capitalize on the national pastime, but for many years have gained for themselves little but contempt and ridicule for their inept tactics. Because the Party lacks the required legal minimum of 75,000 bona fide members, its candidates for public office cannot appear on the ballot. They may, however, announce their candidacy and appeal for write-in votes. None have been successful for over ten years. Party leaders do not expect victory, simply an opportunity to gain attention. Granting the latter as their true motivation, it must be conceded that here they have enjoyed a degree of success. Not only is some attention devoted to their speeches and activities but also to their protests over election frauds when their poor showings are publicly announced by the electoral courts. Such protests were made by Arturo Orona, PCM candidate for governor of Coahuila in 1957, and by Ramón Danzós Palomino, PCM candidate for governor of Sonora in 1961.[75] More publicity was gained in the 1958 presidential elections, particularly with the announcement in February that the PCM candidate was seventy-four-year-old Miguel Mendoza López, who described himself as a socialist and a practicing Catholic. Some observers felt that Mendoza's record as a revolutionary, a Catholic, and a socialist might pull some liberal votes, and that a write-in of 10,000 to 25,000 votes might be considered a "moral victory" of sorts.[76] His campaign could hardly be called vigorous. He spent most of his time in Mexico City, and made a two-week tour of the northeastern states of Coahuila, Nuevo León, and Tamaulipas, delivering about eight speeches in as many towns. He also made a tour of about a week in the western states of Jalisco and Michoacán. The closing speech of his campaign was delivered in the Plaza St. Dominic in Mexico City before about 400 persons.[77] Miguel Mendoza López polled well under 10,000 write-in votes in the

[75] *Ibid.*, August 10, 1958 and July 26, 1961. Because PCM members were allegedly excluded from the voting areas, the Party called on its members at the last minute to boycott the election.

[76] *New York Times*, February 28, 1958, p. 21; *El Universal*, February 16, 1958, pp. 1 and 10.

[77] *El Universal*, March 8, 1958, p. 16; March 12, 1958, p. 6; March 22, 1958, p. 7; April 9, 1958, p. 11; and June 30, 1958, p. 7.

July election and less than 500 in the Federal District. Nonetheless, with its own candidate the Party gained more publicity in 1958 than it had received in 1952 when it tagged along in support of the candidacy of Vicente Lombardo Toledano.

Propaganda production and dissemination constitute the PCM's most vital activities. Foremost among its publications ranks *La Voz de México*, the Party's official organ, founded in 1924 and surviving to the present with a somewhat checkered career. The Party has also published various specialized journals on Communist theory, pamphlets and bulletins on Party meetings, and speeches and leaflets, placards and posters on specific issues. It has also publicized its program and position by word-of-mouth campaigns, speeches, and demonstrations. On occasion Party members have been successful in having their articles on current issues accepted in non-Communist journals.

In the early 1950's *La Voz de México*, scheduled as a weekly, appeared irregularly, but from February 1952 to September 1955 it more often than not met its weekly publication deadlines. This success was followed by the installment of new equipment in the Party print shop and the conversion of the paper to a daily by the fall of 1955. Though initially successful, *La Voz* began to experience increasingly difficult problems. Membership interest could not be sustained on a daily basis with the same intensity as with a weekly. Sales, never sufficiently high to meet the costs of the men and machinery, began to lag. Distribution was difficult and expensive, and mutual recrimination flowed back and forth between Party members and the officials of the paper and print shop. One side condemned the paper as dull and uninteresting, while the paper's editors complained of lack of cooperation and assistance on the part of the membership and the withholding of subscription money by solicitors and local leaders. Despite long hesitation and great reluctance, the Political Committee, the Party's highest council, finally decided to face the thoroughly disagreeable task of reconverting to a weekly.[78] The last daily issue appeared October 16, and the first weekly issue on November 10,

[78] *La Voz de México*, October 16, 1957.

1957. For several weeks the paper appeared generally on schedule, but it experienced difficulties on and off through 1958. For example, from August 10, 1958 to January 3, 1959, the paper appeared on the average of every two weeks. Scheduling improved in 1959 until April, when the paper apparently stopped publication, because of police raids as well as financial troubles. From early to mid-1960 only three issues were published, but from July 1, 1960 to February 3, 1962, inclusive, twenty-eight issues appeared, an average of one every three weeks.

Whether weekly or daily, *La Voz* has been an unimpressive paper. Consisting ordinarily of four to six pages, it is sometimes expanded to include the publication of special reports and speeches of local or foreign Communist meetings. Tabloid in format as a daily (12 in. by 16 in.), it converted to normal newspaper size as a weekly and then reverted to tabloid (16 in. by 24 in.), but the changes did not improve either the presentation of the news or the style. As a rule it has carried no advertising and no feature articles. Its contents have been devoted strictly to Party affairs and interests.

The Central Committee of the Party has long published a theoretical journal of its own for the indoctrination of cadres and other members. *Teoría* fulfilled this function until the mid-1950's, but in February 1957, there appeared the first issue of a new monthly, *Liberación*, subtitled as the organ of the CC (Central Committee) of the Mexican Communist Party. This first issue contained an editorial, two articles by PCM leaders, one by a Russian, and a report on the Eighth Congress of the Italian Communist Party. *Liberación* was replaced in 1960 with *Revista Teórica*, which in turn was replaced with *Nueva Época* in 1962. For the general elections of 1958, both the National Directorate and the Federal District Committee began new publications in the spring of 1958. The former published the first issue of the *Boletín Nacional de la Campaña Económica* in April, and the latter the first issue of its *Vida del Partido* in March. Both were short-lived.

The Party's bookstore and publishing house, Fondo de Cultura Popular A.C., publishes a monthly bibliographical bulletin, *Cultura Popular*, listing books both foreign and domestic that are available in the shop. Its listings are primarily of foreign authorship and origin translated into Spanish. Fondo advertising also lists three other book-shops in Mexico City (La Mercantil, Exposiciones Editoriales, and Librería del Economista), and one each in Guadalajara and Mon-terrey (Librería y Regalos and Exposiciones Culturales) where its listings may be obtained.

The Mexican Worker-Peasant Party (Partido Obrero-Campesino Mexicano—POCM)

LEADERS AND FOLLOWERS

The great purges of the PCM which began in 1940 resulted in a floating population of Marxist and Soviet-oriented intellectuals and working-class people without party affiliations. By the mid-1940's a number of these had coalesced to form the Unified Socialist Action (Acción Socialista Unificada). This group was invited by Lombardo Toledano to participate in his round-table discussions in 1947 which looked to the creation of a new political party in Mexico. The ASU, however, proved to be something of a thorn in the meetings since its delegates rejected Lombardo's concept of a People's Party embracing nationalist bourgeois elements and favored a working-class party. As a consequence, the ASU did not merge with the People's Party when the latter was founded in 1948 but continued to seek unity of "authentic" Marxists.[79]

A second group of PCM expellees organized, in April 1948, a political group called the Movimiento de Reivindicación del Partido Comunista. Shortly thereafter leaders of the Movimiento and the ASU began to hold talks, and these in turn resulted in a pact between them in September of 1948. The pact pledged a joint struggle in behalf of the economic betterment of the lower classes; nationalization of banking; the formation of an anti-imperialist front to oppose the Truman Doctrine, the Rio Pact, and the Marshall Plan; cultural exchange between Mexico and the USSR; and the independence of Puerto Rico. Despite PCM charges of Trotskyism among leaders of the two groups, they pledged themselves to fight the "criminal" activities of counter-revolutionary Trotskyism. Continued cooperation between the ASU and the Movimiento during the next year and a half

[79] *Noviembre*, July 1, 1953.

led to the Congress of Marxist Unity that created the POCM in July 1950.[80] The POCM merged with the PPS in June 1963.

The POCM has never claimed a numerous following and has never applied for registration to the Mexican government as a recognized political party. Peak membership was reached about 1955 or 1956 when the Party could count between 1,000 and 1,500 members. By mid-1962 the Party had at most 1,000 rank and file, of whom perhaps 500 were active. Only 24 members attended the Third National Convention in Morelia in 1960. Statistics on the POCM are even more scarce than on the PCM. A report by Secretary General Alberto Lumbreras to the First National Convention, however, throws some light on the Party composition. He stated that by 1953 POCM cells were organized in thirteen states. Although delegates to the Congress came only from the Federal District, Nuevo León, and five other states, they represented 68 per cent of the cells. He further reported that the urban proletariat constituted almost 60 per cent of the Party membership, peasants almost 20 per cent, and teachers and professional people almost 13 per cent.[81]

Alberto Lumbreras, formerly of the Movimiento de Reivindicación, was POCM secretary general from its founding until 1960, when he was succeeded by Carlos Sánchez Cárdenas. A somewhat shadowy figure, Lumbreras was superseded in fact by Valentín Campa, the recognized head of the Party until March 1960. Campa, prior to 1940, had been second-in-command to Hernán Laborde of the Communist Party until their expulsion. When the POCM was founded, however, Campa was serving what proved to be a three-year jail term for labor agitation and misuse of railway union funds. Nonetheless he was elected to the Party's Executive Committee, the source of power, and on occasion has been called the president of the Party. Upon his release early in 1953 he assumed direction of Party affairs, although his official functions were supervision and direction of Party activities in the field of labor affairs and the direction of the Party newspaper, *Noviembre*. His common-law wife Consuelo Uranga has headed a small group of women members, but they have never formed a women's organization similar to the UDMM of the women members

[80] *Ibid.*, September 16, 1948 and June 22, 1950.
[81] *Ibid.*, November 16, 1953.

of the Communist Party. Until 1959 there had been little or no friction among Party leaders and factions have not appeared. Only the failure of the railroad strike in 1959, in which Campa was deeply involved, and the plan to merge with the PCM in 1960 led to Party disputes and resignations. The POCM National Committee published a list of errors in the Party's conduct in the railroad strike of 1959. Indirectly the finger of criticism was pointed at Valentín Campa. Basically, said the Executive Committee, the strike was ill-planned, ill-organized, launched precipitately, and conducted rigidly without imagination.[82] For many months this conflict simmered within Party circles, but emerged in public with the disclosure of the actions of the Party's Third National Convention in March 1960. Campa was expelled from the Executive Committee and the case turned over to the Central Control Committee for disciplinary consideration. Expelled from the POCM, he joined the PCM, but was arrested in mid-May. Among the six members elected to the new directive committee were Miguel Aroche Parra and Alberto Lumbreras, both serving terms in the Federal Penitentiary in the Federal District; Carlos Sánchez Cárdenas, one of the Party founders; and Consuelo Uranga, Campa's wife.[83] The Party was further weakened by later defections to the PCM, including that of Uranga, and the collapse of negotiations for unity by September 1960.

The long period of stability and rigidity within the Party leadership seemingly prevented few if any younger leaders from receiving needed experience in the direction of national Party affairs. Miguel Aroche, secretary of organization, wrote in 1953 that one of the gravest needs of the Party was professional leaders, i.e., full-time paid leaders.[84] There is nothing to indicate that need has ever been fulfilled either on the national or lower levels in the Party. Campa, himself, was often hard pressed for funds, especially since his ousting from the railway union in 1949 deprived him not only of a job but also of his pension rights. Perhaps it is this sacrifice of economic security that Party leadership entails that has also contributed to the lack of rising younger leaders.

[82] *El Popular*, September 8, 1959.
[83] *Excelsior*, March 25, 1960, p. 21.
[84] *Noviembre*, August 4, 1953.

The Socialist Youth of Mexico, the youth wing of the POCM, was formally organized in 1953 following a call by Party leaders for a national youth organization unattached to any political party.[85] The JSM, however, has always been identified as a POCM appendage. An ambitious program, including sports, theater, radio, and music activities, was planned but did not materialize. Neither did the JSM contribute substantially to the "fight for peace," improved educational and health facilities, or the "independence" of Mexico from foreign economic domination, its stated goals. A few clubs were formed in areas where Party members were to be found, and a group of JSM students at the National University made up part of the membership of the ephemeral Young People's Anti-Imperialist Front formed in 1954 to support the Arbenz government in Guatemala against alleged attacks on it by the United Fruit Company and the government of the United States.[86] The JSM was under the general supervision of a member of the POCM Executive Committee but elected its own officers. The secretary general in 1954 was Valentina Campa,[87] daughter of the Party's president, Valentín Campa. In August 1958 Valentina and her sister Juana were among the leaders of a student group of agitators at the National Polytechnic Institute (IPN). They raided the office of the secretary general, forcing him to flee. Although the officers of the National Federation of Technical Students (FNET), the student organization at the IPN, denounced the seizure and called a general meeting of the student body, the agitators continued to occupy the offices for several days.[88] On the whole, however, the JSM has been ineffective in both propaganda and agitation.

ORGANIZATION

Many similarities are strikingly evident between the organizational structures of the orthodox Communist Party and the splinter Communist Party, the POCM. Although the latter spells out in much greater detail the meaning of its principle of organization, that principle is still "democratic centralism," as it is in the PCM, and the

[85] *Ibid.*, June 16, 1953.
[86] *Ibid.*, June 11, 1954 and June 21, 1954.
[87] *Ibid.*, June 26, 1954.
[88] *El Universal*, August 28, 1958, p. 1, and August 29, 1958, p. 1.

basic ingredients are identical: strict party discipline and absolute majority rule, election of party organs from below, obligation of governing bodies to report periodically to party meetings, and authority of higher party organs over lower level groups.[89]

The basic unit of the Party is the cell, consisting of at least three members, and organized either by place of work or residence. Cells, scheduled to meet once a week, are responsible for carrying out the Party program, while daily tasks are committed to an elected Directive Committee, the size of which depends on the size of the cell. Cells of many members in large business enterprises may be divided into groups by departments or shifts. Each group has its own secretary or Directive Committee and meets separately once a week; the whole cell in such cases meets monthly. However, there is no evidence that such groups and cells have ever been organized. In enterprises which have work centers in various parts of the country, as many cells as possible are to be formed. These cells may meet in local, regional, or national conferences, together with isolated members, on the call of the sectional, regional, or national committees involved.[90] In fact, however, there is no record of such conferences of cells on any level.

Immediately superior to the cells are the sectional conventions and committees which correspond to the municipal level of the PCM and PPS. Sectional conventions are to meet every six months. The regional conventions and committees, corresponding to the state levels of the other parties, are superior to the sectional. Regional conventions are to meet yearly. Both sectional and regional conventions elect their committees, the size of which is determined by individual circumstances in each case. Each committee names a secretariat from among its members to carry out the daily tasks of the party.[91]

The highest authority in the POCM is the National Convention, made up of delegates representing at least a majority of the cells. Scheduled to meet every three years, the National Convention is the sole organ with powers to modify the Declaration of Principles, the Program, and the Statutes. It also lays down the general Party line, resolves problems of organization and discipline in final instance,

[89] *Declaración de Principios, Programa, Estatutos*, pp. 47–48.
[90] *Ibid.*, pp. 48–50.
[91] *Ibid.*, pp. 52–53.

and examines the reports of the National Committee and the Central Control Committee. The National Convention also elects the National Committee which directs Party business between conventions. The National Committee, scheduled to meet every four months, has the specific duties of seeing to the fulfillment of the Program, representing the Party in meetings with other organizations, and managing Party finances. The National Committee also elects from its members the Executive Committee and the Central Control Committee. The latter has charge of internal discipline, protects the Party from hostile external infiltration, and reviews the accounts of the Executive Committee and the Party's periodical publications. The Executive Committee, scheduled for weekly meetings, appoints the editors of the Party's periodicals and elects from its members a secretariat charged with carrying out the Party's day-to-day business.[92]

With its small membership and concentration in Mexico City, the only regional organization of any importance within the POCM is the Region of the Valley of Mexico, centering in the Federal District. Isolated cells and several scattered sectional organizations have been organized in a few railroad centers, such as Monterrey, Veracruz, Nuevo Laredo, Jalapa, and Acapulco, where the Party has kept its followers.[93] As with the PPS and PCM, the actual power structure bears little resemblance to the theoretical organization provided by the statutes. The National Committee exercises little power.[94] Made up of the members of the Executive Committee resident in the Federal District and delegates from different parts of the country, it has proven to be an unwieldy group. Instead of meeting thrice yearly, it averages between one and two meetings per year. Real power consequently rests with the Executive Committee, whose membership changed but slightly between 1950, the year the Party was founded, and 1960. The first two meetings of the National Convention proved to be rather perfunctory affairs that confirmed in power the current national leaders and approved their policies. The third meeting

[92] *Ibid.*, pp. 50–51.
[93] For references to these organizations see *Noviembre*, November 13, 1954; August 4, 1953; and August 16, 1953.
[94] In reports of its activities the National Committee is frequently called the Central Committee, the analogous organ of the PCM.

(March 6–9, 1960) had far-reaching consequences for the Party in that it overturned the Party leadership and replaced the office of secretary general with a committee of six, thereby introducing the theory, and perhaps the practice, of collective leadership into the Party.[95]

PRINCIPLES, PROGRAMS, AND PROPAGANDA

The theme of the POCM, officially adopted in the Party statutes, indicates the Party's general goal: "Through the Mexican Revolution, to Socialism." Furthermore, the opening sentence of the Party's official Declaration of Principles states that its every activity "is founded on the scientific certitude of the general and definitive crisis of the Capitalistic system, of its necessary substitution by the socialist regime, and of the possibility of accelerating that substitution by means of a struggle based upon the popular masses, under the direction of the proletariat."[96] There next follows a résumé of Marx's interpretation of the history, development, and final destruction of capitalism, the rise of the proletariat, and the construction of a socialist society. But, says the Declaration, the socialist regime is only the first phase of the Communist society. This process is already well under way in Europe and Asia, as witness the creation of socialist regimes in the USSR, China, and the "democratic republics" of eastern Europe. Final victory will not be won without further struggles for "Yankee imperialists" are marshalling reactionary and imperialist forces all over the earth and using military measures to defeat nationalist revolutions in colonial countries, to suppress workers trying to improve their standards of living, and to destroy the USSR and "popular democracy" in China and Europe. To counter this aggressive capitalism the Soviet Union has undertaken a campaign for peace, democracy, peaceful coexistence, self-determination for subject peoples, reduction of armaments, overthrow of tyranny, and constant improvement in the well-being of the working masses.[97]

Mexico, continues the Declaration, as an integral part of the world process in the development of human societies, has been transformed

[95] *Excelsior*, March 25, 1960, p. 21.
[96] *Declaración de Principios*, p. 3.
[97] *Ibid.*, pp. 3–6.

from a primitive communism to modern capitalism, having passed through periods of slavery and feudalism. Just as certainly, socialism will be substituted for the current regime, but capitalism will not fall of its own internal contradictions in Mexico. Socialism will come principally as the fruit of the Mexican Revolution, from the maturity and political training of the proletariat, from their organization and revolutionary struggle.

Before this socialism may be attained, however, Mexico must achieve complete national independence and liquidate feudal remnants; independence can be achieved only by linking its struggle with those of other oppressed peoples in the world, and by obtaining the aid of the international working class and the "democratic camp" against the imperialistic monopolists. With this help China achieved her goals; without it Iran failed. Mexico must take this road, according to the Declaration, and the Mexican people must group themselves around their working class. For the working class to succeed in its mission as vanguard, it must have the guidance of a proletarian revolutionary party. The task of the POCM is to overcome the present division of the Mexican Communist movement and give unity to Communism and the working class.[98] To achieve this unity, POCM leaders have made clear on many occasions that they are willing to submerge their Party within the PCM, provided the latter accept them en masse. To mid-1962 the PCM was unwilling to unite on these terms because it desires to exclude some POCM leaders and members. However, by mid-1960 some POCM leaders were accepting the PCM offer, now interpreted broadly by the latter's new leaders to include even Valentín Campa.

Based upon the above set of principles, the POCM has drawn up a seven-point program that embodies their principal immediate objectives. The first, the attainment of "national independence," assumes that Mexico is dominated by the United States, if not politically, then economically and culturally. "Yankee imperialism is our principal enemy" states the Program of the Party, and the means to overcome it lie first in the creation of an "Anti-Imperialist Democratic Front" consisting of "workers, farmers, the industrial and agrarian bour-

[98] *Ibid.*, pp. 6–8.

geoisie not associated with imperialism, the urban petty bourgeoisie, and democratic intellectuals and professionals." The "Front," once established, should then fight for the nationalization of: Yankee mining companies, all metal smelting and refining plants, the extraction and distribution of sulfur, electrical industry, and all air lines, communications, and public services in the hands of foreign capital enterprises. The Party's second objective is to remove political power from the hands of those persons allegedly allied with U.S. imperialists: "the financial oligarchy, the bureaucratic bourgeoisie, the reactionary upper clergy, and the feudal remnants." They are to be replaced by those groups which are to compose the Anti-Imperialist Democratic Front. Thirdly the POCM calls for the defense of the national economy from foreign interference and competition. Specifically, the Program demands the abolition of further foreign investments, the rejection of foreign loans, and severe curtailment of foreign enterprises already established. Furthermore, it advocates government control of foreign exchange and commerce and the nationalization of banks to eliminate importation of all items but basic necessities for the development of the economy, to obtain the best prices possible on the sale of oil abroad, and to expand the economy. The Program also seeks an indefinite moratorium on present loans, abolition of indirect taxes, and heavy progressive taxes on foreign and mixed enterprises. The fourth Party objective, "the liquidation of latifundism," includes not only the destruction of the remaining large agrarian properties but also assistance to the *campesinos*, especially the Indians. State aid is sought in the form of technical assistance to increase production through better fertilizers, seed, and insecticides and in the providing of increased credit, credit facilities, and price guarantees. Special Indian aid proposed includes more land and water for the villages, protection against middlemen who buy Indian products, cultural development, enjoyment of political and social rights, and special government administrative machinery to supplement the Program.

Like all opposition parties in Mexico, the POCM constantly inveighs against the lack of democracy because of the political manipulations of the official party, the PRI. The POCM calls for proportional representation, municipal government for the Federal District, and the establishment of municipal freedom as the Constitution provides. This fifth objective also demands equal rights for women and greater benefits for infants, children, and youths, including lowering the voting age to eighteen. Lamenting the poor standards of living throughout Mexico, the Program next insists upon greater benefits for the working class in the form of higher wages and salaries, price controls, a forty-two-hour work week, improvement and extension of social security, better living quarters. The Party also demands the divorce of labor from government, the inclusion of bank employees and civil servants under the general labor law, and respect for the right to strike, as guaranteed in the Constitution.[99]

To implement the above six objectives, the POCM proposes the creation of a great party of the working class. In effect, this seventh and last objective of the Program is a plea to the PCM (named directly) for unity and acceptance:

Communist unity can be attained if the leaders of the PCM cast aside the prejudicial method of branding the POCM and its affiliates with every kind of calumnious adjective, totally unfounded, and accept the necessity of common action between both organizations, each one of them weak in isolation but capable of strengthening and developing the Communist movement rapidly if they coordinate their activities, and, later, unite in organic form.[100]

The Party organ, *Noviembre*, has applied this line without variation. It has been insistent in its call for Marxist unity, the formation of a great revolutionary "Party of the Working Class" to liberate Mexico from Yankee imperialism and to liquidate the remnants of feudal and reactionary forces within the country. These latter are identified as the holders of large properties and those bankers, industrialists, and merchants who are associated with foreign capital.[101] In bidding for unity, *Noviembre* has also denied the repeated PCM charge that the POCM is Trotskyist; in 1954 the paper bitterly attacked the friends of Trotsky's widow, accusing them of receiving

[99] *Ibid.*, pp. 9–40.
[100] *Ibid.*, p. 41. Cf. also *Carta del Partido Obrero—Campesino Mexicano al Partido Comunista: Proposiciones para la unidad orgánica o la realización del Frente Único.*
[101] *Noviembre*, Issue No. 1, September 16, 1948.

money from Washington and Wall Street to infiltrate the workers'
movement in Mexico.[102]

The Third National Convention in 1960 did not add a single new
concept to the Program. Except for specific complaints, such as one
against government imprisonment of the 1959 railway strikers, and
for specific demands, such as aid for Castro's Cuba, the themes discussed and the resolutions passed have a familiar ring. As always, the
need for unity of action among Communist groups and the need for
eventual unity in organization were the themes most strongly
stressed.[103]

ACTIVITIES

The activities of the POCM are broadly similar to those of the
other two parties, but some vary considerably in emphasis. Fund
raising and dissemination of propaganda materials seem to occupy
proportionately less time among POCM members than among those
of the PPS and PCM. Believing in "direct action" techniques, the
POCM, small and weak though it is, joins enthusiastically in labor
and political disturbances wherever they appear. It is unsparing in
its criticism of the government and the official Party, at times in a
more extremist manner than is the PCM. On the other hand, the
POCM is similar to the PPS and PCM in its interest in elections and
the opportunities they afford for agitation and propaganda, and also
in its failure to capitalize upon or create opportunities for building
strength from the grass roots.

The statutes of POCM provide that new members pay an entrance
fee of one peso to the National Committee, in return for which they
receive their credentials. Credentials are renewed in January of each
year, at which time all members are to pay their dues. The quota for
dues is proportionate to a member's income, ordinarily 1 per cent
of his monthly wage. In special cases the cell may increase or de-
crease the percentage. The quota for rural workers is set by the cell,
which is instructed to consider the economic condition of each member. The income from dues is divided among the various Party levels,

[102] *Noviembre*, February 16, 1954.
[103] *Excelsior*, March 25, 1960, p. 21. See also *Noviembre*, October 1960, for
resolutions of the XVI Plenum of the National Committee.

30 per cent going each to the cell and the National Committee and 20 per cent each going to the sectional and regional committees. If sectional and/or regional committees are not organized, their respective amounts are divided between the cell and National Committee as the latter provides. The statutes also encourage fund raising through special grants by members or friends of the Party and by means of social functions.[104] It appears that in practice regular dues contribute insignificantly to the upkeep of the Party. A number of Party leaders receive little or no pay, contributing their time and often their money to Party activities. Valentín Campa was especially anxious to get reinstated in the railroad workers' union to qualify for his pension, part of which at least he planned to use to support the Party. The POCM newspaper, *Noviembre*, has generally supported itself. It is known that the POCM has issued nonredeemable "bonds" to raise money and has held social functions for the same purpose.[105] The success of these ventures has not been reported.

Recruitment campaigns have been desultory affairs. In 1952 the Party secretary of organization, Miguel Aroche Parra, announced a goal of 1,500 new members to be enlisted during May, June, and July, and in 1954 the Regional Committee of the Valley of Mexico sponsored another such campaign. It may be presumed that these efforts had, at best, limited success, since Party affiliations have seldom if ever exceeded 1,500. The Party statutes provide for the training, indoctrination, and discipline of members, but no information is available on their implementation.

Since POCM membership is drawn largely from among the railroad workers, its principal agitation measures have been directed toward government labor policies. In this effort its leaders have sought and gained some support from the leaders of the Communist-affiliated Confederation of Latin American Workers (CTAL), particularly Lombardo Toledano. Campa himself has spoken favorably of the CTAL. The most spectacular cooperation in labor agitation among the Communist parties occurred during the 1958–1959 unrest among the railroad workers. Lombardo Toledano reported that the PPS, PCM, and POCM held tripartite talks prior to and during the

[104] *Declaración de Principios*, pp. 55–56.
[105] *Noviembre*, May 1, 1952 and December 16, 1953.

railroad strike in the spring of 1959. Differences of opinion as to tactics and strategy led to bitter recriminations when the strike failed in April. Lombardo criticized the PCM and POCM leaders for pushing too hard without support except that of the railroad workers. This condition, he argued, presented the government with the opportunity to break the strike and impose new leaders on the union. Contrary to the belligerent attitude of the POCM and PCM, the PPS counseled making peace with the government, criticizing its errors, and assisting it to benefit the masses and the national interests.[106] Lesser forms of agitation have included participation in the "peace" movement, sending of protest messages over alleged attacks by government agents on the Party newspaper, and a Grand Assembly to protest the imprisonment of agitators.

Electoral activities of the POCM have always been at a minimum. Lacking the required 75,000 bona fide members, the Party can register its candidates on the ballot only in alliance with the PPS. It sometimes has allied with the PCM, but until the presidential-congressional elections of 1958 it resticted cooperation to the PPS because of the bitter hostility of the PCM. For the general elections of 1952 the POCM signed a formal pact with the PPS by which the former accepted the PPS presidential candidate and platform in return for which PPS ran POCM members as its candidates for Congress (one senator, three deputies, and two alternate deputies). In 1954 the local branches of the Party in Guerrero signed an electoral pact with the PPS for the election of state deputies from the state's fifth district and presented a joint slate of *regidores* for the Municipality of Acapulco. In Monterrey in that same year, a POCM professional worker reported relations with the PPS were of the best.[107] In 1958, however, the POCM broke with the PPS and joined the PCM in pesenting an opposition candidate for President. The POCM contribution to these various campaigns has been consistently insignificant. No member of the POCM has been known to hold public office in Mexico as a representative of his Party.

Published propaganda of the POCM has not been extensive, and

[106] *El Popular*, May 2, 1959.
[107] *Noviembre*, February 27, 1952; November 13, 1954; November 20, 1954; December 4, 1954.

word-of-mouth campaigns have probably been more important than the written word. *Noviembre* has been published since 1948 by current leaders of the POCM, who transformed it into the Party's propaganda organ in 1950. During the mid-1950's the Party also published several pamphlets, among which was the *Declaration of Principles, Program, Statutes* (1955) and Carlos Sánchez Cárdenas' *Crisis of the Mexican Communist Movement* (1956). The Party also sells Spanish translations of Russian Communist works in its bookstore, the Librería Nacional, opened in 1952 as the Servicio de Librería de "Noviembre."

Noviembre first appeared on September 16, 1948 in an eight-page edition, scheduled biweekly. That first issue set the tone for succeeding numbers. It contained some news on international events, but devoted by far most of its space to national affairs. It also ran some cartoons, drawings, and photos, but no ads. By 1953 the Party claimed to be printing about 4,000 copies, almost all of which were said to be sold. At the Party Congress held in October of that year it was decided to convert the paper to a weekly. On April 1, 1954 *Noviembre* became a ten-day publication and in June a weekly, but after mid-August 1955 it was forced to revert to a biweekly. From June 1957 to February 1960 the paper averaged about one issue a month. With the difficulties attending the Party because of the desertion of Campa and his followers to the PCM, no issues appeared for almost eight months. With the resumption of publication in October 1960 the paper's director, Alberto Lumbreras, announced the intention to publish the paper semimonthly. Since that time it has appeared irregularly.

The Socialist People's Party (Partido Popular Socialista—PPS)

INTRODUCTION

The Mexican "left" has never been truly unified since the Revolution began in 1910. Its greatest cohesion was probably achieved during the administration of Lázaro Cárdenas (1934–1940) when reformers, revolutionists, and radicals (even the Communists temporarily) worked together to transform Mexico politically, socially, and economically. Disintegration of the left began slowly about 1940, when Cárdenas stepped aside for a more conservative successor, whom he himself had picked to consolidate his reforms. In the face of successive moderate administrations in Mexico, disintegration has continued to the present. Since 1948 Vicente Lombardo Toledano, labor leader under Cárdenas, has attempted to reunify the left through his political organization, the Socialist People's Party (Partido Popular Socialista—PPS), called simply the People's Party prior to 1960. He has failed signally, in large part because of his domineering personality that brooks no opposition or competition within his Party or within any movement in which he participates. Probably the only person who could unify the left today is Lázaro Cárdenas himself. However, Cárdenas seems unwilling to assume the active leadership of any group, although he will lend his name and support to various reform organizations.

Interest in leftist unification dates from the mid-1940's. Narciso Bassols, Victor Manuel Villaseñor, and other professional men founded the League of Political Action (Liga de Acción Política), but it foundered shortly after Bassols went to Moscow as Mexican ambassador. From November 1943 to February 1944 a group of intellectuals and journalists including Enrique Ramírez y Ramírez, Rodolfo Dorantes, and José Revueltas propounded the idea of a new party of the left in their journal *El Partido*, and in September 1944 Lombardo Toledano and his collaborators at the Workers' University (Universidad Obrera) established the Mexican Socialist League (Liga Socialista Mexicana). The League was originally designed as a study group, but Lombardo soon oriented it toward political action for the unification of Mexican Marxists. Like Bassols' League it soon died as its founder became involved in other matters. In 1945 two disgruntled political leaders, Octavio Véjar Vásquez and Vitoriano Anguiano, organized the Independent Democratic National Party (Partido Nacional Democrático Independiente) and won a seat in the Chamber of Deputies in the 1946 elections. Both men were among the founders of the PPS.

Shortly after the inauguration of President Miguel Alemán in December 1946, Lombardo Toledano became convinced that the new government would move farther to the right than its predecessor. Early in 1947 he began to advocate the founding of a new party of the left committed to social and economic reform and to independence from foreign control, whether economic, political, or military. For this purpose Lombardo attracted an impressive number of leftist intellectuals, labor leaders, and politicians to a series of round tables to discuss the possibilities of such a party, and attempted to carry over with him his old labor organization, the Confederation of Mexican workers (Confederación de Trabajadores Mexicanos— CTM). He failed in the latter endeavor and his influence throughout labor was undercut by the government and by the top labor leaders, most of whom remained loyal to the official party, the PRI. Nevertheless, Lombardo proceeded with his plans for the new party, concluding as a result of the round tables that for maximum success it should be democratic, popular, and anti-imperialist, as wide as possible in its social composition, independent of the government, but not in systematic opposition. On this premise the party was founded June 1948 as the People's Party (Partido Popular—PP). In 1960 it changed its name to Partido Popular Socialista—PPS.

With the defense of national independence as its primary purpose, the PPS attracted a heterogeneous following, including some anti-Marxists, such as Vejar Vázquez. Marxists, including Lombardo, dominated the organization and held most of the governing positions, but dissatisfaction with Lombardo's cooperation with the government, limited though it was, led to the defection of certain intellectuals in 1949. The Party continued to grow until the election of 1952, but then leveled off as it failed to incorporate the supporters it had gained in the election campaign. With the beginning of bitter intra-party strife in 1955, the Party began an absolute decline. The public conversion of the Party since 1960 to socialism, Marxism, Leninism, and its position in the vanguard of the working class has not attracted back those intellectuals who advocated such a policy years before. Lombardo's iron control and the Party's failure to organize politically at the grass-roots level has continued to impede its growth even among those on the left.

LEADERS AND FOLLOWERS

The PPS has been a legally registered party since its founding in 1948. Its peak strength was probably reached just prior to the presidential and congressional elections of 1952 when it put on a concerted drive to attract members to vote for the PPS presidential candidate Vicente Lombardo Toledano, the Party leader. In the July election of that year, Lombardo polled 72,482 votes by the official count.[108] Less Party enthusiasm was engendered for the congressional elections of 1955, and by the elections of 1958 the Party was badly split by the dissension between Lombardo and his immediate family and close friends on the one hand and a faction of disgruntled intellectuals on the other. Despite these problems, the Mexican government recognized as bona fide members the 75,000 names the Party submitted to retain its registration and the right to have its candidates listed on the ballot. Despite Lombardo's claim of 230,000 members early in 1958 and his pledge of 500,000 by the end of that year, membership by mid-1962 was probably between 50,000 and 75,000.

Although in absolute numbers the lower-class members predominate in the PPS, the Party has attracted a proportionately larger number of students, teachers, artists, and other types of intellectuals than has the PCM.[109] Lombardo himself and most of his chief collaborators fall into one or another of these groups, giving the PPS not only more competent leadership but the respectability that the PCM has never been able to achieve in Mexican society. In fact, the PPS has profited by the PCM purges of the 1940's, since several leading intellectuals, including Enrique Ramírez y Ramírez, for several years second-in-command to Lombardo, found in the PPS a political outlet for their Marxist and Communist inclinations. The PPS also has a proportionately larger number of women than has the PCM, although the PPS has not organized a women's group such as the Communist Party's affiliate, the Democratic Union of Mexican Women (UDMM). Lombardo's daughter, Adriana, has long played an important role in the Workers' University (UO), and Hortensia Rojas, a faithful adherent of Lombardo, was a member and served

[108] *Diario de los Debates de la Cámara de Diputados*, Forty-second Legislature, Vol. I, No. 13, September 13, 1952. This issue gives a breakdown of the votes by state.

[109] Fuentes Díaz, *Los Partidos Políticos en México*, II, 137, gives the following breakdown for 1956: *campesinos*, 60 per cent; workers, 9 per cent; and students, intellectuals, and middle class, 31 per cent.

as secretary of finance of the National Directorate for many years. In 1956 Rojas, Adriana, and Leslie Paz de Zelaya composed a committee to promote women's Party activities.[110] In that same year and again in 1959 the Party also sponsored a conference for working women.[111] None of these met with any notable success in expanding women's membership in the Party or their influence in the community.

Many PPS members, including some of the intellectuals, are by no means Communist in the sense that they wish to see created in Mexico a regime on the model of the Soviet satellite states. Many accept Lombardo's definition of the PPS at its face value as a purely national party of the left. Such people are motivated primarily by desire for more rapid and radical social changes, for greater government intervention in the economy, for less reliance on foreign capital for economic development, for greater democratization of the political regime than can be expected from the government party. It is doubtful, however, that many PPS leaders fall into this category. Some members are also motivated by deep-seated antipathy for the United States, growing out of hostility for past aggressions and out of fear and jealousy of its present dominant political and economic position vis à vis Mexico.

Just as in the PCM, membership in the PPS is concentrated in one urban area, the Federal District, and in one rural area, the northwestern state of Sonora, which is the stronghold of the Party's labor wing, the UGOCM (*q.v.*). Until late 1956 the state of Veracruz ranked with Sonora as a leading PPS area, but defections in that state disorganized the Party there. During the past several years the PPS has claimed to be making headway in Veracruz, but its status in that state cannot be determined. Other states of secondary importance to the Party are Jalisco, Sinaloa, México, Guerrero, Tamaulipas, Michoacán, and Zacatecas. With the exception of Guerrero, Party strength in the south and on the Yucatán Peninsula is negligible.

The leadership of the PPS contrasts favorably with that of the

[110] *El Popular*, February 7, 1956.
[111] See Chapter IV on organized labor.

PCM, although at several critical moments of the PPS' history the leaders committed serious errors that have resulted in weakness and near disaster for it. Lombardo Toledano has directed the Party since its founding in 1948, as president until 1955, and as secretary general since 1955. Well-educated, independently wealthy, he still commands the respect of some non-Communist leftists in and out of the government. He has taught law and philosophy at the National University and has served the government at various levels. Perhaps his greatest claim to fame was his reorganization of labor under Cárdenas into the Confederation of Mexican Labor (CTM) in the 1930's. An excellent public speaker with a magnetic personality, he has a tendency toward vanity. He cannot tolerate opposition to his views within the Party or threats to his leadership.[112] Lombardo's assessment of the power and tolerance of the official government party has generally been accurate. Consequently, PPS leaders have seldom been arrested or molested and Lombardo himself still enjoys the privilege of a diplomatic passport. On occasion, however, he has seriously miscalculated, for example with respect to the student agitation of 1956 which ended with the loss of control by the PPS of powerful youth and student organizations and the imprisonment of PPS youth leaders. Lombardo also demonstrated poor leadership qualities by provoking a quarrel with Enrique Ramírez y Ramírez, his second-in-command in 1955, a quarrel which resulted in major defections of intellectuals and professionals from the Party. Lombardo's choice of a successor to Ramírez was also unfortunate. Vidal Díaz Muñoz, an opportunist with little respect in or out of the Party, proved a nonentity, but his withdrawal from the Party in late 1956 led to further defections. His successor as undersecretary general, Jacinto López (1957–1960), proved to be a leader of courage, tenacity, and resourcefulness, but in a limited area, that of farm labor and peasant agitation in northwestern Mexico. The other members of the National Directorate have lacked forcefulness and imagination, and reshuffling the Directorate at the Third National Assembly in 1960 did not appreciably strengthen it. Many of the writers and journalists who once worked industriously for the Party have abandoned Lombardo.

[112] *Communism in Latin America*, a *Visión* special report, December 1958, p. 14.

Except for the resignation in 1949 of Narciso Bassols,[113] a leading writer and economist, together with several of his followers, the PPS presented a solid front to its political opponents from its inception in 1948 until the holding of the Second National Assembly in November 1955. From that time on, the Party has been wracked with open dissension which has led to the expulsion of several leading members, the virtual inactivity of an important group of Party intellectuals, and to the withdrawal of the most important labor organization within the UGOCM, the Party's labor wing.

When the Party assembly opened in November 1955 all appeared serene among the leaders, including President Vicente Lombardo Toledano and Secretary General Enrique Ramírez y Ramírez. By clever political maneuverings within the assembly, however, Lombardo had the office of president abolished (though the statutes were never formally amended), had himself elected to the now top post of secretary general, and Vidal Díaz Muñoz of Veracruz, head of the important National Federation of Sugar Cane Workers (Federación Nacional de Cañeros—FNC), elected to the number two spot as undersecretary general.[114] Enrique Ramírez y Ramírez and all of his close associates except one were excluded from the National Directorate of the Party. Delegates to the assembly were stunned, and possibly would have rejected the arrangement had the issue been permitted to come before the congress for a vote. But it did not come before the assembly because that body had earlier voted to delegate this power to a special committee which Lombardo had picked.

---

[113] Despite his resignation, Bassols continued his ties with Lombardo until his death in 1959. It has been claimed that Bassols was one of the principal contacts of the Soviet Embassy. For a brief biography see *El Popular*, July 25, 1959.

[114] Vidal Díaz Muñoz was given a considerable buildup during the late winter and spring of 1956 when he was nominated and then ran for the office of governor of Veracruz on the PPS ticket. Lombardo and three other top leaders attended the state nominating convention, and a high-ranking representative of the Communist splinter party, the POCM, spoke in behalf of unity of all "revolutionary forces" in Veracruz. In May and June, Díaz Muñoz stumped the state, and when the elections were declared against him and his associates running for the state legislature, they set up a rival government for a few days. No one took all this activity seriously, but it was good publicity. Cf. *El Popular*, February 20, 1956 and June 17, 1956.

Various theories have been advanced to explain the demotion of
Ramírez and his followers. A semiofficial Party explanation was that a
dispute had arisen between Lombardo and Ramírez over tactics.
Ramírez had long advocated placing emphasis upon recruitment
among urban workers; Lombardo felt that the Party should emphasize work among the *campesinos*. This interpretation may be true in
part since the number two spot in the party has been occupied by a
campesino leader since that time, but it does not explain the under-
handed methods Lombardo used to oust Ramírez. Furthermore there
has been no evidence of a new, determined drive to recruit and organize *campesinos* on a large scale. A second explanation, and one
that rings true, is that Lombardo feared the growing popularity of
Ramírez and wished to demote him before Ramírez became powerful enough to take over Party leadership. A third explanation, and
one that is no more than a rumor, is that the demotion of Ramírez
and associates represents the victory of the Lombardo family, Federico and Adriana de Silva primarily, over their personal and political
opponents within the Party. Whatever the explanation, this dissension
has weakened the PPS.

During the first half of 1956 at least, some hope of reconciliation
between the factions appeared possible. In several open letters to
Mexico City publications Ramírez denied rumors and allegations
that he had formed a Ramirista group within the PPS, insisted that
he was not complaining of the fact that he had lost his official position,
and said he still had a high regard for Lombardo Toledano. He did
emphasize, however, that he objected to the methods used to demote
him, that he refused to follow Lombardo blindly, and that he believed in frank and open discussion of principles, not in *persona-
lismo*.[115] More bitter was José Alvarado, a friend of Ramírez and a
member of the National Directorate prior to November 1955. Alvarado launched an unrestrained attack on the new undersecretary general, Díaz Muñoz, accusing him not only of being unlettered but of
enriching himself, currently as a labor leader and formerly as a
deputy and senator in the National Congress.[116] Alvarado's untemp-
ered remarks resulted in his expulsion from the PPS in 1957,

[115] *El Popular*, January 21, 1956; February 16, 1956; and March 3, 1956.
[116] *Ibid.*, February 17, 1956.

but against the rest of the Ramiristas, Lombardo refused to take action. At the same time he made no gestures toward reconciliation; rather, he demanded their unconditional surrender.

The student disturbances from the spring to the fall of 1956 revealed the depths of the split within the PPS. As Ramírez' reconciliation efforts apparently were getting nowhere, his adherents on the newspaper *El Popular* and in the Confederation of Mexican Youths (Confederación de Jóvenes Mexicanos—CJM) began to criticize the student leaders, particularly Nicandro Mendoza, PPS member and close associate of Lombardo. With the government victory over the strikers in the fall, the CJM practically cut its ties with the PPS. *El Popular* continued to drift free and by 1957 was hardly recognizable as a onetime mouthpiece of the Party.[117] The paper continued to take a far-left position on most issues, but with the continuing fragmentation of the left and growing government hostility it finally ceased publication on November 30, 1961.[118]

Within two months of the student fiasco the Party was rocked by the resignation of Vidal Díaz Muñoz from his position as undersecretary general. Díaz Muñoz thereupon withdrew from the Party and pulled his labor organization, the FNC, out of the UGOCM, CTAL, and WFTU. He took the bulk of the Party members in Veracruz into a new Veracruz Independent Socialist Party, which he himself headed.[119] Officially, he resigned for "economic reasons and for reasons of health," but rumors circulated that he was disgruntled at the treatment he received from Lombardo and other Party lead-

[117] *El Popular* began to print Free World labor news, enthusiastically received U.S. Ambassador Hill when he visited the plant, and moderated its tone toward the United States. Cf. *El Popular's* friendly editorial of June 28, 1957 on a speech made by President Eisenhower on the disasters of modern war.

[118] In a lengthy editorial in its last issue, *El Popular* announced it was ceasing publication after 23½ years because of deterioration of equipment, declining advertising lineage and subscription list, and difficulties with the government over newsprint.

[119] Isaac R. Sánchez, secretary general of the PPS State Committee in Veracruz, formally announced the dissolution of the PPS apparatus and its reincorporation into the new Party on January 10, 1957. Lombardo disavowed the resolution, but the state delegates insisted on the right to secede. The PPS has since reorganized in Veracruz, but has not recovered its former strength. Cf. *El Universal*, January 11, 1957, p. 17.

ers.[120] Whatever the reason, the resignation further weakened the Party, and Lombardo hurriedly called for a meeting of the National Executive Committee for mid-January to discuss Party problems and to elect a new undersecretary general.

Prior to the meeting, Ramírez and Alvarado indirectly attacked Lombardo by complaining of the Party's organizational weaknesses, but in the National Executive Committee no holds were barred. Ramiristas accused Lombardo outright of practicing the "cult of the personality," while Lombardistas returned with the charge that their opponents were "traitors delivered over to U.S. imperialism."[121] Amidst the hubub Jacinto López, leader of the UGOCM, was elected undersecretary general.[122] This Executive Committee meeting of January 1957 appears to have been a turning point in the dispute between Lombardo and Ramírez.[123]

According to some observers the lineup among leading elements in the PPS early in 1957 was as follows:

Followers of Lombardo: Adriana Lombardo de Silva, Francisco Figueroa Mendoza, Lic. María Teresa Puente, Nicandro Mendoza, Antonio García Moreno, Indalecio Sáyago, Jacinto López, Federico Silva;

Followers of Enrique Ramírez: Rodolfo Dorantes, Celerino Cano, Raul Moncada, Macrina Rabadán, Manuel Alcaraz, Alberto Beltrán, Leopoldo Méndez;

Conciliators: Manuel Marcué Pardiñas, Jorge Carrión, Leopoldo Ancona, Constancio Hernández.

In total numbers the Ramiristas were swamped by the loyal and even fanatic followers of Lombardo. Fence sitters and compromisers were forced to choose sides. Dr. Jorge Carrión and Manuel Marcué

---

[120] Although in April 1958 Díaz Muñoz cooperated with PCM agrarian leader Arturo Orona in land seizures and agitation, he led several political and labor organizations into the official Party, the PRI, in August 1959. These were the Socialist Party of Veracruz, the Revolutionary League of Workers and Farmers, and the Union of Mexican Agricultural Workers. The FNC, although no longer under his control, did not return to the CTAL. See *El Popular*, April 13, 1958; August 10, 1959; and August 11, 1959.

[121] *El Popular*, January 17, 1957.

[122] *La Voz de México*, January 17, 1957.

[123] Cf. *El Universal*, January 8, 1957, p. 12.

Pardiñas, both intellectuals, remained with Lombardo, though they continued their attempts at conciliation as late as April 1958. However, the staff of *El Popular*, the CJM, and the artists of the People's Graphic Arts Shop (Taller de Gráfica Popular—TGP) became virtually inactive. Macrina Rabadán, the Ramirista leader of the Party in Guerrero, all but withdrew the state organization. At the Party's Tenth National Council meeting in May 1957 the Ramiristas made only feeble attempts at obstruction. They said that in principle they accepted Lombardo's *Tesis sobre México* as the basis for the PPS presidential election campaign, but they objected to the fact that it was being railroaded through without proper consideration and discussion. The delegates approved the *Tesis* overwhelmingly.[124] In November the Party held its Second Extraordinary National Assembly, at which unreconciled Ramaristas, including Macrina Rabadán, PPS leader in Guerrero, were summarily removed from all national offices. In July 1958 the Party directorate unsuccessfully petitioned the Federal Electoral Commission to remove from the registry of candidates the name of Macrina Rabadán and Eladia Salgado de Figueroa, on the charge that they had violated Party statutes. Rabadán won and accepted her seat in the Chamber of Deputies. In September she, Ramírez, and a number of their followers were finally expelled from the Party.[125] It was probably the weakness resulting from these conflicts that led Lombardo to the decision not to run for the Presidency in the elections of July 1958. As it was, PPS campaign efforts were weak, workers were not enthusiastic, and scant propaganda success marked the Party's participation.[126]

---

[124] Cf. the extensive reports on the Council in *El Popular*, May 28–31, 1957; also *El Universal*, May 31, 1957, p. 1.

[125] Macrina Rabadán was expelled from the National Executive Committee for adherence to the Ramírez faction. She was expelled from the Party in September 1958 for accepting, contrary to Party directives, a seat in Congress, to which the Electoral College of the Mexican Congress had confirmed her. Ramírez was finally expelled (at the same time as Rabadán) as a traitor to the Party's principles and discipline. He was also accused of planning to take over Party leadership by subverting state organizations and calling an Extraordinary National Assembly. See *El Popular*, September 20, 1958.

[126] In a review of the PPS electoral campaign of 1958, the Party's Eleventh National Council confirmed that the only candidate for deputy who mounted an intensive campaign was Dr. Jorge Carrión. Candidates for the districts of

No further disturbances of this magnitude have shaken the PPS. The Third National Assembly revealed that there was some criticism of Undersecretary General Jacinto López within the Party, but no serious crisis occurred.[127] The position of undersecretary general was abolished but López retained his position in the National Directorate and Central Committee. Several other persons were replaced in the National Directorate but were retained in the Central Committee. *El Popular* listed the following:[128]

Vicente Lombardo Toledano .	Secretary General
Jacinto López	Secretary of Campesino Policy
Rafael Estrada Villa . . .	Secretary of Organization
Jorge Kruickshank [sic] . .	Secretary of Propaganda
Isidoro Gámez [sic] . . .	Secretary of Trade Union Policy
Antonio García Moreno . .	Secretary of Relations
Jorge Carrión	Secretary of Political Education
Lázaro Rubio Felix	Secretary of Electoral Affairs
Indalecio Sáyago	Secretary of Finances

Manuel Marcué Pardiñas refused to accept his election to the Central Committee because of the press of his duties as director of several publications, including the lively *Política* and the respected *Problemas Agrícolas y Industriales de México*. He announced that he would remain simply a member of the Party. Unity has been maintained, but the price has been high, with the loss of many intellectuals and the continued fragmentation of the left.

The official youth wing of the PPS, the People's Youth (Juventud Popular—JP), conforming with Party policy added *Socialist* to its title in 1960. The stated purposes of the organization are to raise standards of living materially, intellectually, and morally for Mexico's young people, and to contribute to the advent of a new Mexico.[129] In reality the Party's youth wing has been used to recruit

---

Veracruz, Ixtepec, and Tonalá were not registered because of the failure of Salvador Bojórquez to perform his duties. Rabadán's campaign was not mentioned. Cf. *El Popular*, July 29, 1958.

[127] *El Popular*, October 16, 1960.
[128] *Ibid.*, October 17, 1960.
[129] *Ibid.*, June 18, 1956.

young people and to supply PPS-directed leaders to youth and student organizations throughout the country. To this end some successes have been achieved.

The JP has claimed many thousands of members in all parts of the country, but it is probable that membership has never exceeded 2,000 to 3,000, limited mostly to the Federal District and a few other places where the Party has enjoyed some concentration. The Constituent Congress of 1954 formulated a program and drew up a series of statutes for the organization, but growth was slow. In the spring of 1956 a call was issued for its First National Ordinary Congress, which assembled from July 13 to 16 inclusive. The principal speaker at the opening session was the Party secretary general Vicente Lombardo Toledano, who outlined the tasks to be undertaken by the organization. Principally, Lombardo called for scientific studies of national problems and a search for solutions and the unity of all Mexican youth to attain their economic, political, and cultural progress. He also told them to fight for citizenship rights for eighteen-year-olds, for a modification of the government's agricultural policy which favors cash crops over local food crops, and for termination of the bracero program. The JP passed resolutions in line with these suggestions,[130] but there is no evidence that it has persistently taken steps to implement the program. In fact the organization has appeared rather inactive for the past several years except for the convening of an Extraordinary Congress in September 1957 in which a new slate of officers was elected and a resolution passed to affiliate with the Soviet-sponsored youth international, the World Federation of Democratic Youth (WFDY).[131] In October it finally published the first issue of a long-projected periodical, *Juventud Popular*, an eight-page tabloid. The first issue was dated August 31, but it is not known by this writer how regularly the paper has appeared since that time. A Second Ordinary Congress met in December 1958, but its only significant action was the formation of the Pioneers of the People's Youth for boys aged eight to twelve. The twelve charter members were headed by a grandson of Lombardo Toledano. The financial situation of the J.P. was so precarious during 1959 that, despite the

[130] *Ibid.*, July 13, 1956; July 14, 1956; and July 15, 1956.
[131] *World Youth*, January 1958, p. 3.

offer of some financial assistance from the Festival's preparatory committee, the organization could not participate in the Seventh World Festival for Youth and Students held in Vienna during July and August. Early in 1960 the group made a perfunctory protest over the presence of troops in the National School for Teachers.[132] In January 1962 about twenty members demonstrated for a few minutes in front of the U.S. embassy in behalf of Fidel Castro, and in February one of its officers, Miguel Castro Bustos, led about two hundred students on a wild rampage through the National University and Mexico City protesting the University's stiff entrance requirements. On one occasion the mob threatened Rector Ignacio Chávez with violence. Castro was suspended temporarily from the University and then arrested for four days when he attempted further agitation in Mexico City. His attempt in March to gain control of the student organization at the National University failed miserably.

ORGANIZATION

The PPS issued its first set of statutes in 1948, the year that the Party was formally organized and recognized by the government to have sufficient strength to place its candidates on the ballot for election to public office.[133] Until the Second National Assembly in November 1955, Party organization closely approximated the structure provided in the statutes. At the Assembly, however, Party president Vicente Lombardo Toledano shook up the organization at the top level and introduced some minor changes in terminology and organization at all levels. The Third National Assembly in October 1960 introduced further changes.

The original statutes define the Party's organization as "democratic." Although they do not use the term "democratic centralism" to describe the structure, the statutes' four principles of Party organization result in a political institution strikingly similar in practice to the PCM. These principles are: (1) election of Party organs from below; (2) authority to be exercised by the higher organs over the lower; (3) submission of minorities to the will of the majority; (4) single discipline within the Party for leaders as well as members.

[132] *El Popular*, February 25, 1960.
[133] *Razón Histórica, Principios, Programa y Estatutos del Partido Popular.*

Article 23 stipulates further that higher Party organs have the power to approve or disapprove plans and activities of lower organs and to suspend or revoke their resolutions; and Article 24 states that higher directive committees may refuse recognition of lower directive committees but may not appoint new ones, since they may be elected only by their respective assembly of Party members.[134] On the other hand, Article 20 provides that delegates to higher Party organs (assemblies) are to be elected by the lower assemblies. When the National Council meeting of August 1960 adopted the proposal to reorient the Party openly toward Marxist-Leninist materialism, the leaders concluded that the structure of the Party would be modified in accord with the principle of democratic centralism. By so stating, the leadership simply recognized publicly what had been the practice of the Party since its founding.[135]

The basic organ of the Party, the Local Assembly, called the Neighborhood Cell or Unit since 1955, should normally consist of at least ten members and take its name from their common place of work or residence. The Second National Assembly voted to permit cells of at least three members to form in factories, unions, and other work centers. In Sonora, at least for a time, the novel procedure was followed in certain *ejidos* of establishing separate cells for *ejidatarios,* day workers, youths, and women. The Local Assembly meets at least biweekly, the work of the group being conducted between sessions by an elected Local Executive Committee of at least three members. The primary functions of a Local Assembly are to carry out higher Party directives and recommendations within its sphere of activity, to pass suggestions of its own members upward, and to accept or reject the report of its Executive Committee. The Local Assembly also receives new members and enforces discipline. According to the 1948 statutes the Local Assembly was also granted the power to elect delegates to the next-level Party conference, the Municipal Assembly, but the 1955 National Assembly decreed that cell electors should elect

[134] In April 1959 the National Directorate dissolved the Provisional State Committee of Baja California, denied recognition to its candidates for public office, and dispatched a delegate from headquarters to organize a new committee. For the text of the order see *El Popular*, April 19, 1959.

[135] *Excelsior*, August 28, 1960, p. 11.

the delegates. It was not made clear at the time how the electors were to be chosen nor is there information available how or if the procedure is operating. The Local Executive Committee is charged with reporting to its Assembly and, monthly, to the Municipal Committee. Although the statutes make no provision for isolated Party workers, many members belong to no cell organization. While the PCM permits and even seems to encourage this practice for some of its members, PPS policy is designed to persuade such members to attach themselves to local units.

The State Assembly meets ordinarily every two years to carry out the Party lines and directives at the state level, to approve or reject the reports of its Executive Committee, and to elect a new Directive Committee of at least nine members: president, secretary general, and secretaries for organization, education, propaganda, finance, the People's Youth movement, electoral affairs, and cultural action. As in the Municipal Committee, this requirement is not always met. The State Directive Committee (called Federal District or Territorial in the Federal District and Territories), meeting ordinarily biweekly, carries on Party work at its level between sessions of the State Assembly. The Directive Committee, in addition to reporting to the State Assembly, also reports monthly to the National Executive Committee on Party problems and organization in the state. Although the statutes do not specify the procedure, in practice either the National Directorate or the State Committee may call a state convention for the purpose of nominating candidates to state offices, to the national Congress, or to the state legislature. In such conventions every Party member in the state or electoral district, as the case may be, has the right to vote on the choice.[136] Because of the imbalance of Party strength, state by state, the PPS Central Committee (formerly the

---

[136] In April 1956 the National Directorate convoked the State Assembly of the Party in Durango to name candidates for state governor and state legislators. Party discipline was maintained by Jacinto López, delegate of the National Directorate, who presided over the Assembly. Cf. *El Popular*, April 27, 1956. In Veracruz the State Committee called a state convention for the same purpose in February 1956. Cf. *El Popular*, February 2, 1956. In Tamaulipas in June 1956 the State Committee called a meeting of municipal committees under its jurisdiction to discuss the calling of a state convention to nominate a gubernatorial candidate. Cf. *El Popular*, June 9, 1956.

National Council) resolved early in 1961 to replace the state organs by zonal or regional bodies.

The National Assembly, the supreme Party organ, should meet in ordinary session every three years to determine the Party's program, political lines, and organizational procedures.[137] The Assembly also decides upon the Party's participation in presidential elections, its campaign platform, and the Party candidate. Finally, the Assembly elects members to a new National Executive Committee and hears and decides upon the reports of the outgoing Committee. By statute the National Executive Committee consists of thirty-two members and three alternates, and holds supreme authority between National Assembly meetings. It consists of the following positions:

President
Five vice presidents
Secretary General
Undersecretary
Secretary and two members of Committee for Organization
Secretary and two members of Commission for Political Education
Secretary and two members of Commission for Propaganda
Secretary and two members of Commission for Finance
Secretary and two members of Commission for Technical Studies
Secretary and two members of Commission for Cultural Action
Secretary and two members of the Commission for the People's
    Youth Movement

The National Executive Committee does not function according to the statutes. The Second National Assembly in 1955 abolished the presidency, the five vice presidencies, and reorganized several commissions, leaving the secretariat general as the highest office. Lombardo had himself elected secretary general and a hand-picked follower as undersecretary general before the convention understood the full implications of the change. The amendment to the statutes seemed motivated more by internal Party politics than by a desire for needed organizational reform, because, through this maneuver, Lombardo

[137] In the first fourteen years of the Party's life there were three national ordinary assemblies and two extraordinary assemblies. The latter were held to determine the Party's program and activities in presidential elections.

effectively removed from high Party office his potential rival Enrique
Ramírez y Ramírez, until then his second-in-command as secretary
general. At the Third National Assembly the position of undersecretary general was abolished, but its holder retained his position as a
national leader.

The National Executive Committee is scheduled to meet monthly
in ordinary session to set up the tasks for the above commissions, to
carry out the resolutions of the National Assembly, and to see to the
permanent functioning of the Party. It also administers the funds and
property of the Party, hires office personnel, and names the directors
of the national organs of propaganda. With the abolition of the offices of president and vice president and undersecretary general,
the secretary general and the secretaries of the national commissions
now make up the Political Directorate (more frequently called the
National Directorate), "the organ immediately inferior to the National Executive Committee." The Directorate exercises authority between Executive Committee meetings and convenes at least biweekly.
The size of the National Directorate has varied, with the Third National Assembly setting it at nine members.[138]

Keeping state and national officers in formal contact between Assembly sessions is the Central Committee, consisting of the National
Executive Committee and the president and secretaries general of the
State and Federal District Committees. Prior to the Third National
Assembly (and according to the original statutes) this body was
called the National Council. This organ hears and advises the National Executive Committee and approves changes in membership
on the various national commissions. It appears that forty-two members attended the twelfth meeting of the Council in February 1959,
but the new Central Committee was established with fifty members
and thirteen "candidate" members, some of whom do not appear to
meet statutory requirements.[139]

[138] For the list of the officers and their positions in late 1958, see *El Universal*, September 11, 1958, p. 12; for the list in October 1960, see *El Popular*,
October 17, 1960.
[139] *El Popular*, October 17, 1960. The Tenth National Council met in May
1957, the Eleventh in July 1958, and the Twelfth in February 1959.

Despite a membership many times larger than that of the PCM, the PPS is organized in depth in only two areas: the Federal District, the center of all political life in Mexico, and the state of Sonora, where the Party has been able to organize the *campesinos* under the able leadership of Jacinto López. Party organizations have been established in about half the states, but municipal committees and assemblies tend to be scattered in the larger towns. A number of these are little more than paper organizations with a minimum of activity and few if any cells.

As in the PCM, power is exercised neither democratically nor according to the stipulations of the statutes. Rather it is concentrated in the hands of Vicente Lombardo Toledano and a group of his relatives and close friends. Potential rivals are eliminated and opposition is not tolerated. Organizationally the nucleus of power is the Political Directorate, not the National Executive Committee or the National Assembly, nominally the superior bodies.[140] The weakness of the latter was clearly demonstrated when Lombardo manipulated it to remove his rival Enrique Ramírez from power within the Party in 1955. Similar situations prevail in state, municipal, and local Party organs, where the "committees" dominate the assemblies.

PRINCIPLES, PROGRAMS, AND PROPAGANDA

Published formal documents of the Partido Popular Socialista frequently appear nonrevolutionary though left-of-center in modern

[140] At the Fourth Ordinary Assembly of the PPS Federal District Committee (November 1959) a new directive board was elected for a two-year term. According to reports, the new board was nominated by the Party's National Directorate. In response to a request for the offering of another slate, Lombardo Toledano, who was presiding, opposed the move. The vote was then taken, with 78 in favor, 8 abstaining, 0 opposing. Cf. *El Universal*, November 2, 1959, pp. 1, 7, and 20. There is no authorization in the 1948 statutes for the National Directorate to nominate in the manner described above. In addition, the various changes adopted formally by the Third Assembly in October 1960 were first approved by a meeting of the National Council in August, upon presentation by the National Directorate. The new National Directorate chosen at that same Assembly was elected within five minutes of the presentation of names by Lombardo Toledano. Cf. *Excelsior*, October 16, 1960, p. 29, and October 17, 1960, p. 5.

Mexico, and until 1960 were only slightly Marxist despite Lombardo's frank admissions that he is a Marxist in his economic views. From the first publication of the Party's program and principles in 1948 to its electoral campaign platform for 1958, the *Tesis sobre México*, its stated goals and position changed little. Then as later it saw the three fundamental problems of Mexico as the "physical poverty of the national territory, the regime of exploitation of the people . . . and the evil influence of the forces of foreign imperialism in our domestic life."[141] The Party takes the position that little or nothing to strike at the roots of these problems was done for one hundred years after the first declaration of independence by Hidalgo, but that the Revolution, inaugurated in 1910 and continuing to 1940, made great strides in attempting to find solutions. However, not only does much more remain to be done, but since 1940, the PPS alleges, the government and the official party (the PRI) have slowed down, if not reversed, the Revolution. One-party dictatorship; electoral frauds; rising influence of big business; slowdown in land distribution, educational development, and labor gains; and the increasing economic ties with the United States all attest, according to the PPS, to the need for a party of the Mexican people which will strive to attain the goals and ideals of the Revolution of 1910.[142]

For twelve years the PPS consistently disclaimed any predilection for particular ideologies or social classes:

Formed by men and women of different philosophical opinions, of distinct religious beliefs and social classes; by campesinos and by workers, by artisans, and by small merchants and small industrialists; by civil servants and by private employees; by school teachers; by professional people; by intellectuals and by artists; by men of science, and by all Mexicans in general who agree fully and loyally with the transcendental objectives of

[141] *Razón Histórica*, p. 5.
[142] *Ibid.*, pp. 10–13. In September 1957 Jorge Carrión, member of the National Directorate and a candidate for the Chamber of Deputies in 1955 and 1958, listed the Party goals as: (1) a higher standard of living for the Mexican people, (2) democracy in political life, and (3) absolute respect for the independence and sovereignty of all countries (*El Universal*, September 30, 1957, pp. 1 and 20). In January 1959 Lombardo demanded "rectitude" in national politics and improvements in education, which he insisted was presently deficient in every sense (*El Universal*, January 19, 1959, p. 1).

the historical struggles of our people and in their concrete program of
action, the People's Party will be one of the most vigorous and purest con-
structive forces of Mexico.[143]

Notably absent from the list are landholders, big-business men, military officers, and the clergy.

The first PPS program was drawn up at the Party's National Constituent Assembly in June 1948 for the purpose of achieving its goals
and implementing its principles. A lengthy document consisting of
eighty-four articles divided into fourteen chapters, the *Programa* may
conveniently be discussed under four main policy headings: national
political, national social and economic, international political, and
international economic. Although national political problems and the
PPS' program for improvement occupy a prominent position in the
Programa by being treated first and last, political matters are in fact
given slight attention when compared with economic and social matters.[144] Politically, the PPS demanded a democratic regime in Mexico, separation of powers, and the operation of a federal system, all
of which are provided by the Constitution but none of which, the
Party claims, prevail in practice. Changes which the PPS sought were
a new electoral law to prevent election frauds effectively,[145] establish
proportional representation,[146] and give the vote to women; and a
new law to guarantee municipalities the freedom which the Constitution provides but which they have never enjoyed.[147] PPS plans concerning domestic economic and social matters called for increased
purchasing power and therefore improved standards of living for
the masses, extension of social security, government-sponsored national health and sanitation programs, increased educational benefits,

[143] *Razón Histórica*, p. 11.

[144] Twenty pages are devoted to social and economic questions and only five
to political and international matters. This imbalance is somewhat redressed
by the amount of publicity given to PPS political propaganda in the daily
Mexico City press where the Party's political squabbles as well as political program are given greater attention than its economic affairs.

[145] On the eve of the 1958 elections Lombardo expressed the hope that there
would be less electoral fraud than in the past (*El Universal*, July 6, 1958, p. 1).

[146] At the Party's Tenth National Council in May 1957 Lombardo opened the
session with a call for proportional representation and freedom of voting (*El
Universal*, May 20, 1957, p. 1).

[147] *Razón Histórica*, pp. 15–19.

integration of the Indians into national social and economic life, equal rights for women, protection of rights guaranteed to workers,[148] protection of small landowners and small-business people against their more powerful competitors, continuation and improvement of the land distribution program, more and easier agrarian credit, more irrigation, more conservation, and more rural schools.[149] They also demanded equality of opportunity in the armed forces regardless of social class, government aid to science and art, and government direction of and assistance to industrial development. In addition to the above specific policies, spelled out in greater detail than here indicated, the PPS program also laid down some general principles of national economic policy. It insisted that the state should coordinate and regulate the national economy to guarantee to the great majority of the people who live from their labor an ever increasing standard of living and to stop the process whereby wealth tends to concentrate in the hands of a privileged few. The program maintained that this goal should be achieved by a constant development of the economy through industrialization and the modernization of agriculture and that the state should assist private enterprise but should prevent undue profits, monopoly, and privileges. It felt that this could be accomplished by a tax on profits which exceeded an equitable return on capital.[150]

The PPS position on international relations was, on the whole, moderate. The Party in 1948 called for support of the United Nations, continued vigilance against the revival of fascism, and a "fight for international peace and condemnation and systematic denunciation of every act of governments, institutions, or persons tending to provoke a new war." The Party also urged that the basic international policy of Mexico consist of friendship with all countries and con-

[148] For the PPS' response to labor agitation, 1956–1960, see Chapter IV on organized labor.

[149] These aims are frequently repeated in Party documents and speeches. Cf. the conference given by Lombardo on August 13, 1959 entitled "The Economic Development of Mexico and the People's Standard of Living," *El Popular*, August 18, 1959. In this same article Lombardo said that "the PPS considers itself the vanguard party in the struggle of the Mexican people and no one can challenge this place of honor."

[150] *Razón Histórica*, pp. 24–25.

demnation of antidemocratic regimes, recognition of the right of self-determination of people in the formation of their own government, and solidarity with colonial and semicolonial people in their efforts to secure political and economic independence.[151] This spirit of moderation, however, departed from the Party program when inter-American relations came under discussion. The thirteenth chapter, which deals with this subject, opens thus: "The expansionist policy of North American imperialism constitutes the principal threat to the sovereignty of the countries of Latin America, as well as the major obstacle to their rapid and adequate industrialization and to their full economic development."[152] To counter this alleged threat, the Party called for Mexican adherence to the doctrine of nonintervention, opposition to monopolies, support of freedom for Puerto Rico, and demand for United States' abandonment of military bases in Latin America.[153]

As a basic principal for Mexican international economic policy, the PPS declared that the country must never tie itself to international agreements which would restrict its freedom to regulate imports and exports. Furthermore, foreign investments should be excluded from basic elements of the national economy but encouraged to enter areas where expansion is still feasible. Foreign capital should also be regulated with regard to mixing with domestic capital, reinvestment, transportation costs, taxes, and production for Mexican consumption. Ideally, foreign capital should be excluded from basic industry, but when sufficient domestic capital is not available, foreign capital may be invited to participate, but only if it is to be subject to "the national sovereignty." Intergovernmental loans are preferable to direct private investment.[154]

[151] *Ibid.*, pp. 38–39.

[152] *Ibid.*, p. 36.

[153] In its call for a "National Patriotic Front," the National Directorate of the Party softened this hard anti-U.S. line in November 1957 at the Second National Extraordinary Assembly. Among the Party objectives was "an international policy, based on sincere friendship with the United States of America and with the peoples of Latin America as well as with other countries of the world *without discrimination of an ideological or political character* [emphasis mine] which permits Mexico the fullest dispersion of its foreign commerce." *La Situación Política de México: El Partido Popular Frente a la Sucesión Presidencial* in *Problemas de México*, I, No. 4 (July 15, 1958), 93–94.

[154] *Razón Histórica*, pp. 25–26.

From June 1948 to May 1957, when the Party's *Tesis sobre México* was presented to the public, the PPS program changed somewhat
in emphasis, but not strikingly except in a few matters. The *Tesis* is
more detailed and specific in its statement of Party positions and
objectives for Mexican political and economic affairs both at home
and abroad. Consisting of 250 articles divided among thirty chapters,
the *Tesis* begins with international problems, particularly world
peace, condemning the formation of aggressive regional blocs, U.S.
guided-missile bases in other countries, and the continuance of the
armaments race. The Party recommended that Mexico, among other
things, establish cultural and diplomatic relations "with all peace-
loving countries," and commercial relations with all countries, while
refusing to participate in regional pacts or blocs which threaten
peace, democracy, or the nation's independence. In Latin American
relations the Party upholds the Estrada Doctrine[155] as a recognition
policy, and encourages the country to assist the peoples of Latin
America in their attempts to counter the activities of imperialist
and traditionally reactionary forces.[156] Economic matters follow
problems of international relations, and the first of the major changes
occurs in this field. Where in 1948 the Party had advocated only
control, in 1957 it recommended the nationalization of basic industries and credit institutions as a principle of national economic
life. The *Tesis* repeats the earlier program in its call for protection
of national industry against foreign competition and for limitations
on investment of foreign capital. A second but lesser change is to be
noted on the latter issue. Whereas in 1948 the Party program supported intergovernmental loans as the least obnoxious form of foreign
capital, in 1957 it advocated loans from international credit institutions as preferable to any others.[157] The *Tesis* next examines various

[155] This doctrine was enunciated by Genaro Estrada in 1930. Estrada maintained that recognition should not depend on the origin or ideology of the regime to be recognized. Mexico does not follow this doctrine consistently, e.g.,
in the cases of the People's Republic of China or Franco's Spain. It does at
times give lip service to the theory of Estrada.

[156] *Tesis sobre México: Programa del Partido Popular* in *Problemas de
México*, I, No. 4 (July 15, 1958), 23–27.

[157] *Ibid.*, pp. 27–33. The Federal District Committee of the PPS requested
the government to nationalize the electrical industry (*El Popular*, August 5,

sectors of the economy, setting forth the Party's suggestions for improvement and functioning.[158] The *Tesis* virtually repeats the earlier program in those chapters dealing with the rights of women (omitting the political aspect since women now have the right to vote), laboring men, *campesinos*, youth, soldiers, Indians, civil servants, and the middle class.[159] The *Tesis* also calls for establishment of the free municipality, a greater outlay for education, the introduction of proportional representation, and the raising of the general standard of living. A new problem introduced since 1948 is that of the bracero, and the Party roundly condemns the economic situation in Mexico which causes these thousands of laborers to seek work in a foreign country. The Party expresses its fears over the loss of some of those workers who remain in the United States and over the new ideas which the returning workers bring back to Mexico. "They are being converted [through propaganda], without wishing to be, into supporters of perpetual submission of our country to the nation of the north."[160] To eliminate the need for braceros, the Party recommended new schools and industries in affected areas, further land reform, resettlement of some families, establishment of cooperatives,

1958); at the National Agrarian Congress of Toluca in October 1959 (*El Popular*, October 29, 1959) Lombardo called for the nationalization of private banks. The PPS National Directorate was critical of the President's 1959 report to the nation for its failure to provide for nationalization of public credit, further diversification of international markets [meaning increased bloc trade], or stronger control of foreign investments. The Directorate was also critical of the government's announced plan to use international credits to expand the government petroleum corporation, commonly called PEMEX. See *El Popular*, September 10, 1959.

[158] *Tesis sobre México* in *Problemas de México*, I, No. 4 (July 1958), 34–41.

[159] *Ibid.*, pp. 62–78. The Twelfth National Council of the PPS in February 1959 proposed laws to revise education, grant municipal autonomy, increase state intervention in the economy, and create a National Commission on Minimum Salaries with power to keep salaries in line with price rises (*El Universal*, February 23, 1959, pp. 1 and 25). In the course of the PPS electoral campaign of 1958, various candidates urged more and better food, clothing, and living conditions for children, increased salaries and the 40-hour week, social security, longer vacations for workers, and freeing of the unions from corruption and control by political parties (*El Universal*, June 2, 1958, p. 14). With regard to the last point, no evidence is available that the PPS took any steps to end its control over the UGOCM.

[160] *Tesis sobre México* in *Problemas de México*, I, No. 4 (July 1958), 48.

and the creation of a commission to study the problem and make further suggestions. To implement these basic goals, it called for the creation of a "National Patriotic Front of democratic forces," to support a common platform and a common slate of candidates. This front was to be composed of some elements within the government and the PRI, all the members of the PPS, the Mexican Communist Party, and "other minor groups." The front was also to include "the nationalist industrial bourgeoisie who are defending the independent economic progress of Mexico," those intellectuals "of progressive ideas," and great sectors of the middle class "who know that their interests can only be defended by alliance with Mexicans who desire the autonomous progress of their country." In other words the potentially democratic and patriotic forces of Mexico, according to the PPS, are those who have felt adversely the effects of the "semicolonial structure of our country," whether economic or political.[161] The PPS front has had but limited success. In the 1952 and 1955 elections the Party succeeded in concluding alliances with the PCM and POCM, but in 1958 even this small success was not to be achieved. Lombardo attempted to bring the official party, the PRI, into a new alliance by having it accept his *Tesis sobre México,* and tried to persuade the PCM and POCM to accept the candidacy of López Mateos. López Mateos and the PRI rejected the *Tesis,* and the Communist parties rejected López Mateos. As a result, the most the PPS could salvage was its own support of López and a claim that the PPS had contributed to his victory.[162]

From a study of the formal PPS programs published in 1948 and 1957 one could not prove that the Party was Marxist, much less Communist. Only at the Third National Assembly in October 1960 did

[161] Lombardo Toledano, *La Situación Política,* pp. 93–95. Lombardo continued to push the idea of such a front not only prior to the election (Cf. *El Universal,* September 8, 1957, p. 14) but also afterwards (*El Universal,* July 26, 1959, p. 1).

[162] At its Second National Extraordinary Assembly the Party decided not to support López Mateos formally but to urge the members to vote for him "as the necessary first step in the fight for the establishment of the National Patriotic Front." *Dictamen del Partido Popular sobre el Informe de la Dirección Nacional y la Participación del Partido en las Elecciones Federales de 1958* in *Problemas de México,* I, No. 4 (July 15, 1958), p. 127.

Lombardo formally add Socialist to the Party name. When he had proposed an openly socialist orientation for the Party at its 1955 National Convention, he encountered such widespread opposition that he quietly dropped the matter. The change of the Party's name in 1960, the description of the Party as the vanguard of the working class in the class struggle, and the policy of working toward a "people's democracy" and a socialist regime in the meaning of Marx and Lenin is the first formal Party declaration of adherence to international Communism.[163] Specific immediate objectives of the PPS have not changed drastically from early years; they still describe a Party that is strongly nationalist, reformist, and perhaps neutralist, but one that works within the context of the Mexican Revolution and advocates use of accepted liberal and democratic political machinery to implement its program. At the 1960 Party assembly the resolutions adopted called for restrictions on foreign capital, freedom for political prisoners, and the abolition of the crime of "social dissolution," a catchall phrase for the apprehension of persons who provoke disorders of all kinds.[164] These old themes were accompanied, however, by demands for the nationalization of civil broadcasting. The latter demands were departures from the *Tesis sobre México* in that they named specific industries to be nationalized.

In PPS propaganda the infernal regions are Wall Street and the Pentagon, the highest orders of devils are U.S. bankers, industrialists, and military officers with interests in Latin America, and their subordinate demons are Catholic clergy, of whatever nationality, and those Mexican businessmen and politicians who are friendly to the United States. Eden and its delights are represented by the Soviet Union and its satellites and their faithful adherents and friends everywhere. In its attitude toward the President of Mexico and toward many basic policies adopted by him, the PPS has, however, demonstrated much greater moderation in criticism than has the PCM or POCM. It is not clear whether he is regarded as a possible convert or a heretic, too powerful to challenge. Seldom is the President severely castigated while in office, though once he steps down he is fair

[163] *Excelsior*, August 28, 1960, p. 11.
[164] *Ibid.*, October 15, 1960, p. 14.

game.[165] At the same time the Party has attempted to increase its
popular prestige by taking credit for government action similar to
that advocated in its own program and by blaming Cabinet officers
and PRI officials for departures from "Revolutionary principles."

The Party pursues its goals through whatever media are available,
whether spoken or written. When the government created the Mexican Nuclear Energy Commission in early 1956, *El Popular* (then still
allied with the Party) hailed it as the "Protection and Safeguard of
Our Radioactive Material" from foreign exploitation, and the Party
platform for the Veracruz election of 1956 contained planks on increased production in various sectors of the economy, continued land
reform, higher standards of living, minimum salaries, education,
health, social security. Various speakers in the campaign condemned
lack of freedom in the municipalities, fraudulent elections, the "doc-
ile" press, the enormous volume of North American investments, and
the bracero situation.[166] Commenting on the White Sulphur Springs
meeting of the U.S., Canadian, and Mexican heads of state in the
spring of 1956, Lombardo Toledano impugned U.S. motives with
regard to Mexico by insisting that the United States tried to enlist
moral support from Mexico, a nonimperialist nation, for U.S. penetration in the Near and Far East and in Africa. At the same time the
PPS-dominated editorial board of *Problemas de Latinoamérica* accused the U.S. government of planning to conclude some form of
military agreement with Canada and Mexico.[167] Addressing the
Party's Federal District organization in January 1959, Lombardo berated the United States for intervention in Guatemala five years before, and defended the firing-squad operations of the new Castro gov-

[165] These generalizations were well illustrated at the 1960 New Year's dinner
at which Lombardo Toledano analyzed the current situation in Mexico. He
praised President López Mateos for stabilizing the peso and checking the rising
cost of living, for carrying out an enlightened labor and agrarian policy, and
for improving international relations through his recent trip to South America.
However he criticized the Administration for continuing to hold under arrest the
railroad strike leaders and the leaders of the PCM and POCM, for failure to
improve government efficiency, and for continuance in office of some of the
followers of former President Ruiz Cortines. Cf. *El Popular*, February 7, 1960.
[166] *El Popular*, February 16, 1956; February 21, 1956; and February 22,
1956.
[167] *Ibid.*, March 20, 1956.

ernment.[168] Furthermore, Lombardo, in his bid to establish a national patriotic front with the PRI and parties of the left for the presidential elections of 1958, claimed that a common program and a single candidate were needed to avoid the outbreak of revolt which could give an opportunity to the clergy and the agents of Yankee imperialism to seize power. When the PRI rejected his bid and the PPS suffered overwhelming defeats then and again in 1961, Lombardo blamed his setbacks in part on the influence of the clergy, as well as on the machinations of the government to prevent a fair tally of the votes. Lombardo's friends in the Problems of Latin American Society accused the United States of so building its relations with Mexico as "to impose its will as a peremptory law." The Party's National Directorate, in its report to the Second Extraordinary National Assembly, in November 1957, proclaimed that the gravest danger to the "progressive ideas and institutions of our country" lay in the new relationship between the Mexican clergy and the Vatican on the one hand and the governing class in the United States on the other.[169] The report states further that "Cardinal Spellman and other high chiefs of the Catholic Church in the United States, are those who are intervening in the political orientation of the Mexican clergy."[170] Finally the Resolutions Committee of the Assembly reported the following:

. . . North American imperialism, which . . . has suffered reverses of a military, economic and political character, is reinforcing its pressure on the countries of Latin America, trying to make true satellites of them, to lead them as it wishes, to exploit their natural resources and their working masses, and to impede their free relations with other nations who could cooperate in their economic development. This fact explains the anxiety of the monopolists of the United States to intervene more than in the past in the life of Mexico, with the pernicious effects that all our people feel and which are growing year by year.[171]

168 *El Universal*, January 19, 1959, p. 1.
169 Lombardo Toledano, *La Situación Política*, pp. 103–104.
170 *Ibid.*, p. 105.
171 *Dictamen del Partido Popular*, in *Problemas de México*, I, No. 4 (July 1958), 122. The dissidents on *El Popular*, while adhering to the official Party line for the most part, have not demonstrated quite the hostility toward the United States as has the Lombardo group. They also appear to be even more moderate than Lombardo in their criticism of the government and deplore vio-

The dispute between the United States and Cuba, beginning in early 1959, has also provided the PPS with abundant materials to attack the United States. As early as October 1960 Lombardo was predicting an invasion of Cuba and called upon the OAS and the UN to investigate the preparations being made in Guatemala with U.S. assistance. Following the April 1961 attack on Castro, Lombardo alleged that new plans were being laid for overthrowing the Cuban revolution. In November 1961 he protested to the UN that Guatemala and Swan Island were again being used as staging areas for an attack on Cuba and accused President Ydígoras of Guatemala and President Kennedy of the United States of plotting new moves against the island.[172] Some striking similarities are evident between the PPS and the Castro movement. The Party's new name, Socialist People's Party, is almost identical to the Cuban-Communist People's Socialist Party (PSP); and the adoption of the Marxism-Leninism, dialectical materialism, and the advocacy of a "people's democracy" is common to both the PPS and Castro's government. The editorial and news policy of *Política*, edited by PPS officers, often parrots Castro's attacks on the United States and its citizens.

Finally, PPS propaganda is Soviet oriented to the extent that Party leaders have unwaveringly adhered to Moscow pronouncements. They have repudiated no Kremlin doctrine nor criticized any Soviet activity unless the Soviet regime itself had engaged in prior self-criticism. The first issue of *Polémica*, an art magazine published by Federico Silva, son-in-law of Lombardo, contained an article advocating "Socialist realism in Mexico," a "Cantata on the Rosenbergs," and a poem by Lombardo entitled "Present and Future," a poem to the Sino-Soviet Bloc.[173] In 1956 Party leaders belatedly ad-

lence and agitation as means to legitimate goals. Cf. editorials in *El Popular* on February 21, 1959 on the Eisenhower-López Mateos meeting at Acapulco and on April 1, 1960 on current agitation against the government. See also the article "Curación del Antiyankismo" by Sadot Fabila H. in *El Popular*, October 18, 1959.

[172] *El Popular*, October 30, 1960; November 7, 1961; and November 21, 1961.

[173] *Polémica*, I, No. 1 (July 1954). The magazine announced as its purposes: (1) to develop an art which expresses national and universal reality, ie., man's disintegration in the capitalist world, (2) to expose and combat as

mitted errors of the Stalinist regime, but only after Khrushchev had publicized them at the Twentieth Party Congress of the USSR earlier in the year.[174] The 1957 report of the National Directorate gave a number of clues on the PPS attitude toward the Soviet Union and its allies. The opening paragraphs of the document treated of the threats to world peace in the postwar era. Ranking high among those dangers were "imperialist" adventures of the Western powers in Indo-China, the Near and mid-East, and Africa. The Egyptian War of 1956 was singled out for special mention, while the report held that "the imperialist governments, by every means have been pressuring the other Arab peoples to force them to accept their tutelege." Significantly, the Soviet suppression of the Hungarian revolt in 1956 was not mentioned. The report also maintained that "the cold war has dislocated the internal life of the United States and of the capitalist nations of Europe," but again omitted any mention of similar developments in the Soviet bloc. Optimistically stating that the danger of war was receding daily, the report pointed out that the "catastrophe would be provoked if an irresponsible government in the United States or one of its allies committed an unexpected act of aggression against one of the socialist countries or another, to dominate it, under the pressure of hysteria on the part of the captains of the great monopolies." Nothing was said of the possibility of similar acts on the part of the Soviet Union.[175]

To this point the evidence for a pro-Soviet position consists of obvious omissions, but in 1956 the Hungarian revolt provided a situa-

---

the greatest enemies of the nation the forces of Yankee imperialism and the local reactionaries who support them. The third stanza of Lombardo's poem literally translated reads as follows:

> How they shine in the new world
> the stars of the Soviet Union of
> China liberated
> and of the other people's democracies
> —an aurora borealis which announces the
> new day for all men
> of the five continents of the earth.

[174] The question might well be raised as to why the leader of a purely Mexican party felt that he had to explain to his followers these political events in the Soviet Union.

[175] Lombardo Toledano, *La Situación Política*, pp. 85–90.

tion where lines were clearly drawn and devotees of international
Communism could hide behind a mask of nationalism only by silence.
So shattering was the Soviet repression in Hungary that longtime
Communists in Europe denounced the action and abandoned their
support of the Soviet Union. Not so in Mexico. Not only the Communist Party but also the Socialist People's Party fully justified the
action, with no discernible repercussions among their cadres or rank
and file. The revolt in Budapest seemingly caught the Mexican Communists by surprise. With no instructions to follow and with the equivocal attitude at first adopted by the Soviet Union, the Mexican
Communists remained silent for nine days. Then on November 1 the
Mexico City dailies, including *El Popular*, reported an address given
by Lombardo Toledano the preceding evening at the Universidad
Obrera. Lombardo maintained that the revolt was the work of anti-
socialist reactionaries aided by Western imperialist agents. Soviet
intervention, he said, had been undertaken at the request of the Hungarian government under the terms of the Warsaw Pact. Enrique
Ramírez y Ramírez, then leader of the dissident faction within the
PPS, addressed himself more to the errors committed by Soviet and
Hungarian Communists which had led to a revolt sponsored by reactionaries. He did not commit himself on the justice of the Soviet
repression but called on all patriotic Mexicans to preserve their independence, work for world peace, and seriously reflect on the present
situation.[176] On November 4 *El Popular* published the official Soviet
statement. The most interesting remarks came from Lombardo himself in the November 18 issue of *El Popular*, as a response to an
anti-Communist meeting held two days previously to denounce the
Soviet action in Hungary. Calling the anti-Communist protest
"shameful and ridiculous," he alleged that the revolt in Hungary was
led by the Catholic bishops to restore the Hapsburg empire, an idea
"always agreeable to the Vatican." It was for this reason that Cardinal
Mindzenty requested Western intervention, and it was on Vatican
orders that clericals and reactionaries in Catholic countries had taken
up the fight against international Communism. Lombardo's attack
ended with a reminder to the Mexican people that reactionaries and

[176] *El Popular*, November 3, 1956.

the clergy have never defended oppressed peoples or the independence of small countries.[177]

To the Tibet revolt of 1959 and the Sino-Indian conflict from 1959 to the present, the PPS has given scant attention. Lombardo Toledano has refrained from public comment, but the dissidents who control *El Popular* have tried to explain away both embarrassing incidents. From March 27 to 29, 1959, *El Popular* ran daily reports on the Tibet uprising. At first it treated the news of fighting in Tibet with skepticism, but finally accepted the fact of revolt. Thereafter, *El Popular* indicated strong sympathy for Red China, and ignored the flight of the Dalai Lama. The Chinese-Indian dispute *El Popular* called a "pseudo-conflict" and designated Nehru and his people "true fighters for world peaceful coexistence."[178] Despite his strong public commitments to peace, Lombardo Toledano ignored the Soviet rupture of the nuclear-test halt in the fall of 1961. On October 24, the day following the Russian detonation of the greatest nuclear explosion the world had witnessed to that time, Lombardo lectured at the National University on international problems that threaten world peace. He talked of the Berlin and Congo problems, advocated a treaty between East and West Germany, urged all nations to fight for disarmament, called for the dismemberment of the OAS and NATO, and censured the UN as an organization that served only the imperialist countries. He failed to mention the resumption of nuclear testing by the USSR.[179]

ACTIVITIES

Basically, PPS activities follow the same pattern as those of the PCM, with shifts in emphasis here and there. Party meetings and conferences, electoral campaigning, agitation, and publication of views constitute primary Party activities. Recruitment and training, organizational problems, and finances constitute support measures for continued effective Party operations.

Finances are a constant problem, and in some respects the PPS has

[177] *Ibid.*, November 18, 1956.
[178] *Ibid.*, December 10, 1959.
[179] *Excelsior*, October 25, 1961, p. 14.

appeared worse off than the PCM. The Party has had but indifferent success in operating its own newspaper (*El Popular* was never the official Party organ), and the frequent moving of Party headquarters in the past few years gives indication that rentals could not be managed. Party funds appear more plentiful at election time, possibly owing to special donations of friends and sympathizers who choose the opportunity to support political opposition to the government party, the PRI. From time to time PPS headquarters announces special fund-raising drives, usually far in excess of what normally might be expected. In March of 1957 the Party opened a campaign to raise 500,000 pesos for PPS participation in the forthcoming election races. A common technique is to sell Party "bonds" which are not redeemable. Funds are also needed for travel of members within Mexico and abroad. In the latter cases the individuals involved usually attend meetings not as PPS members but as delegates for other associations or organizations such as labor, the peace movement, or professional societies. As such, they apparently receive the same sort of aid from Soviet-sponsored international organizations as do members of the PCM.

Party statutes stipulate that Party support comes from ordinary and special assessments on the members, gifts from Party sympathizers, public collections, and proceeds from Party activities organized for the purpose. The last method probably refers to fund-raising dinners, socials, and raffles held by the Party from time to time.[180] The statutes also forbid the acceptance of gifts or subsidies from the national or state governments in Mexico or "from any foreign organization." Monthly dues are assessed on the ability to pay, according to the following schedule:

Income per Month		Dues per Month
Over	*To*	
0	150 pesos	10 centavos
150 pesos	200 "	20 "
200 "	300 "	50 "

[180] "Análisis de la Linea Estratégica y Táctica del Partido Popular," *IV Asamblea General Ordinario del Partido Popular en el Distrito Federal que se celebrará en la Ciudad de México, los días 30, 31 de Octubre y 1º de Noviembre de 1959,* p. 17.

300 pesos	400 pesos	1 peso
400 "	500 "	2 pesos
500 "	600 "	3 "
600 "	800 "	5 "
800 "	1,000 "	10 "
1,000 "	1,500 "	20 "
1,500		Set by the National Committee

Dues are paid by the member to his local Committee, which retains 40 per cent. The Municipal, State, and National Committee receive 30 per cent, 20 per cent, and 10 per cent respectively. In the Federal District the Local Committee retains only 30 per cent while the National Committee receives 20 per cent. Special dues are assessed only by the National Executive Committee.[181]

Although the PPS statutes are silent on the recruitment of new members, Party leaders, especially Lombardo, refer repeatedly to the need for lengthening the Party rolls. If Party membership figures are any indication, there is no sustained, concerted effort to attract new members. The most vigorous drive apparently was launched in the first year of the Party's organization (1947–1948) when Lombardo and his friends signed up 35,000 members, the minimum number then required to obtain entry of Party candidates on the official ballot. Enrollment climbed steadily for several years so that the Party was able to meet the new requirement of 75,000 members for the presidential-congressional elections of 1952. It has been estimated that membership may have gone to as high as 100,000 at that time, but internal troubles probably reduced it to less than 75,000 by 1960. Even prior to the troubles, Enrique Ramírez complained of poor organization and lack of discipline in the Party. In the past few years Lombardo has announced drives to raise total membership anywhere from 250,000 to 1,000,000, but no one seems to take these announcements seriously. When the Veracruz organization defected late in 1956, the Party attempted not only to recoup its losses in that state, but to compensate for them by recruiting in the northwest states of

[181] *Razón Histórica*, Articles 10, 11, 12, 13, 14, 15, and 16, pp. 45–56.

Sonora, Sinaloa, and Baja California, Norte. No spectacular results have been apparent.

The PPS statutes provide that each Party organ provide "a center of political education" to teach their members the history of Mexico, the economic, political, social, and cultural problems of the country and of their particular region, and the means of solving these problems in accord with the Party program. The National Executive Committee is charged with the responsibility of coordinating these activities.[182] In view of the confusion resulting from Lombardo's speech on "socialism" at the Second National Assembly in 1955, it does not appear that these "centers" had been particularly active or successful. Subsequent meetings and conventions of the Party have emphasized the constant need of indoctrination,[183] but training and indoctrination of PPS members appear to be carried on primarily in an informal manner. The Federal District Committee reported in 1959 that its Circle of Studies (Circulo de Estudios) was functioning regularly but that it was insufficient to train all Party cadres. The Committee stressed that more Circles were needed but there is no evidence that the problem has been met.[184] While there are lectures and speeches and documentary films from time to time, especially in the Federal District,[185] the rank and file are kept informed of Party activities and viewpoints more through informal discussions and the reading of Party literature, such as news sheets and special publications. An excellent example of the latter was the Party's *Tesis sobre*

[182] *Ibid.*, Articles 17 and 18, p. 47.

[183] The Eleventh National Council meeting in July 1958 listed as its first and second resolutions: (1) the training of new members, and (2) revival of the permanent work of training all members—*El Popular*, July 29, 1958.

[184] "Análisis de la Linea," *IV Asamblea General Ordinario del Partido Popular*, p. 18.

[185] The PPS Regional Committee for the Federal District organized a series of conferences, June 9–13, 1958, on the general theme: "The People's Party and the National Action Party." Speakers included Lombardo, Lázaro Rubio Felix, Jorge Carrión Villa, Anselmo Mena, and Antonio Pérez Elías—Cf., *El Universal*, June 7, 1958, p. 14. On August 13, 1959, Lombardo gave a conference on "The Economic Development of Mexico and the People's Standard of Living"—Cf., *El Popular*, August 18, 1959. In late 1959 the Federal District Committee, in its "Análisis de la Linea," reported that the Cine Club Popular, an integral part of the Party's educational program, was functioning regularly on Sundays.

México, the PPS campaign program for the elections of 1958 which got wide distribution. In 1960 Lombardo announced that the *History of the Communist Party of the Soviet Union* was required reading for Party leaders. Published in the USSR and covering the period 1883–1959, the work explains the new strategy and ideology of the twentieth and twenty-first Party congresses of the USSR. The principal center for training PPS junior leaders is unquestionably the Universidad Obrera. Recognized by the government as a bona fide educational institution, it has no formal connection with the Party. However, the Lombardo family both controls and uses the UO as a Marxist training institute.

Since the organization of the PPS in 1947–1948, the Party has had scant success in leading the urban masses in agitation programs. First of all, Lombardo's protégés in the labor movement, Fernando Amilpa (now deceased) and Fidel Velásquez (currently secretary general of the CTM) renounced Lombardo's leadership of Mexican labor in the mid-1940's. Not only did they refuse to carry the CTM into an alliance with the PPS but they withdrew the union from its affiliation with the CTAL. Lombardo's attempts to retain his influence among the independent unions of the petroleum, electrical, mining, and railroad workers has likewise failed. Today PPS influence is strongest in the National Teachers' Union, where Marxist doctrine became deeply entrenched in the 1930's.[186] Although the PPS does not control the teachers, PPS members have held and currently hold official positions in the union. There appears to be a tacit agreement of "live and let live" between Communist and non-Communists in the highest level of the teachers' union, in sharp contrast to the anti-Communist national leadership in Mexico's other labor organizations.

For nine years Lombardo was also a power among student groups in Mexico City and some of the states. However, he overstepped himself in 1956, with the result that PPS influence has been all but obliterated in that sector. Possibly owing to these serious reverses among urban groups, the PPS has recently concentrated its agitation energies among the *campesinos*, especially in Sonora. There the Party

[186] For what appears to be an exaggerated estimate of PPS strength in the teachers' union, see the monthly organ of Section IX of the teachers' union, *Unidad Magisterial*, V, No. 7 (August 1, 1954), 2.

found a readymade situation in the Cananea Cattle Company, owned by an American family but incorporated under Mexican laws. The Party agitated for the expropriation of the land by the government and its distribution among landless peasants. PPS and UGOCM leaders also conducted groups of _campesinos_ to squat on the lands of the Cananea Cattle Company and other large properties in northwest Mexico for several years. Although the government ousted the squatters and protected the property holders, the agitation attracted wide publicity and considerable sympathy in Mexico—the Revolution is not completely forgotten. Finally in 1958, when the government expropriated the Cananea Cattle Company, PPS activity shifted from agitation to the organization of the _campesinos_ who acquired the company lands, but successes have been moderate.

The most common form of PPS agitation has been the spoken or published protest directed generally at governmental authorities in Mexico and at PRI officials. On June 29, 1956 Lombardo and other PPS leaders held a mass meeting of protest in Tepic over the disappearance of Miguel Echauri, described as a _campesino_ leader. Lombardo claimed to have documentary proof implicating the state authorities in the disappearance. He also promised to start legal action within ten days if neither the state authorities nor the national Secretary of Agriculture reported satisfactorily on the matter.[187] But nothing further was done. In March of that same year, the PPS National Directorate published some "Declarations" in connection with the forthcoming visit of President Ruiz Cortines to the United States. Reminding the President of the strong nationalist current in the country, the Party leadership "expressed its confidence that the patriotism and grave historical responsibility of the President . . . 'would reject compromises for Mexico which lessen its sovereignty, its international liberty of action and democratic principles . . .' "[188] Following the arrest of Railroad Union Leader Demetrio Vallejo for provoking a nationwide railroad strike in April 1959, the PPS participated in the formation of a committee of intellectuals to secure his release, and in 1960 Lombardo raised objections to Project Mercury, a missile-tracking installation in Sonora. He questioned the wisdom

[187] _El Popular_, February 2, 1956.
[188] _Ibid._, March 24, 1956.

of Mexico's cooperating with a country having technical difficulties in rocketing.[189] In the summer of 1958 the Party unsuccessfully petitioned the Congress to intervene in Sonora on the grounds that the governor was forced upon the state against the will of the majority.[190]

Electoral campaigns are used for both agitation and propaganda purposes, but unlike the PCM, the PPS has made some serious efforts to elect its members to office, especially in the national legislature. Many Party members wish the PPS to give full opposition to the PRI and all its candidates, as does the PCM, but Lombardo has steered the Party on a more moderate course. The President, while in office, is usually free from serious attacks by the PPS although Cabinet members are not exempt. The PRI high command, the Central Executive Committee, has been caustically attacked by Lombardo, who on one occasion said that government disregard of the popular will was worse under the PRI than in the times of Porfirio Díaz. On another occasion he predicted that civil war would result if the PRI prevented the people from voting freely in the 1958 presidential elections. PPS members have protested the vote count for various offices in every election since the founding of the Party. In fact the first election in which the PPS participated (the congressional in 1949) caused an internal crisis. In accordance with a practice that has now become custom, the PRI "awarded" a few deputy seats to opposition parties, with the PPS obtaining two. Despite protests, Lombardo permitted the members to take their seats, but Narciso Bassols, one of the Party founders, and a few others resigned in protest. Lombardo permitted it in 1952, and again in 1961, but not in 1955 and 1958; members who took their seats in those years, despite Party orders to the contrary, were expelled. In 1958 the PPS also refused to participate in the Electoral College of the Congress on the grounds that it did not want to be an accomplice of a "gigantic electoral fraud." On other occasions in local, state, and national elections the PPS has supported PRI candidates. The most important such event was the Party decision to recommend to its members the PRI presidential candidate of 1958, Adolfo López Mateos. Lombardo's attempt to swing the PCM and POCM into a broad-based "democratic and patri-

[189] *New York Times*, May 22, 1960, p. 33; *Política*, May 1, 1960, pp. 8–9.
[190] *El Popular*, August 13, 1958.

otic national front" signally failed.[191] The PCM and POCM refused
to compromise with the official party or with other parties. The Nationalist Party of Mexico (Partido Nacionalista de México—PNM),
describing itself as Christian socialist, rejected outright Lombardo's
proposal, the PRI refused to cooperate, and the PRI candidate,
Adolfo López Mateos, rebuffed Lombardo's invitation to accept a
separate nomination by the PPS. Since Lombardo felt his Party was
too weak financially and organizationally to run its own candidate, he
attempted to salvage some prestige by continuing to support López
Mateos. Several months after the election he claimed that López
Mateos won the Presidency because during his campaign he had
formed a "national front" which was supported by the PPS masses.[192]
There is no evidence that the PPS received special rewards for its
efforts by the government or by the PRI, or that it materially advanced any of its objectives by its campaign. At best, Lombardo has
held his own. His position was so weak that he had no choice but to
support López Mateos. Recent government repression has touched the
PPS but slightly, but Lombardo knows that an all-out attack would
lead to the Party's direct immediate repression. He sees his Party's
role as one of replacing the PCM as the Soviet representative in
Mexico. As a result he criticizes the government moderately.

Propaganda activities play a vital role in the Partido Popular Socialista, but not quite so exclusively as in the PCM. The Party has
established an official bookstore, the Librería Popular, but the PPS
has had difficulty in publishing a national Party newspaper. One of
its more recent ventures, entitled *El Mexicano*, published its first
issue, an eight-page tabloid, in October 1957 under the directorship
of Indalecio Sáyago, then national secretary of propaganda and a

---

[191] Lombardo broached the subject of such an alliance as early as September
1956. He repeated his proposal in the summer of 1957, but at its National Assembly in November the PPS decided not to support any candidate formally because of López Mateos' attitude. The Assembly did urge the members to support
López "as the necessary first step in the fight for the establishment of the National Patriotic Front." Cf., *El Universal*, November 24, 1959, pp. 1, 5, and 38.

[192] *El Universal*, January 19, 1959, p. 1. This was a speech addressed to
Party members of the Federal District on the occasion of their occupancy of
new offices. It should be noted that Lombardo does not state that López won
because of PPS support, but he clearly implies it. This is typical of the tactics
used by Lombardo.

member of the National Directorate. *El Mexicano* was published, although irregularly, until early 1959 at which time the Party leaders drew up plans to substitute for it a monthly magazine on Marxist theory. More important was the journal of the PPS organization in the Federal District, the *Boletín Informativo del Partido Popular en el Distrito Federal*, which first appeared in 1956. After publishing four issues between April and September, the *Boletín's* staff announced that the paper would appear irregularly thereafter as a general Party newspaper.[193] Seven more issues of the *Boletín Informativo* were published up to April 1959, when the police raided the headquarters of the Federal District Committee.[194] Publication was then suspended. In July there appeared, for Party members only, the first issue of *Correo del Partido Popular en el Distrito Federal* and in August a second issue.[195] No further issues were published, although in the summer of 1960 the Party was trying to raise money to publish it once more. In the wake of the Third National Assembly, October 1960, the PPS began to publish *Avante* as the organ of the Central Committee and *El Popular Socialista* as the general Party newspaper.[196]

Other media are also used to advertize the Party's views. Handbills and pamphlets expressing Party policies are widely distributed at election time.[197] PPS materials, particularly speeches and articles by Lombardo,[198] and Party documents have been published by Manuel Marcué Pardiñas, a Party member, in his various periodicals, *Problemas de Latinoamérica, Problemas Agrícolas y Industriales de México, Problemas de México*, and *Agronómica*. The boards of editors and the collaborators on all four publications are dominated by PPS

[193] *Boletín Informativo del Partido Popular en el Distrito Federal*, No. 4, September, 1956.

[194] "Análisis de la Linea," *IV Asamblea General Ordinario del Partido Popular*, p. 15. No. 11 was never distributed because of the raid.

[195] *Ibid*, p. 15.

[196] *El Popular*, April 4, 1961; June 29, 1961.

[197] Jacobo Escobedo Zárate, PPS candidate for deputy from the second district in the Federal District, protested that this kind of campaign literature in his behalf was removed by employees of the Cleaning and Transport Department, allegedly at the orders of the chief of the Federal District. Cf. *El Universal*, July 3, 1958, p. 26.

[198] See Bibliography for some recent works by Vicente Lombardo Toledano.

members although the second includes some non-Communists as well as members of the PCM. Marcué Pardiñas and Jorge Carrión also began editing a confidential newsletter, *Política Mexicana*, in September 1958. This was expanded to a semimonthly news magazine of excellent format and substance in May 1960 and is called simply *Política*. Although cable and photo service are obtained cheaply, the quality of the venture presupposes a considerable subsidy from sources other than the Party, which is chronically in debt. PPS propaganda themes have also found outlet through *Ahí Va El Golpe*[199] (now defunct), directed by dissident member Alberto Beltrán of the Taller de Gráfica Popular; *Paralelo 20*, directed by PPS sympathizer Jesús Alejandro Martínez; and *Guión de Acontecimientos Nacionales e Internacionales*, a monthly founded in 1956 by Narciso Bassols Batalla, whose father, Narciso Bassols, was a founder of the PPS. Despite the resignation of the elder Bassols from the PPS in 1949, the family has continued to sympathize with Lombardo and the broad objectives of the Party. *Guión* has also run articles by members of the PCM and POCM.[200] Lombardo also finds outlets for personal and Party views in the non-Communist press. José Pagés Llergo, director of *Siempre*, has opened that periodical to Lombardo articles on many occasions in the past few years; leading Mexico City dailies publish news and views on the PPS, especially at election time; and both *Excelsior* and *El Universal* accepted as paid advertising the PPS *Tesis sobre México*, the Party campaign program for 1958.

Until 1957 the most important outlet for PPS propaganda and views was the daily Mexico City newspaper, *El Popular*, believed by many to be the official Party organ. *El Popular*, however, was never owned nor controlled by Lombardo Toledano. Founded in 1938 as an organ for the labor movement, the Marxist owners and publishers of *El Popular* joined the PPS when the Party was founded in the late 1940's. Until 1955 the paper nicely filled the role of an official news sheet, though it never became such formally. With the split between Ramírez and Lombardo in November 1955, the staff of *El Popular* sided with the former. The estrangement of the paper from the Party leadership first became apparent in the summer of 1956, when it se-

[199] *Ahí Va El Golpe* ceased publication in 1959 for lack of funds.
[200] Cf. *Guión*, Vol. III, 1958.

verely criticized the student strike leaders, all Lombardo men. As the bitterness of the feud between Ramírez and Lombardo intensified through late 1956 and into 1957, *El Popular* more and more showed sympathy for Ramírez, though it continued to publish information on the Party. Until its demise in November 1961,[201] *El Popular* could be considered an independent leftist newspaper with sympathies for the objectives of the PPS but with hostility to the leaders. Thus, the schism of the intellectuals from the PPS accounts for the continuous attempts to found a national official Party newspaper.

In organization, general activities, and propaganda themes all three parties are roughly similar. In membership, leadership, and tactics, however, they have varied to a marked extent. All three parties are highly centralized, although a small degree of collective leadership was introduced into the PCM and POCM about 1960. All have spent much time and energy in propaganda activity, but the PCM has been the most successful in publishing viable party periodicals. The themes of all publications are directed toward enhancing the position of Communist countries in Mexico and in undermining U.S. influence. While PCM and POCM members come from primarily lower-middle- and lower-class origins, PPS members are more distinctly professional middle class. Perhaps this accounts in part for the more militant nature of the PCM and POCM attitudes and activities, and the PPS' more moderate response to the ruling party and the government. Of the three parties, the PPS has enjoyed the greatest success in attracting members and in obtaining concessions from the government, limited though these gains may be.

[201] The last issue of *El Popular* was November 30, 1961.

III. Communist-Front Organizations in Mexico

Introduction

A Communist "front" is an organization which pretends to be independent of Communist control in order to attract and manipulate non-Communists who are sympathetic to the stated goals of the group. Such groups are "fronts or facades behind which Communism operates."[1] They may be purely national and directed solely by the local Communist apparatus. On the other hand, they may be affiliated with an international organization. In the latter event, general policies, programs, and propaganda will be outlined by Moscow with national implementation left to local Communist leaders.

Of the thirteen international fronts with headquarters in various parts of Europe, six (including the five largest) have affiliates in Mexico. By far the most important in terms of influence, numbers, and organization are the World Federation of Trade Unions (WFTU) and the World Peace Council (WPC); their Mexican affiliates are among the most important fronts in that country. The World Federation of Democratic Youth (WFDY) and the International Union of Students (IUS) have had little influence in Mexico since the government broke the back of a Communist-led student strike in 1956. The Women's International Democratic Federation (WIDF) has been able to attract few Mexican women,[2] and the In-

[1] *Facts about International Communist Front Organizations*, p. 5.
[2] The WIDF sponsored a Congress of Latin American Women in Santiago,

ternational Organization of Journalists (IOJ), one of the lesser international fronts, has had only a small following dating from 1955.

Front organizations, as their titles indicate, may be divided into two general types: those directed to the populace at large, and those directed to specific target groups. Among the former may be classified the several Bloc-Mexican friendship and cultural exchange societies, the "peace" movement, and lesser organizations designed to attract support for revolutionary or leftist movements in neighboring Latin American countries. Special targets at which fronts are aimed include women, students, labor, farmers, and professional and intellectual organizations. Few fronts have enjoyed any real success either in attracting large numbers of adherents or in influencing private and/or public action in behalf of their goals. At most they can strengthen or reinforce prevailing attitudes in Mexico. They cannot impede or pose serious obstacles to official government policy.

Of minor interest are numerous front organizations that are quickly formed, and as quickly abandoned, to meet a specific situation from which Communist leaders expect to make political propaganda. In this category fall the Alliance of Patriots of Latin America against Colonialism and Imperialism. Founded in January 1957 following the Bandung Conference, the Alliance proposed the linking of Latin American and Afro-Asian nations in "anticolonialist and anti-imperialist activities." Nothing further has been heard of it. From a similar mold came the National Committee for the Liberty of Political Prisoners and the Defense of Constitutional Liberties.[3] This Committee was founded in June 1959 to protest the imprisonment of the railroad strike leaders who had been seized in April. Since some of these people are still held by the authorities, the Committee publishes

---

Chile, in November 1959. Three women from Mexico attended. The WIDF also scheduled a Congress for Women of the Western Hemisphere for July 1962 in Cuba. With respect to the latter, a forum of women from Mexico, Central America, and the Caribbean met in Mexico City in April 1961 to discuss the problem of unifying the women of Latin America and of participation in the Congress. Cf., X.X., "Actividades comunistas en América Latina," *Estudios sobre el Comunismo*, Año VIII, No. 29 (July-September 1960), p. 80; and X.X., "Actividades comunistas en Iberoamérica," *Estudios sobre el Comunismo*, Año X, No. 35 (January–March 1962), p. 68.

[3] *Excelsior*, October 8, 1959, p. 12.

a bimonthly journal, *Liberación,* issues an occasional protest, and held a national congress in the summer of 1960.[4] Organizations in Mexico other than those discussed here have from time to time been accused of Communist control, infiltration, or manipulation. That Communists hold membership in such organizations cannot be denied, but care must be taken not to assume undue influence on their part for activities taken by the group. National feeling runs high in Mexico, anti-U.S. sentiment is strong, and admiration for Soviet technical and industrial achievements is widespread. Frequently the goals of nationalists and Communists coincide. When they do, personal contacts and unified actions between the groups occur. In this manner the fronts can often attract temporary support from non-Communist individuals and organizations.[5] Two such nationalist groups, frequently accused of being under powerful Communist influence if not outright control, are the University Student Federation (Federación Estudiantial Universitaria—FEU) at the National University, and the National Chamber of the Transformation Industry (Camara Nacional de la Industria de Transformación—CNIT), a highly nationalistic employers' association. Neither is Communist-controlled or even measurably Communist-influenced, although both have cooperated at times with Communist groups and organizations to a degree that would be unthinkable in the United States. The Mexican milieu permits such action without serious social, economic, or political reprisals.

The National Liberation Movement (Movimiento de Liberación Nacional—MLN)

The Movimiento de Liberación Nacional constitutes the most vigorous and influential Communist front in Mexico today. Founded in 1961, primarily to unite the Mexican left, which has been severely fragmented, the MLN enjoyed some initial success in attracting widespread attention and a degree of popular interest. Its founders succeeded in enlisting the support of former President Lázaro Cárdenas,

[4] H. Lara, "México: El anticomunismo conduce al fascismo," *Problemas de la Paz y del Socialismo,* Año III, No. 12 (December 1960), pp. 96–97; and X.X., "Actividades comunistas en Iberoamérica," *Estudios sobre el Comunismo,* Año IX, No. 32 (April–June 1961), p. 97.

[5] *Excelsior,* January 19, 1960, p. 17.

and adopted a program of considerable nationalist appeal that included advocacy of closer ties between Mexico and Castro's Cuba, opposition to U.S. imperialism, the freeing of political prisoners, redistribution of national wealth, and the socialization of land.[6] Members from all three Communist political parties and from numerous Communist-front groups have participated in the organization from its inception, but no single group has appeared to dominate it. Following some initial cooperation, a struggle for control ensued among the contentious and diverse leftists comprising the organization. Unable to dominate the MLN, Vicente Lombardo Toledano disassociated himself and his political party (PPS) from the movement in June 1962. PCM influence appeared to be increasing, but the Communist Party obviously does not dominate the movement.

The ideological origin of the MLN dates back many years to the Soviet call for colonial and semicolonial countries to liberate themselves by throwing off the yoke of imperial rule. Nikita Khrushchev spoke of the success of the "National Liberation Movement" at the Twentieth Party Congress in 1956, and the Thirteenth Congress of the PCM in 1960 proposed the creation of such a movement in Mexico.[7] None of this propaganda contained basically new ideas that had not been repeated for some years by the PCM, PPS, and POCM. Then in March 1961 the World Peace Council sponsored in Mexico City the Latin American Conference for National Sovereignty, Economic Emancipation, and Peace, a meeting designed primarily to rally wide support for the Castro regime in Cuba. The Mexican delegation included members from a large cross section of Mexican leftist and Communist organizations, and in the euphoria of international sponsorship and common goals they laid plans to unify the Mexican left. Their efforts resulted in the creation of the National Liberation Movement at the First National Assembly for National Sovereignty, Economic Emancipation, and Peace, held August 4–5, 1961 in Mexico City.[8]

During its first year the MLN pursued a vigorous recruitment and

[6] *New York Times*, March 6, 1961, p. 2; March 26, 1961, p. 32.
[7] Edelmiro Maldonado L., *Informe al V Pleno del Comité Central sobre el Tercer Punto del Orden del Día (7–13 Dic.—61)*, pp. 34–35.
[8] *Política*, September 15, 1961, pp. i–xvii.

organization campaign. In 1962 it claimed to have established over 300 committees and to have attracted over 500,000 members.[9] Both figures unquestionably represent gross exaggerations, but it cannot be denied that the movement has attracted wide interest, particularly since Cárdenas has openly supported it. Most of the membership, however, appears to be drawn from Communist and Communist-front organizations whose leaders simply enrolled their total membership. Political parties as such cannot affiliate with the MLN, but their youth, labor, and women's groups are permitted to join and have done so.

The MLN is highly centralized in organization despite its regional, state, and municipal committees. The seven-man governing board, called the Executive and Coordinating Commission, includes Communist leaders such as Manuel Terrazas, an officer of the PCM, but appears to be dominated by pro-Communist and leftists such as Alonso Aguilar and Narciso Bassols who have a long history of front-group participation without open party affiliation.[10] In January 1962 the following persons comprised the Executive Commission: Alonso Aguilar, Narciso Bassols, Enrique Cabrera, Cuauhtémoc Cárdenas, Enrique González Pedrero, Braulio Maldonado, Manuel Terrazas. A larger advisory body of twenty-eight, called the National Committee, includes the members of the Executive Commission in addition to representatives of a wide variety of political groups and organizations.[11]

The basic question concerning the MLN revolves around the degree of success it has enjoyed in serving as a vehicle for leftist unification in Mexico. The idea of unity was greeted with enthusiasm at the March 1961 conference, and all groups worked in a generally cooperative spirit to organize the August meeting at which the MLN was officially launched. The only major difference to appear involved the representation of political parties on the National Committee. The PCM advocated such representation, but the majority vetoed the proposal.[12] For about the first ten months all seemed to go well with

[9] *Ibid.*, November 1, 1962, p. 9.
[10] *Ibid.*, January 15, 1962, p. 37.
[11] *Ibid.*, September 15, 1961, p. xviii.
[12] Maldonado, *Informe al V Pleno*, p. 35.

the movement. Leaders and factions that had been squabbling for years apparently were working harmoniously in the new organization. However, the old dissension erupted into the open in June 1962 when Vicente Lombardo Toledano withdrew his support and ordered all PPS members to break their ties with the MLN.

The immediate source of the discord rested in disagreements over the control and leadership of the Mexican delegation to the World Conference on Disarmament and Peace scheduled for July in Moscow. The MLN and the Mexican Committee for Peace, the latter long dominated by the PCM, slighted the PPS in drawing up the list of delegates, with the result that Lombardo ordered his followers to withdraw from both groups. He also renounced his cooperation with *Política* and with its editor Manuel Marcué Pardiñas, a member of his own party, because of its strong support of the MLN. On the other hand, Lombardo announced that the PPS would continue to support the World Congress on Disarmament and Peace by sending its own delegation.[13] The action of Lombardo again illustrates one of the basic problems of the left in Mexico: the high degree of personalism that infects the movement. Although ideological differences obviously separate the various groups, they seldom constitute the major obstacles to unity. Whether or not to include the national bourgeoisie in the parties and fronts, whether or not to cooperate partially with the government, whether or not the Cuban road to revolution can be followed by Mexico today—all these have been debated vigorously and bitterly by the leftist factions, but they are secondary to the drive for dominance by the various Communist leaders. Lombardo on earlier occasions broke his links with the peace movement when he could not lead it. He did so again in June 1962. It remains to be seen how long the PCM can tolerate collaboration with the MLN without exercising control, or how long other groups can tolerate the PCM if it gains control of the National Liberation Movement.

The Mexican Peace Committee (Comité Mexicano por la Paz— CMP)

The Mexican peace movement grew out of the International Peace Conference held in Paris in April 1949 and the American Continental

---

[13] *Excelsior*, June 17, 1962, p. 7.

Peace Conference held in Mexico City in September of that same
year.[14] A Mexican group dominated by members of the PCM and PPS
established a national organization during 1950 and called the First
National Peace Conference in Mexico City, May 16–20, 1951. It has
been estimated that between 800 and 1,000 membership credentials
were issued at that time. During the remainder of 1951 and into
1952 a concerted campaign was undertaken by the organization to
collect signatures endorsing the Stockholm peace declaration. A
high-water mark of 300,000 signatures was reported by April 1952.[15]
The initial success of the movement is attributable to the fact that the
peace campaigners successfully concealed for many months the movement's Communist character from thousands of Mexicans who sin-
cerely and anxiously desired a settlement of international disagreements. The movement began to decline rapidly by the end of 1952
with the emergence of effective anti-Communist counterpropaganda
and exposure. Despite repeated attempts to stir up interest and enthusiasm in succeeding years, the movement has been reduced to
impotence on the national political scene although within the Communist movement it continues to be one of the primary front groups.
By the mid-1950's only the Communist press gave any space to its
activities, including meetings of congresses and conferences. The
notable exceptions to the rule of silence occurred when former President Lázaro Cárdenas accepted the Stalin Peace Prize in a Mexico
City ceremony in February 1956 and when he cosponsored the Hemispheric peace conference of March 1961. The latter was given limited attention, however, by the news media, on the advice of the
government.[16]

The Mexican peace movement began under the auspices of both
the PCM and the PPS. In its initial stages Vicente Lombardo Toledano appeared to be the leading figure. He clearly dominated the

[14] *Cultura Soviética*, X, No. 59 (September 1949), 1.

[15] *Ibid.*, XV, No. 90 (April 1952), 6.

[16] Communist attempts to capitalize on these events were not entirely successful. Most of the Mexican papers were critical of Cárdenas for accepting the
foreign award, although *El Popular*, February 25, 1956, headlined an article
defending Cárdenas in accepting the Prize: "No Doubt about the Mexicanism
of Cárdenas." Much more hostility has greeted Cárdenas in the aftermath of
the March 1961 conference.

Mexican delegation to Paris in 1949, although Dionisio Encina, secretary general of the PCM, also attended. Lombardo, and Cárdenas *in absentia*, were elected international officers, the former organizing the Continental Peace Congress held later that same year for the purpose of arousing interest in the creation of national movements everywhere in Latin America. In line with his policy for conducting the PPS, Lombardo desired to keep the peace movement from becoming openly Communist, as was urged by several speakers at the Congress. He chose to play down the leading "peace" role of the Soviet Union in favor of a running attack on Yankee imperialism, a theme of vital significance for Latin Americans of various political persuasions. Within the Mexican peace movement a rivalry that involved both politics and tactics soon developed between PPS and PCM members. For some years there appeared to be a fairly even balance and an alternation in control of the organization. For the past several years, however, PCM members have dominated the directing board, and the PPS members, though still proclaiming Soviet peace goals, have tended to disassociate themselves from the movement's activities. The struggle flared into the open in 1962, with the PPS formally withdrawing in June. This conflict is but another example of the general struggle between Lombardo and PCM leaders to lead the Communist and extreme left movements in Mexico.[17]

The peace movement still attracts some non-Communists, a few of some importance, and attempts to exploit them whenever possible. Its most notable recruits have been retired General Heriberto Jara, president of the movement, and former President Lázaro Cárdenas. The movement has not been entirely happy with Cárdenas since he has refused to identify himself exclusively with the "peace" partisans and has even on a few occasions had some kind words for the peaceful intentions of the United States. Nonetheless, Cárdenas has never disavowed his election to an international peace office, and he accepted the Stalin Peace Prize. In his acceptance speech Cárdenas

[17] *Noviembre*, December 4, 1954, commenting on the recent World Peace Council meeting held in Stockholm, noted that the "fight for peace" in Mexico was narrow and limited. *Noviembre* laid much of the blame on the PCM for treating the peace movement as its personal property and causing its internal conflicts.

again disappointed the Communists by his failure to regard the peace movement as the sole agent for world peace. His oration was a masterpiece of caution and noncommitment. He gave the Prize to charity.

Mexican peace propaganda follows slavishly the international line. During the late 1950's the peace partisans demanded the abolition of nuclear tests and weapons, made emotional appeals against atomic war, and insisted upon the establishment of peaceful coexistence. These general proclamations were frequently supplemented by accusations that Yankee imperialism in Latin America is a threat to peace and that the United States is plotting to drag Latin America into future wars. Peace propaganda, however, has consistently failed to note Soviet nuclear tests and stockpiling of nuclear weapons, and in the March 1961 Hemispheric peace conference, all nuclear testing was entirely ignored. Peace propaganda was directed against all forms of U.S. aid to Latin America, including the Food for Peace program, and against U.S. control over Puerto Rico. The conference also called for the return of the Canal Zone to Panama, the renunciation of all treaties that support the Monroe Doctrine, and an increase in diplomatic and cultural relations between the Soviet Bloc and the countries of Latin America.[18]

The Mexican peace organization has been known under several names. In the early 1950's it was called the National Committee for Peace (Comité Nacional Pro-Paz), but through most of the decade it was known as the Mexican Peace Movement (Movimiento Méxicano por la Paz). The group reorganized in 1959, since the peace organization had virtually disappeared, and a new name was adopted: the Mexican Committee Impulse in the Struggle for Peace (Comité Mexicano Impulso de la Lucha por la Paz). The reorganized movement participated in the Latin American Peace Conference held in Havana March 1960, hosted the Latin American Conference for National Sovereignty, Economic Emancipation, and Peace held in Mexico City March 1961, and sponsored the National Peace Congress held in Mexico City June 1962. However, at the Hemispheric peace conference of March 1961 the movement adopted its old name of Mexican Committee for Peace (Comité Mexicano por la Paz) and

[18] *La Voz de México*, February 8, 1957 and July 26, 1958; *Excelsior*, March 12, 1961, p. 12.

participated in a new national organization, the National Liberation Movement (Movimiento de Liberación Nacional—MLN), that was to stress not only peace but also freedom from Yankee imperialism. The relationship existing between the MLN and the peace movement has been close, with considerable overlap among the leaders of the two groups. Because of the titular leadership of Cárdenas in the MLN, that organization has tended to overshadow the peace movement. In actual operations, however, PCM members control only the CMP. Until 1962 the PPS continued to participate in the peace movement as well as in the MLN but in a quarrel, ostensibly over policies, organization, and tactics but probably over control, Lombardo Toledano announced in June 1962 that his Party would not participate in the National Peace Congress and was withdrawing from both the peace movement and the MLN. Lombardo added, however, that he adhered to the international peace movement, that he would send delegates to the forthcoming World Congress for Disarmament and Peace, and that he proposed to found a new Mexican peace organization composed of all adversaries of war.[19] The Directive Board of the peace movement was: Guillermo Montaño; Miguel Mesa Andraca, former PPS member; Ana Reyes; Jorge L. Tamayo, PCM; Ruth Rivera, PCM; José Chávez Morado, PCM; Eulalia Guzmán, PCM; Víctor M. Carrasco, PPS; Adriana Lombardo de Silva, PPS.

The Mexican-Russian Institute of Cultural Exchange (Instituto de Intercambio Cultural Mexicano-Ruso—IICMR)

The Mexican-Russian Institute of Cultural Exchange was inaugurated in June 1944 in the Palace of Fine Arts in Mexico City. In the wartime glow of Soviet and Western collaboration a number of prominent non-Communist Mexicans not only joined the Institute but accepted positions on its governing board. Furthermore, Mexican officials from the Departments of Government, Health, and Education presided jointly with the Soviet ambassador at the opening ceremonies.[20] By the early 1950's, however, most of the non-Communists

---

[19] *Excelsior*, June 21, 1962, pp. 5 and 14, presents a full account of the PCM–PPS quarrel over the peace movement and the MLN and a good résumé of both.

[20] *Cultura Soviética*, I, No. 1 (November 1944), 35, 43. First president was

had withdrawn or become inactive, with the Institute (Instituto de Intercambio Cultural Mexicano-Ruso—IICMR) becoming one of the chief centers for the dissemination of Soviet propaganda in Mexico, for the exchange of visitors, and for liaison between Embassy personnel and key Communists and Communist sympathizers in Mexico.[21]

Since 1951 branches have been established in Guadalajara, Monterrey, Saltillo, and Morelia, the last in July 1958. For some time in the mid-1950's the Guadalajara and Saltillo groups were inactive, but at the end of 1959 all the branches were operating, although on a modest scale.[22] The main unit in Mexico City has remained active since its founding, but the enthusiasm of the first years has waned; a low point was reached following the death of the director in 1956. For the past few years the Institute has continued to function primarily because the Soviet Embassy has taken a keen interest in its program and unquestionably has contributed to it financially.

A burst of activity marked the first six months in the life of the Institute. Not only were 3,300 pesos in dues collected from members, but over 27,000 pesos in gifts poured in for its support. Materials on Mexican culture were collected to exhibit in the Soviet Union and 600 books and numerous toys displaying Indian arts and crafts were shipped abroad. Soviet culture was represented in Mexico by a display at the book fair held in Mexico City in the summer of 1946, a photo exhibit of Soviet life displayed in five cities, and the publication of three books by Soviet authors.[23] Finally the first issue of *Cultura Soviética*, the official journal of the Institute, appeared in November

---

Luis Chávez Orozco, economist and historian; Alfonso Reyes, one of the leading lights of Mexican literature, was one of the two vice presidents. Leopoldo Zea, philosopher and historian, headed the Philosophy Section and Manuel Sandoval Vallarta, later the director of the Mexican Atomic Energy Commission, headed the Exact Services Section. As late as November 1945 the president of the Mexican-North American Institute of Cultural Relations attended a function of the IICMR. Dr. Bentley was photographed chatting amiably with a Soviet Embassy secretary and President Chávez Orozco. Cf. *Cultura Soviética*, III, No. 13 (November 1945), 52.

[21] Subcommittee To Investigate the Administration of the Internal Security Act, *Communist Threat to the United States through the Caribbean*, p. 145.

[22] X.X., "Actividades comunistas en América Latina," *Estudios sobre el Comunismo*, Año VIII, No. 29 (July–September 1960), 88.

[23] *Cultura Soviética*, I, No. 1 (November 1944), 35.

1944. Subsequently the activities of the IICMR settled down into a routine of publication, conferences, and Soviet film exhibits. During the past few years the Institute has acted as agent for the People's Friendship University of Moscow. The IICMR has distributed information on requirements for admission and has received applications of students desiring to attend.

At least eight monographs have been published on life in the USSR and two series of smaller publications were undertaken in the mid-1950's: the Ideas Collection and the Culture Collection.[24] Contributors to these were both Mexican and Russian, but primarily the latter. In 1955 and 1956 the Institute published three issues of a new quarterly, *Ciencia y Técnica*, but was forced to discontinue it for lack of interest. Scientific articles were once more published in the Institute's official journal. By far the most successful publishing undertaking of the Institute has been the monthly *Cultura Soviética*, a handsome work which appeared regularly from 1944 to 1955. It was replaced in February of 1955 by *Intercambio Cultural*, smaller and at first of cheaper material. By early 1957 its quality had improved markedly, but it was still restricted to thirty-two pages. To exhibit and make available its own publications as well as other works on Soviet life and culture, the Institute has opened libraries and bookstores in Mexico City and Guadalajara. In 1945 the Institute sponsored news broadcasts, over radio stations XEFO and XEUZ, daily except Sunday, on cultural life in the USSR, but these were not continued.[25]

The conference program of the Institute has featured lectures by Mexican visitors to the Soviet Union. Some of these speakers have been non-Communists, such as Manuel Sandoval Vallarta, who lectured on "Physics in the USSR." Others have been Communist sympathizers, such as José Mancisidor, who spoke of his trip to the Soviet Union as head of a Mexican delegation to May Day festivities

---

[24] *Intercambio Cultural*, III, No. 15 (May 1956), 29; III, No. 17 (July 1956), 19.

[25] *Cultura Soviética*, II, No. 12 (October 1945), 1. Acting as patrons of these broadcasts were the People's Israelite League (Liga Popular Israelita—LPI), the League of Israelite Ladies (Liga de Damas Israelites), and the Constantine Oumansky Society.

in 1952, and who in 1955 addressed the Monterrey branch on "Soviet Literature."[26]

Soviet motion picture showings have been conducted regularly since the founding of the Institute. A weekly program was attempted with some success in the 1950's although many films were shown repeatedly. At times these viewings have been open to the public, at other times restricted to members. Among the films shown have been *Ivan the Terrible* and *Kutusov*. There have also been still photo exhibits on Soviet accomplishments in the arts and sciences, the ceremonies surrounding the awarding of Stalin Peace Prizes, and life in the Soviet Union.[27]

The Institute in its various publications, art and photographic exhibits, lectures, and motion picture showings has generally avoided political or controversial topics. For the most part it stresses the positive side of Soviet cultural, economic, and social achievements, with little criticism of opposing systems. The IICMR has officially stated that its goal is not to eulogize institutions or ideas, persons, or events in either Mexico or Russia, but to inform each country objectively on artistic, scientific, technical, and cultural achievements of both. It disavows political discussions. For the most part Institute publications have avoided politics except for some support for the peace movement in the early 1950's. Apparently this cost the organization some prominent members, and by 1955 and 1956 such transparent propagandizing was abandoned.[28] In other respects the Institute has not lived up to its stated goals. There is much eulogizing of both Mexican and Russian ideas, persons, and events that advance the cause of the Soviet Union. In his inaugural address as president of the In-

[26] *Ibid.*, XVI, No. 95 (September 1952), 48; *Intercambio Cultural*, I, No. 2 (March 1955), 32.

[27] *La Voz de México*, August 10, 1958.

[28] *Intercambio Cultural*, I, No. 1 (February 1955), 2. Despite its disavowals, this same issue stated: "*Intercambio Cultural* is a vigorous upholder of pacific relations among people. To encourage culture within and outside one's own frontiers is to encourage peace." Cf. also *Cultura Soviética*, III, No. 16 (February 1946), 51, for the high praise extended to the Communist-dominated People's Graphic Arts Shop (Taller de Gráfica Popular—TGP). The engravings reproduced, however, were noncontroversial.

stitute in 1957 the usually volatile and sharp-tongued artist Diego Rivera mildly urged greater cultural exchange between Mexico and the Soviet Union. He emphasized that it was necessary to strengthen peaceful and friendly relations with all people but preferably with "adult peoples" like the Russians. He urged travel to the USSR by Mexican youths, artists, writers, and scientists, and advocated the sponsorship of numerous cultural events so that the Soviet and Mexican people might reach a greater understanding of each other.

According to the statutes of the organization, the highest authority of the Institute rests in a general assembly scheduled to meet once a year. Day-to-day affairs are the responsibility of a large board of directors, each of whom is assigned to a specific field of activity.[29] In practice, however, it appears that the assembly, meeting infrequently, has little power and that the board apparently became inactive after the first year or two. The president and the officer in charge of publications dominate the organization, and the latter's two assistants comprise the administrative staff. What influence the Soviet Embassy has on the direction of Institute affairs cannot be accurately determined.

For several years until his death in 1956, José Mancisidor, prominent leftist historian and writer, presided over the Institute. His writings, translated into Russian, were said to be highly esteemed in the Soviet Union, and in 1955 on a visit to Moscow he presented the Lenin Library with about 100 volumes on Mexican history and literature.[30] During his tenure the IICMR appeared to have close ties with Lombardo Toledano and the PPS because of the close personal friendship between Mancisidor and Lombardo. With the former's death, however, Acting President Efraín Huerta, the Institute's publications officer, directed affairs for almost a year until Diego Rivera, the painter, was elected to the post in July 1957. Both men were members of the PCM. Rivera, however, died in November 1957, and for many months the Institute's affairs were in the hands of an acting president. Operations were once more regularized with the election

[29] For a list of the first officers, cf. *Cultura Soviética*, I, No. 1 (November 1944), 43.

[30] *El Popular*, February 5, 1955.

of Manuel Mesa Andraca, a former PPS member, as president in January 1959. Three other members were elected at the same time to comprise the executive committee. Huerta remained in charge of publications.[31]

The Society of Friends of the USSR (Sociedad de Amigos de la URSS—SAURSS)

The Society of Friends of the USSR was originally founded in the 1920's to foster increased cultural relations between Mexico and the Soviet Union. The Society apparently declined and perhaps disbanded during the years when diplomatic relations were broken between the two countries. It reappeared in the 1940's when diplomatic relations were re-established, but its importance has been overshadowed by the IICMR, which has the open support of the Soviet Embassy in Mexico. As a result, activities of this Sociedad de Amigos de la URSS (SAURSS) have been reduced to little more than an annual celebration of the Russian October Revolution.[32] Members and leaders have been associated with both the PPS and the PCM. Its president for many years, José Mancisidor,[33] who died in 1956, was a close adherent of Vicente Lombardo Toledano. Fausto Pomar, secretary of the organization, assumed control with Mancisidor's passing.

The Mexican Society of Friends with People's China (Sociedad Mexicana de Amigos con China Popular—SMACP)

To further political, economic, and cultural relations between Mexico and Communist China, the Mexican Society of Friends with People's China was founded by members of the PCM in 1953. Its

[31] The officers and staff, January 1959, were as follows: Manual Mesa Andraca, president; Emma Hurtado (widow of Diego Rivera), Executive Committee member; Ester Chapa, Executive Committee member; Jerónimo Baqueiro Foster, Executive Committee member; Efraín Huerta, in charge of publications; Azalia Avila, administrative staff; Noemi Villaseñor, administrative staff.

[32] *Cultura Soviética*, XVIII, No. 108 (November 1953), 5. The SAURSS and the IICMR jointly proclaimed June 1951 Friendship Month between the peoples of Mexico and the Soviet Union. Participants in the Inaugural Act included members of both the PPS and the PCM. *Cultura Soviética*, XIV, No. 80 (June 1951), 1.

[33] *Intercambio Cultural*, IV, No. 19 (September 1956), 12.

membership is concentrated in Mexico City and Monterrey,[34] and the scope of its activities is narrow but sporadically vigorous. It has sent greetings to the people of the Soviet Union and Communist China on the anniversaries of their accessions to power.[35] In 1957 it cooperated with several other groups in celebrating a cultural program honoring Red China[36] and addressed an open letter to President Ruiz Cortines requesting that Mexico enter into diplomatic relations with Communist China and support her entry into the UN.[37] February 1960 was a particularly active month: the Society (Sociedad Mexicana de Amigos con China Popular—SMACP) sponsored a Chinese art exhibit and two lectures. Moisés de la Peña, a co-chairman of its Commercial Exchange Committee, spoke on the Chinese rural communes, and Guillermo Montaño, a co-president of the Society, spoke on the problem of cultural exchange between the two countries.

The directive board of the SMACP, elected annually, is composed of a three-man presidency, a secretary general, and nine chairmen or co-chairmen of committees. The board consists of members of both the PPS and PCM as well as members without known party affiliations. Members of the PCM appear to be in the ascendant.[38]

The members of the directive board elected February 1960 were as follows: Guillermo Montaño Islas, president; Guillermo Haro, president; Eli de Gortari, president; Lorenzo Zelaya, secretary general; Leslie Paz de Zelaya, secretary of finance; Paula Gómez Alonso, librarian; Raquel de Gortari, secretary of radio and publications; Moisés de la Peña, secretary for commercial exchange; Alonso Aguilar Monteverde, secretary for commercial exchange; Celia Cal-

[34] Corporation for Economic and Industrial Research, *United States-Latin American Relations. Soviet Bloc-Latin American Activities and Their Implications for United States Foreign Policy*, p. 86. Hereafter referred to as *Soviet Bloc-Latin American Activities*.

[35] *Cultura Soviética*, XVIII, No. 108 (November 1953), 4; X.X., "Actividades comunistas en América Latina," *Estudios sobre el Comunismo*, Año VIII, No. 29 (July–September 1960), 88.

[36] *La Voz de México*, September 30, 1957.

[37] *Ibid.*, October 4, 1957.

[38] *El Popular*, February 16, 1956.

derón, secretary of arts; Elena Huerta, secretary of arts; Clara Porset de Guerrero, secretary of arts; Ester Chapa, secretary of science.

The Mexican-Czechoslovak Institute of Cultural Exchange (Instituto de Intercambio Cultural Mexicano-Checoeslovaco— IICMC)

The Instituto de Intercambio Cultural Mexicano-Checoeslovaco (IICMC) was founded in 1957 to further Mexican-Czech relations on all fronts, although the emphasis is placed on cultural activities. Thus far its activities have been confined largely to the showing of Czech films.[39] In June 1958 the first issue of a scheduled monthly bulletin appeared, and in August 1961 a branch was established in Monterrey. In late 1960 a group of seventeen Mexican teachers, led by Ignacio Márquez Rodiles, vice president of the IICMC, visited Czechoslovakia.

The Mexican-Rumanian Friendship and Cultural Exchange Society (Sociedad de Amistad y de Intercambio Cultural Mexicano-Rumana—SAICMR)

A society to foster friendship with Rumania was formed in August 1956 during the celebration of the Mexican-Rumanian Friendship Month at the Universidad Obrera. Both the August celebration and the founding of the Mexican-Rumanian Friendship and Cultural Exchange Society grew out of a contact made earlier in the year in Rumania by Federico and Adriana Silva in their tour of the Soviet Bloc area.

This Sociedad de Amistad y de Intercambio Cultural Mexicano-Rumana (SAICMR) may well be regarded as an adjunct of the PPS and/or UO, whose members dominate its board of officers. Federico Silva, Lombardo's son-in-law, was elected secretary and Adriana Lombardo de Silva, Antonio Pérez Elías, and Alberto Beltrán, all PPS members, were elected to the directive board. To avoid the appearance of a PPS monopoly, David Alfaro Siqueiros of the Communist Party and Enrique Arreguín of no party affiliation were also elected.[40]

39 *La Voz de México*, September 4, 1957.
40 *El Popular*, September 1, 1956.

*The Mexican-Bulgarian Friendship and Cultural Exchange
Society (Sociedad de Amistad y de Intercambio Cultural
Mexicano-Bulgara—SAICMB)*

The Mexican-Bulgarian Society was founded by Vicente Lombardo
Toledano in September 1959. Under the terms of the statutes a directive council was elected, with Enrique Yáñez as president and
Adriana Lombardo de Silva as secretary general. The aims of the
Society are the establishment of diplomatic and commercial relations
between the two countries and the fostering of cultural ties between
their peoples.

*The Mexican-Hungarian Friendship and Cultural Exchange
Institute (Instituto de Amistad y Intercambio Cultural
Mexicano-Hungaro—IAICMH)*

This Mexican-Hungarian Friendship Institute was organized in
October 1960, probably under the auspices of the PPS. The organizer
was Clementina B. de Bassols, widow of Narciso Bassols who had
been a friend and longtime associate of Vicente Lombardo Toledano.[41]

*The Society of Friends of the People's Republic of Poland
(Sociedad de Amigos de la Republica Popular de Polonia—
SARPP)*

*The Adam Mickiewicz Patronate (Patronato "Adam Mickiewicz"
—PAM)*

Two organizations are dedicated to the promotion of ties between
Mexico and Communist Poland. The Society of Friends of the
People's Republic of Poland, founded in 1955 by Ignacio Márquez
Rodiles, has been dominated by followers of Vicente Lombardo Tole-
dano. The Adam Mickiewicz Patronate is directed by Germàn List
Arzubide, at one time associated with the Communist splinter party
the POCM, but since the mid-1950's, friendly to Lombardo and his
group. In January 1956 the Patronate ran a paid announcement in
El Popular, then still closely allied with Lombardo, on a meeting of
journalists and illustrators honoring Mickiewicz, the Polish poet and

41 *Excelsior,* October 16, 1960, p. 25.

patriot, on the one hundredth anniversary of his death.[42] In March the organization awarded a prize to Ricardo Cortés Tamayo, feature writer for *El Popular,* and to Alberto Beltrán, of the TGP, both of whom were members of the PPS.[43] Then in June 1956 the Society and the Patronate jointly sponsored a commemorative ceremony, which included Polish dances and music, in honor of Mickiewicz in the San Mateo School in the Federal District. As a climax to the proceedings it was announced that the school's name was changed to Adam Mickiewicz School. Bernard Bogdanski, chargé d'affaires of the Polish Legation, and Eliseo Bandala, director of primary education in the Ministry of Public Education, attended.[44]

The Society of Friends of Guatemala (Sociedad de Amigos de Guatemala—SAG)

The Mexican Society of Friends of Revolutionary Guatemala (Sociedad Mexicana de Amigos de Guatemala Revolucionario—SMAGR)

The Sociedad de Amigos de Guatemala (SAG) was organized in 1953 as hostility was beginning to grow among non-Communists in the United States and Mexico against the Communist-infiltrated Administration of President Jacobo Arbenz of Guatemala. Founded and since dominated by members of the PCM, the SAG has attempted to stir up support for the program of and participants in that Administration. With the outbreak of rebellion against Arbenz in the spring of 1954, the organization agitated within Mexico for Mexican governmental support for the regime, and when Arbenz was overthrown, for the reception into Mexico of Guatemalan exiles. Although the Mexican government granted asylum to supporters of Arbenz, its action cannot be attributed to the agitation of the SAG and other Communist groups but rather to a long-standing position in Mexican foreign policy.

Another group of friends of Guatemala (Sociedad Mexicana de Amigos de Guatemala Revolucionario—SMAGR) was founded by

[42] *El Popular,* January 18, 1956.
[43] *Ibid.,* March 12, 1956.
[44] *Ibid.,* June 29, 1956.

members of the PPS in 1955, within a year of the overthrow of the Arbenz Administration. The organization has carried on less activity than the SAG, and demonstrates the continuing rivalry between the PPS and the PCM to lead the Communist movement in Mexico. With the decline of interest in the overthrow of Arbenz and with the obvious impossibility of his restoration, these two groups have virtually ceased their activities.

The Society of Friends of Cuba (Sociedad de Amigos de Cuba— SAC)

The Mexican-Cuban Institute of Cultural Relations "José Martí" (Instituto Mexicano-Cubano de Relaciones Culturales "José Martí")

The Journalist Friends of Cuba (Periodistas Amigos de Cuba)

The Sociedad de Amigos de Cuba (SAC) was founded by members of the PCM in 1953, following Batista's *coup d'état* of the previous year. Beyond some expressions of sympathy for "oppressed" Cubans and for the Popular Socialist Party (Communist) on the island, the SAC has done little. For several years it was apparently moribund. However, with the victory of Fidel Castro in January 1959, followed by a policy of bitter hostility to the United States and friendship to the Sino-Soviet Bloc, the Society of Friends of Cuba revived. In 1959 it apparently merged with a newly formed association to support the Castro Revolution. In January 1960, with several groups, it attempted to stage a pro-Castro rally but was frustrated by the police.[45] The Society apparently has met with some success in attracting non-Communists, for its president early in 1960 was Francisco Franco Carreño, a justice of the Supreme Court of Mexico.

In July 1961 the Mexican-Cuban Institute of Cultural Relations "José Martí" was founded at a meeting of some 200 persons, including Mexican Supreme Court Justice Franco Carreño and Cuban Ambassador José Antonio Portuondo. The president of the new organization is Agustín Cué Cánovas, an associate of Lombardo Toledano.

---

[45] Cf. the paid advertisement protesting police pressure "¿Es Este un Ejemplo de Democracia?" in *Excelsior*, January 19, 1960, p. 17.

It is not known what the relationship is between the SAC and the new Institute.[46]

A third organization supporting the Castro regime in Cuba is the Journalist Friends of Cuba, founded early in 1961. The group issued a declaration of support for the Cuban Revolution at the time of the invasion by exiles, April 1961.[47]

The People's Graphic Arts Shop (Taller de Gráfica Popular—TGP)

The founders of the People's Graphic Arts Shop (Taller de Gráfica Popular—TGP) are responsible for the present revival of engraving, an art-form widely popular in Mexico during the nineteenth century. Engraving had suffered a decline in the early years of the twentieth century; but by the mid-1920's there was some renewed interest, and in 1930 Diego Rivera, Frances Toor, and Pablo O'Higgins edited a volume of the works of Guadalupe Posada. Simultaneously these same muralists began to use engravings in *El Machete*, the organ of the Trade Union of Revolutionary Painters (Sindicato de Pintores Revolucionarios)[48] and of the Communist Party.

In 1933 these and other artists founded the League of Revolutionary Writers and Artists (Liga de Escritores y Artistas Revolucionarios—LEAR), which secured government aid from President Lázaro Cárdenas. Some of the more fervent "revolutionaries" were soon disgruntled by what they regarded as "opportunism and job hunting" on the part of their colleagues in seeking government commissions. By 1937 LEAR was declining, and its Plastic Arts Section, under the "progressive and revolutionary" leadership of Leopoldo Méndez, broke away and founded the People's Graphic Arts Shop. They carried with them about nine or ten other artists. Younger artists have been recruited until in recent years the shop has included about twenty-five members. The most powerful influence on the group has been Posada, although the younger members have been more directly influenced by Méndez, who himself acknowledges the

[46] *Excelsior*, July 26, 1961, pp. 13–14.

[47] *El Popular*, April 30, 1961.

[48] Eugenio Múzquiz, "Un Arte del Pueblo," *Intercambio Cultural*, II, No. 9 (November 1955), 28–29.

influence of Posada.[49] The TGP is governed by a directive board of
five members elected annually.[50]

The group devotes itself primarily to engraving and lithography.
Within these fields it is dedicated "to the strengthening of peace and
friendship among peoples, and in the national scene to fighting
against the enemies of the Mexican people and to denouncing acts
which injure the nation and the people."

The Declaration of Principles of the TGP define the Shop as a
"collective work center for the promotion of functional production,
the study of the different branches of engraving and painting, and
different means of reproduction." The Principles further proclaim
that "art in the service of the people ought to reflect the social reality
of its time and requires the union of content and realist forms." The
organization is opposed to "abstractionism" and "formalism."[51] As
a result of their principles many of the members work in teams, although much work is produced on an individual basis. Their themes
are concerned primarily with the poverty, sufferings, and oppression
of the Mexican people. The United States as a nation, U.S. capitalists
as a class, and Mexican officials and businessmen as a type come in
for severe and bitter attacks. Alberto Beltrán, the leading younger
member of the Shop, in his inexpensive periodical *Ahí Va El Golpe*,
illustrated his attacks on the United States with engravings demonstrating Yankee capital as the cause of Mexican inflation: natives
kicking capitalists, with the caption "Mexico 1938, Suez 1956," and
an enchained Latin America secured by a lock representing the
United States, the key to which was the dollar sign.[52] As a rule, TGP
productions avoid themes of a patently Communist nature. Beltrán,
however, produced an engraving entitled "The Friendship of Mexico
and the USSR" and made a poster for the Communist-promoted
American Continental Peace Conference in 1949.[53] Furthermore, the

[49] *Ibid.*, p. 29; A. A. Sudorov, "El Taller Gráfica Popular en Moscú," *Inter-cambio Cultural*, I, No. 5 (July 1955), 14.

[50] *El Popular*, January 6, 1956 lists the officers recently elected for the year.

[51] Múzquiz, "Un Arte del Pueblo, "*Intercambio Cultural*, II, No. 9 (Novem-ber 1955), 30.

[52] *Ahí Va El Golpe*, No. 26, second half of August 1956.

[53] Múzquiz, "Un Arte del Pueblo," *Intercambio Cultural*, II, No. 9 (No-vember 1955), 32.

TGP exhibit at the Seventh Mexican Book Fair used paper doves, the Communist "peace" symbol, as its decorative theme. To attract the public TGP members demonstrated engraving techniques and sold their work at very low cost.[54]

The TGP has exhibited widely not only in Mexico but abroad. Angel Bracho, Arturo García Bustos, and Beltrán, to name only a few, have won national prizes. They have also exhibited in the United States, Western Europe, and in the Bloc. A 1955 exposition in Moscow included 300 engravings. On the whole, Soviet critics were laudatory, although they did object to the absence of colors and more seriously to the universally somber and sorrowful themes. Soviet critics complained the Mexican artists never demonstrated the happiness of the people.[55] In 1957 the Sixth World Festival of Youth and Students awarded two gold medals to Mexicans. One went to García Bustos and the other to the TGP as a unit.[56]

Politically, members of the TGP have aligned themselves with Vicente Lombardo Toledano and his Socialist People's Party. Within the Party, however, they formed a close connection with Enrique Ramírez y Ramírez and the intellectuals of his faction. When Lombardo demoted Ramírez in 1955 the TGP joined the dissidents and although its members have not been expelled from the Party, they have withdrawn from active participation. The TGP today may be considered a Communist splinter group.

The Center of Mexican Journalists (Centro de Periodistas Mexicanos—CPM)

The Center of Mexican Journalists was founded late in 1955 for the purpose of organizing a group, including both Communists and non-Communists, to participate in the activities of the Soviet-sponsored International Organization of Journalists (IOJ). In March of 1956 a preparatory committee, dominated by CPM members, was established to plan and organize for Mexican participation at the International Conference of Journalists scheduled for June in Hel-

[54] "La VII Feria Mexicana del Libro," *Intercambio Cultural*, IV, No. 23 (January 1957), 15.
[55] Múzquiz, "Un Arte del Pueblo," *Intercambio Cultural*, II, No. 9 (November 1955), 31.
[56] *La Voz de México*, August 21, 1957.

sinki, Finland.[57] The delegation which attended the mid-June meeting consisted of non-Communists as well as members of the PCM and PPS. At least four of the delegates toured the Soviet Union and Red China following the meeting. They had an interview with Premier Chou En-Lai, and reported to Mexico his denunciation of U.S. aid as imperialistic and his desire to trade with Latin America without conditions.[58] In October 1958 a Mexican, Renato Leduc, a vice president of the IOJ, and a member of the Mexican delegation to Helsinki in 1956, was invited to speak at the Venezuelan National Press Conference. Leduc bitterly attacked the coverage of Latin American news by the commercial news agencies and called for a truly Latin American organization. Probably as a result of this Conference, the Prensa Latina Agency was set up in Cuba early in 1959. Although Prensa Latina has denied Communist sponsorship, Communists did inspire and encourage its organization, have infiltrated it, and have aided it by providing news and utilizing its services.[59]

The People's Israelite League (Liga Popular Israelits—LPI)

The People's Israelite League was founded in the 1940's by a group of Communist sympathizers among Mexico's Jewish community. In October 1945 it cosponsored radio broadcasts on Soviet life with the IICMR.[60] For some years the organization constituted an important prop of the PCM, but in late 1956 it began to break away from the Party because of the latter's biting criticism of Israel and defense of Egypt in the brief war in October of that year. The LPI's present affiliations are unknown. It has published a newspaper in past years and has organized Jewish youth and women's groups in association with the main body.

The National Front of Plastic Arts (Frente Nacional de Artes Plásticos—FNAP)

The National Front of Plastic Arts was founded in 1952 by a group of artist members of the PCM; among them were the well-

[57] *El Popular*, March 5, 1956.
[58] *Siempre*, July 19, 1956.
[59] Subcommittee To Investigate the Administration of the Internal Security Act, *Communist Threat*, pp. 156–157.
[60] *Cultura Soviética*, II, No. 13 (October 1945), 1.

known painters Diego Rivera, Xavier Guerrero, and José Chávez
Morado. In 1956 the two latter artists were members of the National
Committee of this Frente Nacional de Artes Plásticos (FNAP). The
purposes of the organization, apart from its propagandistic value, appears to be to give national unity to various Communist and pro-
Communist artistic circles throughout Mexico, to sponsor Mexican
(usually Communist) art exhibits in Soviet Bloc countries, and to
sponsor Soviet Bloc art showings in Mexico.

During 1955 and 1956 the FNAP conducted an exposition of Mexican art in the Soviet satellite countries of Europe and in Red China.
The show was severely criticized early in 1956 by Diego Rivera for
its failure to include the works of more artists, especially of his wife,
Frida Kahlo. The National Committee of the FNAP responded with
a biting manifesto condemning Rivera. The Committee argued that
Rivera's statement reflected a recent growth of that individualism
which had plagued Mexican art circles and hampered the formation
of a professional organization for thirty years. Such individualism
is highly unsuited to a democratic organization and these prejudicial,
selfish, individualistic practices must be terminated, snapped the
FNAP National Committee.[61] In June 1957 the FNAP was planning
to send a small delegation of young artists to the Sixth World Festival of Youth and Students, scheduled for July in Moscow. The delegation was to exhibit a wide selection of paintings by young Mexican
artists.[62] Despite certain ideological differences, the members closed
ranks in October 1960 by refusing to exhibit their works in the Second Inter-American Biennial for Painting, Sculpture, and Engraving.
The boycott of the Biennial constituted an FNAP protest over the
arrest in August of David Alfaro Siqueiros, who was engaged in
Communist agitation against the government.[63]

*The Circle of Mexican Studies (Círculo de Estudios Mexicanos—
CEM)*

The Circle of Mexican Studies is one of the most successful Communist-front operations in Mexico today. Members of the PCM and

[61] *El Popular*, April 28, 1956.
[62] *La Voz de México*, June 9, 1957.
[63] *Visión*, October 21, 1960, pp. 76–77.

the PPS dominate its directive board and comprise about one third the rank and file.[64] They are the most flexible members of their Party and largely comprise the group that sponsored the founding of the National Liberation Movement (MLN) in 1961. On the other hand, prominent non-Communists of the left have played important roles in the organization, giving it the respectability and influence denied to the other fronts.[65] It has been reported that Narciso Bassols, the founder of the CEM, was, until his death in 1959, the contact man between the leaders of the group and the Soviet Embassy. Bassols' name did not appear among the members, but it was alleged that as the undercover leader of the organization he engineered the election of PCM member Alonso Aguilar to the presidency in 1957.[66] The importance of this election may have been overemphasized since a comparison of officers between 1956 and 1960 indicates that a game of "musical chairs" was played by the members of the directive board.

The officers of the National Directive Committee have been as follows:[67]

	In 1956	*In 1958*	*In 1960*
President	Ignacio González Guzmán	Alonso Aguilar M.	Enrique Cabrera
Secretary General	Jorge L. Tamayo	Jorge L. Tamayo	Jorge Carrión
Vice President	Enrique Cabrera	Jorge Carrión	Elí de Gortari
Treasurer	José Luis Ceceña	Ernesto Rodríguez	Mario Salazar Mallén
Voting Members	Matilda Rodríguez Cabo	Enrique Cabrera	Alonso Aguilar
	Alonso Aguilar M.	Elí de Gortari	Manuel Mesa Andraca

[64] Well-known Communists include Sra. Leslie Paz de Zelaya, Sra. Paula Gómez Alonso, Xavier Guerrero, Carlos Noble, and Rosaura Revueltas. They were listed among the members in *El Universal,* September 11, 1958, p. 13.

[65] *Ibid.* Listed were Leopoldo Zea, Jesús Silva Herzog, and Luis Chávez Orozco.

[66] Ing. Manuel Arcos Fenal, "Paparouv, el Titiritero de Nuestros Comunistoides," *El Universal,* July 13, 1957, p. 2.

[67] Cf. *El Popular,* March 24, 1956; and *El Universal,* September 11, 1958, p. 13; *Excelsior,* July 19, 1960.

Voting Members	Jorge Carrión	Manuel Marcué Pardiñas	Manuel Marcué Pardiñas
	José D. Lavín	Emilio Mújica	Guillermo Montaño Islas
	Francisco Martínez de la Vega	José D. Lavín	Jorge L. Tamayo

The importance of this front group lies in the fact that its membership consists of an elite corps of professionals, artists, intellectuals, and would-be intellectuals in Mexican society. Its purposes are to study and comment upon economic, political, and cultural developments in Mexico. Over half its some 300 members are concentrated in the Federal District, but important groups are to be found in Monterrey, Tijuana, Morelia, Mexicali, Oaxaca, Puebla, Uruapan, and Torreón. Smaller groups exist in about nine other towns and cities.[68]

The secret of the success of the CEM in holding outstanding non-Communists in its ranks and maintaining general respect in the community lies in the moderation of its attitudes and propaganda. Except through its officers, it cannot be linked with the Communist movement. Its postures, while somewhat antagonistic to the United States, socialist in tone, and reformist in spirit, are nationalistic rather than pro-Soviet, evolutionary rather than revolutionary, and critical rather than intransigent toward the government. In other words the CEM resembles the PPS in its general program—if anything it is milder in its political and economic demands—and for this reason is a true front rather than a strictly Communist organization, as are most of the other so-called fronts. Its leadership, however, because of the nature of its Communist ties, must be presumed to be motivated by a desire to advance the Soviet cause in Mexico, and for that reason the CEM must be considered in any study of the Communist movement in Mexico.

The National Directive Committee in July 1960 had the following representation:[69]

---

[68] *El Universal*, September 11, 1958, p. 13.

[69] *Excelsior*, July 19, 1960, p. 10. Party and front affiliations supplied by this author.

President................Enrique Cabrera [member of the PCM]
Vice President........Elí de Gortari [officer of the SMACP]
Secretary................Jorge Carrión [officer of the PP]
Treasurer................Mario Salazar Mallén [former member of the PP]
Voting members:
    Alonso Aguilar [member of the board of the SMACP]
    Manuel Marcué Pardiñas [officer of the PP]
    Manuel Mesa Andraca [director of the IICMR]
    Guillermo Montaño [officer of the SMACP]
    Jorge L. Tamayo [officer of the peace movement]

On the occasion of the meeting of heads of state of Canada, Mexico, and the United States in the spring of 1956, the CEM published an open letter entitled "What the Mexican People Expect from the White Sulphur Springs Meeting."[70] The tone of the letter was nationalistic and slightly hostile to the United States. Its authors strongly opposed the conclusion of any military pact involving Mexico, U.S. dumping of surplus commodities, and U.S. views on territorial waters then under discussion by an inter-American conference in the Dominican Republic. Although all three issues have formed themes for Communist propaganda, they cannot be termed Communist per se. Many non-Communist nationalistic Mexicans have heartily subscribed to them.

A 1958 proclamation covering a wide variety of issues and problems went beyond the above mild remonstrance in the manner and form of its criticism but on the whole continued to steer clear of positions that could be dubbed unmistakably Communist. The occasion for a full-page newspaper advertisement entitled "Call to Sanity,"[71] outlining CEM's position, was police repression of a demonstration and parade through Mexico City of the dissident teacher group led by Othón Salazar. The CEM condemned what it called an unprovoked attack on a peaceful demonstration. It accused the police of responsibility for the death of some and the wounding of hundreds of other persons, and protested the invasion of Salazar's home by secret service agents who came to arrest him. With these statements by way of preface, the CEM then proceeded to review the recent

[70] *El Popular*, March 24, 1956.
[71] *El Universal*, September 11, 1958, p. 13.

unrest in labor circles. It defended the land agitation and squatters' movement, led by PPS and UGOCM leader Jacinto López, on the grounds that the government had abandoned the agrarian program of the Revolution. It accused the authorities of permitting land, water, and other resources to fall into the hands of a small number of farmers, of permitting abuses with respect to "small properties," and of permitting *campesinos* to be despoiled of their lands. The authors of this program, noting that the police imprisoned "one of the most popular leaders," Jacinto López, insisted that the authorities hypocritically called López' followers "thieves" and "Red agitators." The article continued with a criticism of student conditions, of government suppression of strikes and demonstrations by labor, and of the indifference of current labor leaders to the demands of the rank and file.[72]

For the most part this second example of CEM attitudes can hardly be identified as Communist or Communistic. There is much sympathy among non-Communists for labor, *campesino,* and student aspirations, and much criticism of the police, army, and government for their disregard of civil and political rights. Prominent non-Communists have protested the arrest and imprisonment of Communists such as Jacinto López on the grounds that constitutional or legal guarantees were denied. What is disturbing in this CEM complaint is what is left unsaid. Nowhere is López' political affiliation mentioned nor the general policies of his Party. Furthermore, open Communist involvement in the strikes of 1958–1959 is completely ignored, and the moderate attitude of the government on the land question, the labor issues, and the student demand is conveniently forgotten. None of this, of course, proves Communist influence in the CEM, but it does arouse suspicion, which another incident bolsters. At the National Agrarian Congress held in Toluca in October 1959, Dr. Jorge Carrión, a member of the Political Directorate of the PPS and vice president of the CEM in 1958, represented both the PPS and the CEM at the Congress. In the expression of his views it is impossible to distinguish which of the two organizations he more closely represented. In the same manner as Lombardo Toledano he defined

[72] With minor changes, the protests of 1958 were repeated in 1960. Cf. *Excelsior*, April 19, 1960, p. 12; and July 19, 1960, p. 10.

the Mexican Revolution as "a democratic nationalist, and above all anti-imperialist movement." The large landholdings he styled capitalistic, not feudal, but he called for "patriotic unity" in support of President López Mateos. On specific issues, still following the PPS program, he called for the nationalization of private credit and the establishment of a cabinet position with full power over all agrarian affairs.[73] Again, none of these positions is necessarily Communist, although they are all included within the program of the Communist and Socialist People's Parties. As a group, however, that has pretensions to scholarship and intellectuality, the CEM opens itself to criticism because of the one-sided position that it takes. Little can be termed objective in the program of the CEM; its bias is revealed not so much by what it says and advocates as by what it leaves unsaid. This omission, coupled with the affiliation of its officers, places CEM at least on the fringes of the Communist movement in Mexico.[74]

In addition to its use of paid political advertisements in newspapers, the CEM disseminates its views through its own publication, *Cuadernos del Circulo de Estudios Mexicanos*, which has appeared on the average about twice yearly since 1954. The organization also has published occasional pamphlets and booklets.[75]

The Democratic Union of Mexican Women (Unión Democrática de Mujeres Mexicanas—UDMM)

The Vanguard of Mexican Women (Vanguardia de Mujeres Mexicanas—VMM)

Organized about 1950 by and among women members of the PCM, the Democratic Union of Mexican Women is not officially and formally a subsidiary of the Party. Active members number probably less than 100. Nowhere does the group appear to be effective in its propaganda, agitation, or recruitment. Since its founding the organization has been dominated by Paula Medrano de Encina, wife

---

[73] *El Popular*, October 31, 1959.

[74] In 1960 Cabrera announced his acceptance, as president of the CEM, of a gold medal awarded to the organization by the World Peace Council at its Stockholm meeting in October 1959. Enrique Cabrera, "Paz y Liberación Nacional," *Política*, Año I, No. 1 (May 1, 1960), 32–33.

[75] See Bibliography for listing of some of these.

of deposed PCM secretary general Dionisio Encina, and a high-ranking Party officer in her own right. Officers in 1953 were: Mireya B. de Huerta, president; Paula Gómez Alonso, vice president; Paula Medrano de Encina, secretary of organization. In 1953 Huerta attended a "peace" conference in Peking, and afterwards traveled through China, the USSR, and some of the satellites.[76] With headquarters in Mexico City, the UDMM also has branches established in a few other important cities and towns. It is affiliated with the international Communist-front Women's International Democratic Federation (WIDF). Outside Mexico City the group seems most active around Torreón and the Laguna area, where its members have joined in agitation sponsored by the Central Union of Ejido Societies (Unión Central de Sociedades Ejidales—UCSE). In June and again in October of 1957 they participated with farmers of the area in a Hunger March and in demands for more water for irrigation purposes.[77] In August of 1957 the UDMM group in Morelia criticized a local hospital for overcharging patients and underpaying workers.[78] The UDMM has also sponsored the Frida Khalo Art Exhibition, which was directed, in 1956, toward Mexican youth. The affair was billed as an opportunity for new young painters to display their talents. With the growing rift in the PCM, a dissident group of wives and members opposed to Encina formed the Vanguard of Mexican Women (Vanguardia de Mujeres Mexicanas), but in late 1960 Paula Medrano represented the UDMM at the meeting of the WIDF Council in Warsaw, and in 1961 at the founding of the National Liberation Movement (MLN) in Mexico City.

The Confederation of Mexican Youths (Confederación de Jóvenes Mexicanos—CJM)

The National Federation of Technical Students (Federación Nacional de Estudiantes Técnicos—FNET)

The Confederation of Mexican Youths consists primarily of an executive committee elected by a convention held about every three

[76] *Cultura Soviética*, XVII, No. 101 (March 1953), 38; XVII, No. 102 (April 1953), 4–14; XVII, No. 108 (November 1953), 48.

[77] *La Voz de México*, October 12, 1957.

[78] *Ibid.*, August 13, 1957.

years by participating student and youth organizations. The CJM was founded in 1939 under government sponsorship to give unity to the various youth and student associations supporting the Revolution. Its early leaders felt deep bonds of sympathy with Vicente Lombardo. With the swing to the right in Mexican politics and labor, the CJM refused to follow the trend and in fact supported Lombardo in his founding of a new leftist party, the PPS, in 1947. Although the CJM never formally affiliated with the PPS, it was long closely tied to it through its leaders, several of whom have been PPS members and officials. A rift between the CJM and Lombardo appeared in late 1955 with the demotion of PPS Leader Enrique Ramírez y Ramírez. Together with many other Party intellectuals, the CJM leaders became highly critical of Lombardo's highhanded tactics. Although few have disavowed their Party membership, a growing estrangement has taken place since 1956, as more and more the CJM has identified with the Ramírez faction. This split among the PPS youth members became public knowledge during the student strikes and disturbances in the spring and summer of 1956. The Sixth National Ordinary Congress held in April 1957, with about 600 delegates attending, confirmed in power the supporters of the Ramírez faction of the PPS. In accord, however, with its usual policy of sharing offices with other groups, the CJM slate of officers included at least one member of the JCM, the youth wing of the Communist Party, and other persons who were members neither of the PPS nor of the PCM.[79] The CJM is a member of the World Federation of Democratic Youth (WFDY) and the International Union of Students (IUS); a number of its affiliates participate in meetings of one or both of these international Communist-front organizations.[80]

[79] *Ibid.*, April 6, 1957.
[80] The Federación de Estudiantes Campesinos Socialistas, a CJM affiliate, was listed as a member of both the WFDY and the IUS in *Cultura Soviética*, XVIII, No. 108 (November 1953), 47; XIII, No. 78 (November 1950), 8. Samuel Mendoza, "La Reunión del Comité Ejecutivo de la Federación Mundial de la Juventud Democrática (FMJD)," *Estudios sobre el Comunismo*, Año IX, No. 33 (July–September 1961), 75, reported that at the Executive Committee meeting at Santiago, Chile, in April 1961, Manuel Ortega Cervantes of the PCM was a vice president and that in addition to the CJM, which is an affiliate of the WFDY, other organizations were invited to attend, including the Juventud Popular and the Juventud Comunista Mexicana.

The size and influence of the CJM is difficult to gauge accurately, since it is composed of numerous youth and student organizations not all of which are active participants in its programs. In the early 1940's it was estimated that the CJM consisted of affiliated student organizations totaling almost 100,000 members.[81] Today its membership is probably less than half that. After the student strike of 1956 in which one of its affiliates, the National Federation of Technical Students (Federación Nacional de Estudiantes Técnicos—FNET), suffered a disastrous defeat in a conflict with the government, its prestige has declined. It is doubtful that the CJM today could call out the bulk of its affiliates and their student bodies in a political strike. As a result CJM activities since 1956 have been confined to protests or expressions of support.[82]

The largest and most powerful of the CJM's affiliates was, until late 1956, the National Federation of Technical Students, centered primarily in the National Polytechnical Institute (Instituto Politecnico Nacional—IPN) in Mexico City. Like the CJM, the FNET is a holding company of numerous student associations organized primarily in the various schools of the Institute. Some student associations outside Mexico City are also included. The FNET, organized in 1937, early fell under the control of Marxist and Communist leaders. Its powers increased to such an extent that for some years it exercised virtual control over the faculty.[83] At the present time, however, it is subject to a large degree to the government-appointed director of the Polytechnical Institute.

[81] It still claimed 100,000 members in 1956 (*El Popular*, April 30, 1956).

[82] The CJM protested the shooting of students by police in Guatemala (*El Popular*, June 30, 1956) and Mexican police harassment of Juan Pablo Sainz, a member of the PCM Political Committee (*El Popular*, April 3, 1957). Troubles on the bus lines in Mexico City called forth a CJM resolution demanding the city take ownership (*El Popular*, September 26, 1958), and the resignation of the vigorous and forceful director of the National Polytechnical Institute, Alejo Peralta, evoked a CJM analysis of the Institute in which his leaving was greeted with warm approval (*El Popular*, March 2, 1959). With the inauguration of Adolfo López Mateos in December 1958, the CJM promised to support his program (*El Popular*, December 9, 1958) and a month later supported the regime in its quarrel with Guatemala over territorial waters and fishing rights (*El Popular*, January 25, 1959).

[83] *El Universal*, June 15, 1956, p. 1.

Like the CJM, too, the FNET long included among its leaders students sympathetic to the PPS and to Lombardo Toledano, but it never declared a formal affiliation with the Party. By the early 1950's PPS members had entrenched themselves in the boarding section of the Institute. They attracted vagabonds and pseudostudents and, through their control over student subsidies and scholarships, dislodged the legitimate students. With a nucleus of strong-armed supporters, organized, concentrated, and determined in their goals, men like Salvador Gámiz and Nicandro Mendoza, both members of the PPS, gained control over the FNET and used the student organization to further the political ends of their Party. In a bid for increased power, including control over the director of the Institute, the PPS leaders of the FNET led the organization in a series of violent riots and strikes that plagued Mexico City from April to October 1956. The struggle ended in victory for the government and the administrators of the Institute, and disastrous loss to the PPS both in power and prestige.

The student disturbances of 1956 started from a minor strike called on April 10 by the student association in the Higher School of Mechanical and Electrical Engineering of the National Polytechnical Institute. The dispute involved nonpolitical student complaints of long standing over finances, old buildings and equipment, and insufficient staff. On the following day Nicandro Mendoza, president of the FNET and PPS member, stepped into the dispute by calling a general strike. His demands included not only purely student interests such as increased subsidies and improved facilities, but also "a total change of the present general administration of the IPN," including the dismissal of the director, Rodolfo Hernández Corso. Telegrams to student federations throughout the country seeking support brought immediate response from the CJM and from the Federation of Students of Guadalajara, led by the notorious J. Guadalupe Zuno Arce.[84] Members of the Zuno family, long a power in the state of Jalisco, have been friendly with Lombardo Toledano but apparently have never joined his political party. To these first demands

[84] *El Popular*, April 11, 1956; and April 12, 1956. An editorial in *El Universal* (April 17, 1956, p. 3) estimated that the demands would raise the expenditures for the IPN from 52 million pesos to 250 million pesos annually.

Mendoza later added the abolition of the "Columbia Plan," which he had already attacked with success at Saltillo the year before. The plan consisted of an agreement between the U.S. and Mexican governments to carry out a survey of Mexico's technical training needs. The survey itself was conducted by Mexican researchers assisted by experts from Columbia University. The plan was unpopular in Mexico because it was regarded as foreign intervention in Mexican education. The PCM and PPS successfully capitalized upon these sentiments.[85]

Although the government was willing to make concessions in matters of student aid, it was unbending in its refusal to permit the FNET to participate in the School's administration. An impasse was reached and the strike continued. Meetings between the strike leaders and the Mexican Secretaries of Education and of Government produced no solution.[86] In mid-May the first open rift began to appear in student and PPS ranks over the conduct of the strike. *El Popular*, controlled by the Ramírez dissidents of the PPS, reported, in what appeared to be a staged affair, that its correspondents had been unable to locate any student leaders for an interview. They had, however, interviewed several students at the Polytechnic Institute who criticized Mendoza and his lieutenants for inadequate explanation of strike goals. Another student said that there were serious suspicions that FNET leaders were not capable of directing the conflict. Mendoza retorted on the following day that the directors of *El Popular* were antistudent and antirevolutionary; an editorial in *El Popular* denied these charges.[87]

In the meantime the strike had extended beyond Mexico City and to schools other than technical ones. Illustrative of the split between FNET and CJM leaders was the statement of the president and the secretary general of CJM supporting the strike in the Rural Normal Schools and the Practical Schools of Agriculture but ignoring the IPN conflict. In answer to accusations of political involvement the CJM asserted that it was working for student goals and denied that it belonged to any political party; the PPS also denied any connection

[85] *Christian Science Monitor*, June 25, 1956.
[86] *El Popular*, May 4, 1956; *El Universal*, May 8, 1956, pp. 1, 6, 18.
[87] *El Popular*, May 14, 1956; May 15, 1956; and May 16, 1956.

with the strike.[88] By early June the rift between the two factions had broadened into a full-scale battle of words. An article in *El Popular* spoke of a "tremendous division" between the National Committee of the FNET and the student body of the Institute, and accused Mendoza and Gámiz of failing to call a general assembly for fear of being overthrown. A CJM manifesto accusing Mendoza and Gámiz of shattering student unity was published in full in *El Popular* and was reported distributed among students.[89] Despite these attacks on his leadership, Mendoza remained in firm control of the strike. He and his followers instigated and led rowdy and destructive parades through Mexico City and noisy demonstrations before the Department of Education. In the midst of these disturbances Jacques Denis, president of the WFDY, arrived from Paris to talk with student leaders and to recruit Mexican students for the youth festival scheduled that summer in Prague. The government, alarmed by the interference of a representative of international Communism, confined Denis to the Mexico City airport, held him incommunicado, and put him back on the next plane for Paris. Protests were voiced by *El Popular, La Voz de México,* the FNET, and the CJM.[90]

As the duration of the strike approached three months with no end in sight, and with many students and most of the public in Mexico City disgusted with the situation,[91] President Ruiz Cortinez finally stepped in and attempted to restore peace and order. The President offered no more concession on student needs than had his Secretary

[88] *Ibid.,* May 24, 1956 and May 11, 1956. The University Student Federation at the National University, however, accused PPS and PCM leaders of directing the strike and called for a return to order and discipline at the IPN (*El Universal,* May 16, 1956, p. 1).

[89] *El Popular,* June 13, 1956.

[90] *Ibid.,* June 1, 1956 and June 3, 1956. Nicandro Mendoza of the PPS and Diego Rivera of the PCM led the delegations that greeted Denis at the airport. Cf. *El Universal,* June 3, 1956, p. 7.

[91] Typical of public protest was the editorial in *El Universal,* May 17, 1956, p. 1, in which the complaint was raised that the police gave no protection to innocent bystanders against mob violence. On the other hand, Mario Fiorini, "El Comunismo en México," *Estudios sobre el Comunismo,* Año V, No. 15 (January–March 1957), 77, suggested that the police demonstrated forbearance with the students for fear of provoking general student disorders.

of Education and refused to remove the director of the Polytechnical
Institute. The strike leaders were far from satisfied and gave only a
reluctant agreement but realized that they could not stand against
the enormous prestige of a Mexican President. After sixty-six days
the strike came to an end.[92]

Unfortunately the end of the formal strike did not bring peace to
the student community. Sporadic riots and disturbances marked the
summer months of 1956. With the apparent inability of IPN Director Hernández Corso to control the affair, the government finally
dismissed him. His successor, Alejo Peralta, far from fulfilling the
hope of the student leaders for a more lenient policy, proved to be a
staunch supporter of a strong stand. For several weeks Peralta bided
his time, but late in September he replaced the director and assistant
director of the boarding school.

In the face of student opposition, led by Nicandro Mendoza, he
struck swiftly and ruthlessly. On Sunday morning September 23, the
approximately 1,200 boarding students of the IPN were rudely
awakened at 5:00 A.M. by a reveille call sounded by the troops of
the eighth and twenty-fourth Infantry Battalions of the Mexican
Army, accompanied by police of the Federal District. The students,
informed that they had to abandon the school, were ordered to pack
their possessions and load onto the waiting buses. About 200 were
found without proper credentials and were taken to jail, but about
150 of these were able to produce their credentials later.[93] The remainder were transported to various parts of Mexico City and were
dispersed. Police and troops occupied the dormitories, and at least
a token force remained until December 1958 to prevent the students
from reassembling and demonstrating. Alejo Peralta announced the
permanent closing of the dormitories, but promised small monthly
sums for room and board to those who could prove that they were
bona fide students. Within a few days the strike leaders, Nicandro

[92] *El Universal*, June 16, 1956, p. 1.
[93] *El Universal*, September 24, 1956, pp. 1 and 6, and September 25, 1956,
pp. 1 and 6. Of the 200 arrested, about 20 were found to be alcoholics. Others
had arms, liquor, and some marihuana. Of the 53 who could produce no credentials, many were reportedly simply poor unfortunates who had found a home
at the IPN.

Mendoza and Mariano Molina, secretary general of the FNET, were arrested.[94]

With these moves the power of Vicente Lombardo Toledano and his supporters in the FNET was broken. All newspapers in Mexico City, except for *El Popular* and *La Voz de México*, supported the stern measures of the government. Student radicals were overawed, and the moderately oriented students, comprising the usually apathetic majority, were stirred to action. At the annual convention of the FNET in October at which the officers of the National Executive Committee are elected, a moderate anti-leftist slate won an overwhelming victory. The new president, repudiating the intervention of the PPS and its agitators, said that politics had no place at the Institute and promised that all future problems would be resolved in peaceful discussions. A splinter group of FNET supporters of Mendoza elected a counter-Executive Committee purporting to represent the FNET. Although they were accepted as the delegates at a CJM conference in 1957, they had no authority in student affairs at the Institute. Director Peralta officially recognized the anti-leftist group. To the present the PPS has been effectively blocked in its efforts to regain control over the FNET and the split still exists between the JP and the CJM. Furthermore, following the drastic measures used by the government in suppressing these student disturbances, no further outbreaks have occurred to compare with these in scope and violence. Communist attempts to continue the student disturbances in Jalisco and Michoacán flickered out by mid-October.[95] A poten-

---

[94] *El Universal*, September 28, 1956, p. 1. Arrested with Mendoza were his two inseparable "pistoleros," Raúl Lemus Sánchez and Efraín Ruiz López. Molina, Mendoza, and Lemus were eventually consigned to the penitentiary; they were finally released in December 1958 by incoming President Adolfo López Mateos.

[95] Sympathy strikes among students of west-central Mexico appeared shortly after the outbreak of the disturbances at the IPN. José Guadalupe Zuno Arce, leader of the Federation of Students of Guadalajara (Federación de Estudiantes de Guadalajara—FEG), assumed command of these forces. With a small contingent of followers he went to Mexico City to assist in the general uprising there but soon quarreled with Mendoza. He returned to Jalisco and confined his activities largely to expressions of sympathy. With the government victory over the students in September, Zuno teamed up with CJM leader Baudelio Alegría

tially serious outbreak in Guadalajara was put down by martial law in May of 1957,[96] and renewed disturbances at the IPN in February and March 1959 were sternly suppressed. On March 1, 1959, Director Peralta resigned, but his successor, Eugenio Méndez Docurro, followed Peralta's policy of strictness. The CJM expressed pleasure at the removal of Peralta, but it has received little comfort from Méndez Docurro. Its power has been broken within the IPN and its influence limited to the rural normal schools. The Communists have never recovered the strength within the student organizations in Mexico that they enjoyed in 1956, and the failure of a PPS student leader, Miguel Castro Bustos, to stir up trouble over admission at the National University in February 1962 only points up the weakness of the Com-

---

to begin student riots in Guadalajara. When these efforts failed they moved their scene of operations to Morelia, where they experienced some success. Student riots broke out on October 5, accompanied by demands that the troops withdraw from the IPN and the arrested student leaders be released. The disturbances continued for several days, highlighted by Zuno's personal attack on a university professor; Zuno knocked the professor's glasses off and tramped on them. Several opposition students were pistol-whipped by Zuno's armed thugs. By October 10 the police had finally intervened, and Zuno, Alegría, and others fled into hiding. Cf. *El Universal*, October 6, 1956, pp. 1 and 15, and October 10, 1956, pp. 1 and 13.

[96] Zuno Arce apparently masterminded this outbreak too. The trouble began with an attack on May 9, 1957 by members of the FEG on students of the Catholic Autonomous University in Guadalajara. It is impossible to connect Lombardo Toledano directly with this affair, but he was known to be in Guadalajara shortly before the outbreak and was reported to have conferred with Constancio Hernández, PPS leader in Jalisco and ex-rector of the University, as well as with the two Zunos, father and son. Later the elder Zuno, former governor of Jalisco, defended the student riots on the grounds that the attackers broke up an illegal religious ceremony (a procession) among the Catholic students. Governor Agustín Yáñez condemned the Zuno group and accused it of receiving orders from the PPS. By May 15 the city was back to normal, Zuno had again fled, and one of his lieutenants was under arrest for assault. Zuno himself was never brought to justice, because of the political power of his family in western Mexico. In August, Governor Yáñez staved off an attempt by the Communists to elect their candidate as rector of the University of Guadalajara. Cf. Unión Cívica Internacional de México, "Comunismo en México," *Estudios sobre el Comunismo*, Año V, No. 17 (July–September 1957), 125–126; *El Universal*, May 12, 1957, pp. 1 and 3; May 13, 1957, p. 7; May 16, 1957, pp. 1 and 20; and August 15, 1957, pp. 1 and 11.

munists.[97] At that time Rector Ignacio Chávez said there were only about 400 Communist agitators out of 74,000 students at the National University.

Like the Communist political parties, the front groups can expect some limited degree of success if they are willing to abide by the rules of the game as established by the government. Criticism and demonstrations are permitted in the rules, but not violence and prolonged agitation. Two fronts, the MLN and CEM, play by the rules and enjoy some success. The more intransigent groups have been suppressed and those that have been too laudatory toward the Soviet Union have failed to attract large followings. Overall the front movement in Mexico is weak.

[97] *Excelsior*, February 28, 1962, p. 1, and March 1, 1962, p. 1. The rector of the National University estimated that there were only 400 Communist agitators out of a total student body of 74,000. He pointed out that they have achieved nothing and that the University will not tolerate violence. *Excelsior*, May 25, 1962, p. 1.

IV. Organized Labor and the Communists

Introduction

Well over 90 per cent of Mexican workers and labor organizations are non-Communists. Most labor leaders are ardent nationalists, firm supporters of the current administration, and militant anti-Communists, for they recognize in Communism a threat to national independence and to some of the basic concepts and goals of the Revolution. With tight internal organization, and with political support from the government and the official party, almost all labor organizations are well equipped to fight off Communist infiltration and propaganda. Occasionally scattered locals have fallen under openly Communist leadership, and in recent years several national unions have elected Communist or pro-Communist officers. Outstanding examples of Communist victories, though temporary, include elections in the railway workers' union, the petroleum workers' union, and Section IX of the teachers' union.

The success of the Communists, however, must be qualified. Their victories resulted not from their organizational activities, nor from labor's acceptance of their ideology, but rather from forces wholly outside of Communist control. Labor unrest in Mexico had been growing slowly but not alarmingly from the early and middle 1950's, as a result of higher prices unaccompanied by comparable wage increases. By late 1957, however, many Mexican workers were con-

vinced that they had suffered a decline in real wages and that the entrenched leaders in their unions did not adequately represent their
interests. Beginning in 1958 a rash of strikes hit the country on and
off for over a year, the only serious labor disturbances in the administration of President Adolfo Ruiz Cortines (1952–1958). The Communist attempt to capitalize on these outbreaks resulted in some
temporary victories, but ended in ultimate defeat and perhaps a
weakening of the movement. The explanation is twofold: first, the
government granted generous wage increases and fringe benefits,
especially after President Adolfo López Mateos took office in December 1958, thus undercutting the position of rebellious leaders; and,
second, the Communists overplayed their hand in those unions in
which the government permitted the election of dissident leaders,
including some Communists and pro-Communists. When these new
leaders attempted to use their position to further embarrass the government with exorbitant demands and strikes, the government coun-
tered by supporting a new opposition within the unions and by
arresting the intransigent leaders.

Communist-infiltrated Labor Organizations

The first evidence of genuine and deep-seated rank-and-file dissatisfaction in Mexican organized labor manifested itself in the
telegraphers' strike, February 7–22, 1958, launched as a protest not
only against current pay scales but also against union leadership.[1]
The dissident leaders under Ismael Villavicencio rejected outright
Communist offers of assistance and reached an agreement with the
government with a minimum of violence and bitterness. A brief
flurry of unrest in August among the telegraphers led to a temporary
occupation of telegraph installations by the Army, a very brief arrest
of Villavicencio, and a final restoration of order when Villavicencio
ordered the workers to return to their jobs.[2] There were some accusations of Communist leadership in these troubles but the evidence
does not support them.[3]

[1] *El Universal*, February 23, 1958, p. 1; *New York Times*, February 16, 1958,
p. 13.
[2] *El Universal*, August 4, 1958, p. 1, and August 7, 1958, p. 1.
[3] Cf. article by Antonio Lara Barragán in *El Universal*, February 15, 1958,
p. 14.

THE RAILROAD WORKERS' UNION OF THE MEXICAN REPUBLIC
(SINDICATO DE TRABAJADORES FERROCARRILEROS DE LA
REPÚBLICA MEXICANA—STFRM)

Following the failure of its efforts to penetrate the telegraphers' strike in February, the PCM conducted a propaganda campaign in March and April by means of handbills urging the petroleum, electrical, and telephone workers to strike. Despite widespread unrest in these unions, this second Communist effort proved premature. In the meantime pressure from the rank and file under popularly chosen leaders forced the officers of the railroad workers' union to appoint a committee for salary increases whose chairman was Demetrio Vallejo, a onetime member of the Communist Party. When the committee's demands were not met on salary and retirement increases, the union leaders were forced by their followers to call a strike, but before the affair reached serious proportions the President of Mexico himself intervened, authorizing increases somewhat lower than the demands. The strike ended suddenly on July 2.[4] However, the troubles within the unions were just beginning. On July 3 and 4 about twenty locals rallied around Vallejo and through him announced their intention to impeach and possibly overthrow their national leaders. By July 20 the rebellious railroad workers had gained the support of the telegraph workers, the Marxist-led but non-Communist electrical workers' unions, and the petroleum workers. Students from the Polytechnical Institute and the National University, and members of the Communist-front Socialist People's Party and its labor wing, the General Union of Workers and Peasants of Mexico (UGOCM), marched in demonstrations before the National Palace pledging solidarity with the railroad workers and demanding recognition of Vallejo as national union chief. Some demonstrators carried banners demanding the release from jail of Jacinto López, secretary general of the UGOCM who had recently been arrested for land agitation in Sonora.[5]

On July 26 Vallejo, in an apparent attempt to test his strength,

[4] *New York Times*, July 5, 1958, p. 8.
[5] *El Universal*, July 2, 1958, p. 1; July 4, 1958, pp. 1 and 6; and July 20, pp. 1 and 5.

called a one-hour strike. It was effective throughout the railway system. He then proceeded to form a rump national executive committee, but was refused recognition by the Secretary of Labor. Several persons who agitated in his behalf were arrested. Vallejo went into open rebellion against the union leaders, and by indirection against the government, by calling for a general strike on August 2. The Army took over the railroad facilities. In less than a week the government ended the strike by agreeing to permit new elections.[6] Vallejo was swept into office and took up his duties as secretary general on August 27.[7]

For five months Vallejo occupied his position as leader of the railway workers with little cause for apprehension by the government except for the reinstatement into the union of Valentín Campa, a former Communist Party member and then leader of the Communist-splinter Mexican Worker-Peasant Party (POCM). In mid-February 1959, however, he presented to the government a list of demands which even the Campa group reportedly considered too many and too excessive for a state enterprise to accept. When the demands were not met, the union, led by Vallejo and Campa, struck on February 25. The Federal Board of Conciliation and Arbitration declared the strike illegal. The government, however, made some concessions, which Vallejo accepted at the urging of Lombardo Toledano. Railway service was quickly restored, but agitation continued within the union and a month later Vallejo struck again. The Federal Board again declared the action illegal, and this time the government was adamant. Services were seriously curtailed for about a week. On March 29, following charges brought by the office of the Attorney General, Vallejo and about 150 railroad leaders were arrested. In other parts of the country over 800 were taken into custody. Two weeks later Vallejo and 60 others were formally imprisoned, but the others were released. In the meantime opposition to Vallejo within the union had grown considerably among the more moderate elements. By the first of April most of the workers had returned to their

[6] *Ibid.*, July 27, 1958, p. 1; August 1, 1958, p. 1; August 3, 1958, p. 1; August 4, 1958, p. 1; August 7, 1958, p. 1; and August 8, 1958, p. 1.
[7] *El Popular*, August 28, 1958.

jobs, and new elections of officers were held. Campa and his associates were again expelled from the union; amicable relations were once more restored between the union and the government.[8]

The question as to the degree and nature of Communist participation remains to be answered. According to the files of the Mexican Judicial Police, made public the first week of April, Vallejo himself joined the Communist Party in 1950 following a trip to the Soviet Union the previous year. Vallejo admitted that he had been a Communist at one time but claimed that he left the Party in the mid-1940's.[9] Conceivably both reports could be true, but, aside from this problem, it is clear that Vallejo conducted himself as a Communist to the interests of the Communist movement in Mexico. His senseless March demands, which he knew would be rejected, forcefully if necessary, can be explained only in political terms, especially in the light of his brilliant victories in July and August 1958 and February 1959. He had then gained for himself and for his union the maximum economic benefits that the Administration could at that time bestow. His further demands could and did lead only to political conflict and his own destruction. Secondly, the government expelled two Soviet diplomats for alleged involvement, and the Federal Judicial Police made public the information that raids on PPS and POCM headquarters had turned up letters from the Communist Party of the Soviet Union to known Mexican Communists urging general agitation, with specific references to the railways.[10] The accuracy of this report may be questioned but not the presence of Communist agitators in the forefront as well as in the background of the strike. Certainly Campa and leading members of the POCM were among the strike leaders. Gerardo Unzueta, onetime administrator of *La Voz de México*, the official organ of the PCM, was arrested for agitation,[11] and on the day of the February strike all three parties of the Com-

[8] *El Universal*, February 18, 1959, p. 1; February 21, 1959, p. 1; February 25, 1959, p. 1; February 26, 1959, p. 1; February 27, 1959, p. 1; March 26, 1959, pp. 1 and 7; and March 31, 1959, pp. 1 and 9.

[9] *Ibid.*, April 1, 1959, p. 1, and April 3, 1959, p. 11. The Attorney General reported that the police files indicated that some of the state leaders were Communists of long standing. See also *El Popular*, March 31, 1959.

[10] *El Universal*, April 7, 1959, pp. 1 and 9.

[11] *El Popular*, March 30, 1959.

munist movement signed and distributed thousands of pamphlets attacking the federal government and urging the people to rally to the strikers. Finally, in a "post mortem" of the strike failure, Lombardo Toledano blamed the PCM and the POCM because of their intransigence and their failure to follow the moderate councils of the PPS in planning agitation within the railway union.

THE MINING AND METALLURGICAL WORKERS' UNION OF THE MEXICAN REPUBLIC (SINDICATO DE TRABAJADORES MINEROS Y METALÚRGICOS DE LA REPÚBLICA MEXICANA—STMMRM)

Dissatisfaction and rebellion in the petroleum workers' union followed a similar but not identical path as that in the railway union. Having noted the initial success of Vallejo in the spring and early summer of 1958, rebellious leaders under Ignacio Hernández Alcalá forced the creation of a Committee on Salary Increases. Bargaining with the government proceeded peacefully, and Hernández gained substantial benefits without a strike by mid-July. Within two weeks, though, Hernández called a strike to overthrow the union leadership and, following some violence in August and September, eventually gained control of the union.[12] Like Vallejo he proceeded cautiously for several months, but when Vallejo opened his attack on the government, Hernández supported him. For that matter so did several other important unions, such as the electrical workers and the dissident primary school teachers in the Federal District. When the extent of Communist involvement in the railway strike was made known, several unions abandoned Vallejo. Hernández did not and was arrested with the railway leaders. New leaders assumed control of the petroleum workers and announced their withdrawal of support of Vallejo and the railroad strike.

THE MEXICAN CONFEDERATION OF ELECTRICAL WORKERS (CONFEDERACIÓN MEXICANA DE ELECTRICISTAS—CME)

Marxist and Communist penetration exists in the important Mexican Confederation of Electrical Workers (Confederación Mexicana de Electricistas—CME). The CME, one of two electrical workers' labor organizations, is divided into two unions: the Mexican Union

[12] *El Universal*, April 22, 1958, p. 6, and July 17, 1958, p. 1.

of Electrical Workers (Sindicato Mexicano de Electricistas—SME),
with about 8,000 members, until 1959 under the leadership of Agustín Sánchez Delint, who was a self-declared Marxist but an opponent
of Soviet imperialism; and the National Federation of Electrical Industry and Electrical Communications Workers (Federación Nacional de Trabajadores de la Industria y Comunicaciones Eléctricas
—FNTICE), under the leadership of Rafael Galván, who shares the
views of Sánchez Delint. Sánchez and Galvan merged to form the
CME in 1955 in the hope of using the new confederation as a basis
for another labor bloc in Mexico. Sánchez was chosen secretary general and Galván, undersecretary general of the new organization, but
it made little progress with its major objective. With the removal of
Sánchez as leader of the SME in July 1959, the new secretary general,
Luis Aguilar Palomina, succeeded to the position of CME secretary
general in elections held in December 1959.[13]

The question remains as to how much Communist influence has
existed in the CME and its components. Following their merger in
1955, Sánchez and Galván appeared to be planning an alliance with
Lombardo Toledano, specifically with Lombardo's UGOCM. This
relationship suddenly cooled with the Soviet suppression of the Hungarian revolt in November 1956. The SME monthly newspaper, *Lux*,
in several succeeding issues bitterly condemned the Soviet action at
the very time that Lombardo was vigorously justifying it. Even prior
to this disagreement, Sánchez had rejected an invitation to join the
CTAL. In an article in *Lux* he charged that CTAL adherents within
his union (probably PPS members) were opposing the union's leadership and that the CTAL and the WFTU were under Soviet control.

When general labor troubles broke out early in 1958, Sánchez and
Galván supported the striking unionists, but denied, as they had in
the past, the accusations of old-line labor leaders that they were
Communists.[14] They again supported the agitation in midsummer,
but this time opposition appeared within the SME to the electrical
workers' involvement in the agitation of other unions. Sánchez over-
rode the opposition but counseled Vallejo to moderate his demands
and abide by an election carried out according to the constitution of

[13] *El Popular*, December 13, 1959.
[14] *Ibid.*, January 6, 1956; *El Universal*, July 6, 1958, p. 1.

the railway union. Opposition continued to mount against Sánchez within his own union, and in October he and the other directors offered to resign. One report stated that he was under pressure on the one hand from anti-Communists who were disturbed over his association with Communists in the recent labor troubles, and on the other hand by Communists who were dissatisfied with his failure to join the Communists outright.[15] Sánchez was confirmed in his position, and in February and March once more supported Vallejo. The Soviet involvement, however, led to his hasty retreat and condemnation of the strike leaders, but apparently the damage was done. When elections were held to renew the directive board of the electrical workers' union in mid-summer 1959, Sánchez did not stand for re-election. He relinquished his post with some bitterness over criticisms of his tenure and the defeat of the slate that he supported. The new officers who took up their duties early in August stoutly declared their political independence of any party and their rejection of Communism.[16] Nevertheless, some Marxist and Communist influence remains in the SME, as exemplified by the invitation extended by Manuel Tapia Gómez, SME secretary of external affairs, to Czech labor leaders. A four-man team arrived from Czechoslovakia for a week's visit in May 1961 as guests of the SME. They were also received by the new National Worker's Center (Centro Nacional de Trabajadores—CNT) but were ignored by other labor organizations.

THE NATIONAL TEACHERS' UNION (SINDICATO NACIONAL DE TRABAJADORES DE LA EDUCACIÓN—SNTE)

The National Teachers' Union (Sindicato Nacional de Trabajadores de la Educación—SNTE) consists of about 80,000 members of more than fifty sections, or locals, the most important being Section IX, composed of about 15,000 primary school teachers in the Federal District. The teachers were heavily infiltrated by Communists during the Cárdenas Administration (1934–1940), and many of these persons are still teaching.[17] Probably every one of the sections

---

[15] *El Popular*, August 5, 1958; *El Universal*, October 28, 1958, pp. 1 and 6.
[16] *El Universal*, August 2, 1959, p. 6, and August 3, 1959, p. 1.
[17] *El Popular*, April 30, 1959, and August 3, 1959; *El Universal*, July 16, 1959, pp. 1 and 9, and July 28, 1959, p. 1.

of the union has at least a few Communists, but no section is under Communist domination. Some of the editors and members of the directive board of *El Maestro Mexicano*, the official organ of the SNTE, are PPS members and sympathizers. PPS members are also influential in, if not in control of, one of the three factions into which the powerful Section IX of Mexico City is divided. Furthermore, the SNTE is still formally affiliated with the World Federation of Teachers' Unions (FISE), the only truly professional department of the Communist WFTU. In 1957 Enrique W. Sánchez, then secretary general of the SNTE, was still listed as a vice president of FISE, but the Mexican Teachers' Union had been inactive for a number of years.[18]

The most recent threat of serious Communist penetration within the teachers' union began in 1956 when a dissident group in Section IX, at least one of whose members was a Communist, refused to accept the government offer of a 20-per-cent pay increase. The dissidents demanded 30 per cent. Within a week a new and forceful leader, Othón Salazar, assumed control of the rebel group, which took the name of Teachers' Revolutionary Movement (Movimiento Revolucionario del Magisterio—MRM), and has continued agitation despite government compromise and pleas to end the controversy. Although Salazar has denied that he has ever been a Communist or that he has had close relations with the Communists of Mexico, the evidence available indicates that he has sought their support and has worked hand-in-glove with them. By August 1956 the dispute had widened to include demands not only for salary increases, but also for elections of officers of Section IX. The national leader of the SNTE, Enrique W. Sánchez, agreed to the calling of an extraordinary congress for this purpose, provided that the Salazar group first disband. This proposal was put forward September 1, 1956, at a lengthy meeting of four hours in which not only the three factions within Section IX but also the PCM and PPS were officially represented. Juan P. Sainz of the PCM Political Commission and Jorge Cruickshank of the PPS presented the respective views of their parties, while José Reyes Ayala spoke for the Communist group in the pro-

[18] *Facts about International Communist-front Organizations*, April 1957, p. 55.

fessional and higher schools, and Cándido Jaramillo of the PPS spoke as factional leader in behalf of the Revolutionary Bloc of Trade Union Orientation (Bloque Revolucionario de Orientación Sindical— BROS). A second meeting was held on September 4, in which Sánchez repeated his terms. Salazar's rejection was supported by Cruickshank, Jaramillo, and Sainz. Five days later a formal split occurred in Section IX when the Salazar group formed a rump executive committee. PCM members supported Salazar, but the BROS under Jaramillo refused to sanction the break and remained loyal to the legal executive committee. During the next few months the dispute was dragged through the organs of arbitration within the Government Workers Federation (FSTSE) to which the SNTE is affiliated. In February 1957 the Tribunal of Arbitration, the highest court in the FSTSE, confirmed the authority of the national executive committee of the teachers' union over the rebellious sector of Section IX, and ruled that all members of the SNTE are subject to the regulations of its statutes.[19]

The Salazar group, thoroughly disgruntled with the findings of the Tribunal of Arbitration, demanded new elections in Section IX within thirty days. In March a truce was reached between Salazar and the national officers. In return for dissolving his dissident committee, Salazar was admitted to the National Consultative Council of the SNTE and members of his group were given posts on various Section IX commissions charged with cooperating with the national officers on problems in the Federal District. The national executive committee agreed to call elections at a propitious time. The compromise seriously weakened Salazar's position. Many of his followers accused him of selling out "for a plate of beans," but when he responded to this pressure by calling for a rejection of the agreement, those members who were given posts in Section IX abandoned him.

Though the dissatisfaction continued, the Salazar group remained quiescent for almost a year. In April 1958, however, renewed agitation began among the teachers in Section IX, and a strike began in midmonth. PPS and PCM members were reported to be among the

[19] *El Universal*, July 4, 1956, p. 12; July 11, 1956, p. 1; September 1, 1956, pp. 1 and 14; September 5, 1956, p. 11; September 10, 1956, pp. 1 and 10; and February 18, 1957, p. 1.

leaders of the movement, but it is doubtful in the extreme that, given
Salazar's weakened position, Lombardo or his followers were willing
to risk their entrenched status in the SNTE. The strike was disruptive but not 100 per cent effective. In frustration, a band of the strikers seized some of the offices of the Department of Education and
held them for over a month. The government was unwilling to ex-
acerbate the situation by removing them by force. Late in May the
PCM Political Committee publicly demanded that the government
grant the demands of the dissident group.[20]

Early in June agreement was reached between the government and
the dissidents. Pay increases of 10 per cent were authorized for pri-
mary-school teachers, and the national leaders of the union agreed to
call for elections in Section IX. When classes resumed on June 9 all
factions were in agreement, except for a small minority which demanded a further 10-per-cent increase. The congress of Section IX,
called by Enrique W. Sánchez, head of the teachers' union, met in
late August. Its composition, however, was unacceptable to the Salazar group, which called its own congress and elected its own executive
committee. In mid-August Cándido Jaramillo, leader of the BROS
and a member of the PPS, had called for unity in Section IX and had
condemned the Salazar group as divisive.[21] Further, all organized
factions of Section IX resolved to cite Salazar and several of his
lieutenants before the Committee of Honor and Justice at the next
national congress and to request their expulsion from the union. In
an attempt to force recognition, a Salazar group comprising hundreds
of persons wildly demonstrated for about seven hours on September
6 in the streets of Mexico City. Police broke up the demonstrations
with tear gas. Some 300 people were treated for minor wounds and
gassing, and about 50 were seriously injured. Salazar and some of his
companions were arrested.[22]

The use of violence by the police in quelling the demonstrators

[20] *Ibid.*, April 4, 1958, pp. 1 and 10, and June 1, 1958, pp. 1 and 10.
[21] *El Popular*, August 17, 1958. Other PPS members in the SNTE are Jorge
Carrión, a Party official; Jorge Cruickshank; Antonio García Moreno; María
de Jesús Otero; Mariano Molina Rodríguez; and Indalecio Sáyago. Sáyago was
elected a member of the SNTE Executive Committee in 1960, possibly as a
reward for PPS support of the Union's leaders against the Salazar group.
[22] *El Universal*, September 7, 1958, p. 1.

elicited almost immediate response from many groups, including several labor organizations, some of which had recently experienced similar difficulties with the government. A "Manifesto to the President and to the People of Mexico" protested the "aggression" against Salazar and his executive committee of Section IX and likened it to the action against Jacinto López of the UGOCM earlier in the summer. The Manifesto was signed by Demetrio Vallejo, who had just fought his way to the top of the railroad workers' union; Ismael Villavicencio, leader of the telephone workers—who had had similar troubles; the UGOCM, whose leader was still under arrest; and the Confederation of Mexican Youth (CJM), a Communist-infiltrated organization led by former adherents of Lombardo Toledano.[23] UGOCM adherence to the Manifesto did not imply PPS support for Salazar's disruptive activities within the teachers' union, but rather opposition to the use of police force in labor disputes, a cardinal issue in all PPS propaganda.[24]

The use of force turned the tide of battle to Salazar's favor. In October in government-supervised elections Salazar's follower, Gabriel Pérez Rivero, was overwhelmingly confirmed in free elections as secretary general of Section IX, and in November new national leaders were installed in the SNTE. Then on December 5, 1958, just a few days after taking office as President of Mexico, Adolfo López Mateos released Salazar and his followers from prison. The Attorney General issued a statement upon their release that the President's action should not be interpreted as a recognition of their innocence of the crime of "social dissolution" of which they were accused, but as an act of magnanimity. The charges of "social dissolution," however, were withdrawn. Upon his release Salazar emphasized that he would continue the fight against the corrupt leadership of the SNTE not only in the Federal District but throughout the country.[25]

Differences between Section IX and the national leaders erupted once more in March of 1959 with the presentation of the report on teacher needs to the Secretary of Education by the National Execu-

[23] Manifesto published in *El Universal*, September 11, 1958, p. 9.
[24] The National Directorate of the PPS published its own protest of the use of force against demonstrators. Cf. *El Universal*, September 11, 1958, p. 12.
[25] *El Popular*, December 6, 1958; *El Universal*, December 6,, 1958, p. 1.

tive Committee of the Union. Salazar, now supported by the officers of Section IX, announced plans to submit other petitions to the government. Meetings between the elementary teachers of the Federal District and national officers in the spring of 1959 brought no solution, but an open break did not occur at the time. This conflict continued to simmer throughout 1959 and into 1960, resulting first in the suspension of Pérez Rivero by the Vigilance Committee and eventually in his expulsion from the union by the National Council of the SNTE on May 17, 1960. From that moment the MRM went once more into decline, from which it had not recovered by mid-1962. Salazar attempted to organize a strike in June and to lead a demonstration in August 1960, but the former failed and the latter was suppressed by the police with tear gas and riot guns. Several persons were wounded and about 200 arrested. In the following year the MRM held its first congress, but the meeting was assaulted by bands allegedly organized by the police. Little was accomplished, and since that time the MRM has been relatively quiet.[26]

Communist-controlled Labor Organizations

THE WORLD FEDERATION OF TRADE UNIONS (WFTU)

THE CONFEDERATION OF LATIN AMERICAN WORKERS
(CONFEDERACIÓN DE TRABAJADORES DE AMÉRICA LATINA—CTAL)

The World Federation of Trade Unions (WFTU), the Soviet-sponsored international labor organization, is the best organized, the most liberally financed, and potentially the most dangerous of the international Communist fronts. The WFTU was founded in Paris in October 1945 as a result of the interest of the British Trade Unions Congress in founding a worldwide labor organization. At the Paris meeting the Soviet representatives insisted on the election of Louis Saillant as secretary general, the official in whom power would reside. Between 1945 and 1948 the Communists increased their representations on various organs of the WFTU by their victories in Czechoslovakia and China and by artificially inflating membership figures.[27] With the emergence of Communist control and attempted manipu-

[26] *El Popular*, August 5, 1960; *La Voz de México*, July 26, 1961.
[27] *Facts about International Communist-front Organizations*, April 1957, p. 19.

lation of the WFTU for Communist ends, the British TUC, the American CIO, the Dutch NVV, and the Mexican CTM (Confederación de Trabajadores Mexicanos) withdrew in 1949 and subsequently banded together in the International Confederation of Free Trade Unions (ICFTU).

The officers of the WFTU, collectively known as the Executive Bureau, consist of the president, the secretary general, and twelve vice presidents. Latin America has been represented by Vicente Lombardo Toledano of Mexico, Ramiro Luchesi of Brazil, and Lázaro Peña González of Cuba.[28] The Bureau is the policy-making body of the organization and although scheduled to meet quarterly, convenes when the secretary general deems it necessary. Mexicans and other Latin Americans also have had representation on other organs of the WFTU, but all these positions are largely honorary, since the Executive Committee and the General Council have little authority.[29]

The broad objectives of the WFTU were outlined in a speech by S. Dange at the organization's Fourth Congress in 1957. Dange called for the support of the national bourgeoisie against imperialism, opposition to military alliances, support of the peace movement, advocacy of nationalization of foreign enterprises, and promotion of trade-union unity, including peasant-labor alliances within each country. In fact these have been the broad goals pursued by Communist labor leaders in Mexico and other parts of Latin America for the past several years.[30] Although the Chinese Communists have increased their contact with Latin America in recent years,[31] the major orientation for the Communist labor movement in the area still comes from the Soviet Union.

Ninety per cent of the claimed membership of the WFTU represents the Bloc countries; over one-half is from the Soviet Union. At the end of 1958 this claim comprised 90 million workers in fifty-seven affiliates in forty-one countries. For non-Communist affiliates

[28] *Ibid.*, p. 20.
[29] U.S. Department of Labor, *Directory of World Federation of Trade Unions,* pp. 1–13.
[30] Subcommittee To Investigate the Administration of the Internal Security Act, *Communist Threat to the United States through the Caribbean,* p. 151.
[31] "Nuevos horizontes para Mao," *Visión,* May 20, 1959, p. 33.

the WFTU has provided for the establishment of nine liaison bureaus organized on a regional basis in various parts of the world. Up to 1961, however, it appeared that only its Latin American affiliate, the Confederation of Latin American Workers (Confederación de Trabajadores de América Latina—CTAL) was in any way functioning.[32] During 1960 the CTAL had active affiliates in the French West Indies and in five countries of Latin America: Mexico, Costa Rica, Ecuador, Chile, and Uruguay, with a claimed total membership of about 100,000[33]—a sharp decline from the half a million members the Confederation listed in 1958.[34] By mid-1962 the CTAL was virtually defunct.

The CTAL antedates the WFTU: it was founded in 1938 by Vicente Lombardo Toledano, then at the height of his powers as Mexican labor leader. With the organization of the WFTU in 1945, the CTAL soon affiliated with the world movement and subsequently became its liaison bureau for the Western Hemisphere. Headquarters are located in Mexico City and the governing body consists of a president and several subordinate officials from various Latin American countries.[35] Men like Lázaro Peña of Cuba and Roberto Morena of Brazil received training and financial support during their years of service on the directive board of the CTAL. The organization has been in decline for many years now, beginning with the withdrawal of the non-Communist unions in 1949. Lombardo's own Confederation of Mexican Workers defected and he himself has lost much of his former prestige and influence as a result of far-reaching shifts in Mexican labor and political organizations. The lack of success of the CTAL has brought criticism to Lombardo's leadership on several occasions, although his position was long unchallenged as the leading

[32] U.S. Department of Labor, *Directory of World Federation of Trade Unions,* pp. iii–iv.

[33] Corporation for Economic and Industrial Research, *Soviet Bloc-Latin American Activities,* p. 46.

[34] U.S. Department of Labor, *Directory of World Federation of Trade Unions,* p. lx.

[35] *La Confederación de Trabajadores de América Latina (CTAL) y La Federación Sindical Mundial,* 2d ed., pp. 6 ff.; *Directory of World Federation of Trade Unions,* p. 20. Officers in 1958 were: Vicente Lombardo Toledano (Mexico); Ildefonso Alemán Lemus (Chile); Antonio E. Cabrera (Argentina); Víctor Manuel Gutiérrez (Guatemala); Lázaro Peña González (Cuba).

Communist labor leader in Latin America. In 1960, during Latin American Solidarity Week in Havana, he, however, advocated a "third force"—a neutralist Hemisphere labor confederation. It was believed at the time that the abolition of the CTAL was being seriously considered, and Lombardo's announcement in October 1960 that he planned to retire as president of the CTAL lent weight to the argument.[36] But to mid-1962 Lombardo was still president and the new labor organization had not materialized.[37]

The purposes of the CTAL have been to coordinate the labor activities of its national affiliates, to sponsor agitation throughout the Hemisphere in behalf of its labor goals, and to distribute and disseminate propaganda in accord with the current Soviet line.[38] The organization has directed its primary activities to the last of these goals and only occasionally attempts to stir its members to action. There is little or no evidence of its coordinating the activities of its member unions. In pursuit of its goals the CTAL has attempted to avoid any action that may be construed as interference in the internal politics of any Latin American country, but it is not always successful. The Mexican affiliate in 1958 openly attempted to pressure the government to step up its plans to acquire the lands of the Cananea Cattle Company in Sonora, whose owners are largely U.S. citizens. More serious charges of intervention were leveled at the CTAL and Lombardo in late 1957 by the governments of Ecuador and El Salvador. The Ecuadorian Minister of Government and the President of El Salvador presented to the press of their respective countries copies of documents bearing the letterhead of the CTAL and signed by Lombardo Toledano. These documents called for a program of agitation, including strikes and sabotage, in these two countries. Lom-

---

[36] *Visión*, November 4, 1960, p. 24; *El Popular*, October 17, 1960.

[37] "Actividades comunistas en Iberoamérica," *Estudios sobre el Comunismo*, Año X, No. 35 (January–March 1962), 67; *El Popular*, February 18, 1961. In February 1961 Lombardo Toledano attended a meeting of the Executive Committee of the WFTU in East Berlin. At the same time a CTAL protest over the murder of Congolese Leader Patrice Lumumba was sent to the UN over Lombardo's signature as president of the CTAL.

[38] Alexander, *Communism in Latin America*, p. 348. The CTAL was given the task of issuing and distributing all Spanish-language publications of the WFTU at the Peking meeting in December 1949.

bardo vehemently denied their authenticity, calling them "provocations" instigated by his "political enemies." He labeled the charges "grotesque and ridiculous," claiming that the acts existed only in the heads of FBI agents. Adhering closely to his position, announced repeatedly in other contexts, he insisted: "To think that we could consider paralyzing productive activities and communications systems would be to take us for fools and enemies of national progress."

Generally the CTAL is more circumspect in its advocacy of agitation or in its representations to various governments of Latin America. More common than the above circulars were a call early in 1956 to workers of the world to support the employees of a cement company in Bucaramanga, Colombia, in their drive for higher wages; protests to the governments of Colombia (April 1956) and Honduras (March 1956) over the imprisonment and mistreatment by the authorities of labor leaders in their respective countries; and a protest to the government of Guatemala (September 1956) over the imprisonment of a former judge of the Arbenz regime.[39] The CTAL also took credit, because of its agitation, for the freeing from prison of two leading figures of the Arbenz regime who had been sent into exile by the Guatemalan government early in 1956.[40] The CTAL during 1956 was also rumored to be assisting the Cuban plotter, Fidel Castro; the Associated Press reported that Lombardo and the Cuban Communist Lázaro Peña, an official of the CTAL, endorsed Castro's entry into Mexico.

In public statements of its position and attitudes the CTAL has attempted to give the impression that it is a "third force," a middle ground, beween the Communist and non-Communist segments of world organized labor. It has not been able to convince non-Communist labor leaders and organizations that such is its role. Rather, they view the CTAL as an integral part of the Communist movement and shun contacts with it. Despite constant rebuffs, Lombardo continues in his attempts to gain recognition from non-Communist unions, including the Inter-American Regional Labor Organization, the American Federation of Labor-Congress of Industrial Organiza-

[39] *La Voz de México*, September 18, 1956; *El Popular*, March 8, 1956, and April 9, 1956.
[40] *El Popular*, March 26, 1956.

tions, the International Confederation of Free Trade Unions, and the International Confederation of Christian Trade Unions. The CTAL sends greetings to them on various occasions, invites them to send observers to CTAL or affiliate functions, and requests their cooperation in achieving various labor goals.[41] CTAL's known success in recent years was receipt of an invitation to send observers to the Second Congress of the Bolivian Labor Central (Central Obrera Boliviana—COB) in June 1957 in La Paz. The CTAL also gained some favorable publicity for itself by donating funds, as did other labor organizations, for aid to those hurt by the earthquake in Mexico City in August 1957. More impressive than these gestures at solidarity with the non-Communist organizations are CTAL's very solid ties with the WFTU and known Communist groups in Latin America. In his New Year's message to the workers of the world in January 1956, Lombardo called for support of the Soviet-sponsored Workers' Trade Union Charter and the approaching World Conference of Workers, as well as for such popular goals as the maintenance of peace, the triumph of the "Geneva spirit," and the lessening of international tensions. He also sent fraternal greetings to the WFTU, "whose unifying policy has oriented the struggles of the workers of the whole world to achieve their most deeply felt goals." He also greeted "the workers of the Soviet Union who are now successfully facing the great tasks which the construction of Communism entail; the workers of People's China and the People's Democracies of Europe, in whose countries the working class is directing with success the march of society toward the construction of socialism . . ." Later that same year the CTAL sent greetings to the Central Council of Soviet Trade Unions on the occasion of the thirty-ninth anniversary of the October Revolution.[42]

To carry out its propaganda activities the CTAL has published some of its own materials and has distributed material supplied to it by the WFTU. It has also used local newspapers for announcements and news stories. The official organ of the CTAL is the *Noticiero de*

[41] *Christian Science Monitor*, March 31, 1956, p. 2; *El Popular*, April 13, 1956, and January 12, 1956.
[42] *El Popular*, January 2, 1956; January 17, 1956; February 19, 1956; *La Voz de México*, November 8, 1956.

la CTAL (*CTAL News*) a monthly tabloid ordinarily about twenty pages; its size and format have varied from time to time and special editions have been published frequently. Contents of the periodical consist largely of labor news throughout Latin America, particularly that pertaining to the CTAL, its affiliates, or its interests. A lesser amount of space is devoted to labor activities outside Latin America, especially the activities of the WFTU. The CTAL also publishes special reports from time to time such as *The Confederation of Latin American Workers and the Pan American Conference of Caracas* in 1954, mimeographs or prints speeches and reports of WFTU leaders, makes posters to advertise meetings and conferences, and prints handbills for wide distribution to supplement its agitation activities. In the past the newspaper *El Popular* was the most widely used of local periodicals to advertise the CTAL and its activities. With the growing estrangement between the staff of *El Popular* and Lombardo, growing out of the dissension within the PPS, CTAL news was seldom publicized from 1958 to the demise of *El Popular* in 1961. Occasionally the PCM organ, *La Voz de México*, has been used, but the continuing rivalry between Lombardo and the Communist Party precludes that paper as a regular outlet. Finally, the CTAL with Lombardo as editor has published the Spanish edition of the WFTU's monthly *World Trade Union Movement* (*El Movimiento Sindical Mundial*).

THE GENERAL UNION OF WORKERS AND PEASANTS OF MEXICO
(UNIÓN GENERAL DE OBREROS Y CAMPESINOS DE MÉXICO—UGOCM)

This Mexican affiliate of the CTAL and WFTU, Unión General de Obreros y Campesinos de México (UGOCM), was founded in 1949 by Vicente Lombardo Toledano to replace the non-Communist Confederation of Mexican Workers, which had withdrawn from the CTAL into which Lombardo had led it some years earlier. The UGOCM has an estimated membership of 20,000 divided into about fifteen state federations, which in turn are composed of a number of regional and local unions. Agricultural workers make up the bulk of its membership.[43] Until late 1956 its strongest subgroup was the National Federation of Sugar Cane Workers (Federación Nacional de Cañeros—

---

[43] "Actividades comunistas en Iberoamérica," *Estudios sobre el Comunismo*, Año IX, No. 32 (April–June 1961), 97–98.

FNC), with headquarters in Veracruz. With the withdrawal of the FNC in December 1956, the UGOCM center of strength shifted to the northern state of Sonora. Other concentrations of lesser importance exist in Sinaloa, Chiapas, Michoacán, and Guerrero. Although the UGOCM has no formal affiliation with the PPS, in reality it is the labor wing of the Party, and an interlocking directorship has long existed between the Party and the Union. For example, from 1955 to 1956 the undersecretary general of the PPS, the number two official in the Party, was Vidal Díaz Muñoz, the secretary general of the FNC, and with the resignation of Díaz Muñoz, the position of undersecretary general was held from 1957 to 1960 by Jacinto López, secretary general of the UGOCM since its First National Congress in 1951.[44] Prior to that promotion López had long been high in Party circles, while his second-in-command, Lázaro Rubio Felix, had also been a longtime member of the National Directorate, the governing inner circle of the Partido Popular Socialista. Both are still members of the PPS National Directorate. The Mexican government has never recognized the UGOCM as a bona fide labor union; consequently it has no powers of collective bargaining. Furthermore some of its subunits appear to be largely paper organizations, while one of its strongest affiliates, the Central Union of Ejido Societies (Unión Central de Sociedades Ejidales—UCSE), dominated by the Communist Party, is not subject to the national leaders. As a result, the activities of the UGOCM have been limited largely to agitation and propaganda. However, the UGOCM has no propaganda organ of its own and uses those outlets available to the PPS and the CTAL. National headquarters are located in Mexico City.[45]

With the collapse of the PPS in Veracruz and the removal of Díaz Muñoz, Jacinto López was free to pursue vigorous union activity in his home area of northwest Mexico, principally in the state of Sonora. Since 1957 López and his followers have agitated for government

[44] For a list of the officers elected at the First Congress, see *Cultura Soviética*, XV, No. 85 (November 1951), 7, and for a brief report of the Congress, see *Noviembre*, November 25, 1951. The Third National Congress was held May 1960.

[45] U.S. Department of Labor, *Directory of Labor Organizations, Western Hemisphere*, Chapter 26, p. 37.

expropriation and division into *ejidos* of lands allegedly held in violation of the agrarian laws and the Constitution with regard to size or, if foreign owned, proximity to the border. In 1957 and 1958 the primary target was the Cananea Cattle Company, owned by the Greene family of the United States but incorporated under Mexican law. The Administration of President Ruiz Cortines had been interested for several years in the eventual acquisition of the estate and the owners were not opposed to its sale, but the negotiations proceeded slowly. During 1957 the UGOCM complained that government officials were not following up the "presidential order" for the nationalization of the property, and for much of the year carried on agitation to this end. In the first week of February 1958 a band of men led by Jacinto López and local Communist Party leader Ramón Danzós Palomino, recently returned from Moscow, seized control of the radio station in Cananea and announced their intention to invade lands of the 400,000-hectare Cananea Cattle Company in the area. They added that they had at their disposal twenty-three trucks to transport those *campesinos* who desired to participate in the land seizure. Federal troops and the Judicial Police repelled them, but López shifted his attack to the Culiacán Valley in Sinaloa, to the south, where some properties were invaded by squatters. Dislodged by federal forces, López then shifted his operations westward to the Mexicali region in the neighboring state of Baja California, Norte, where he was again repulsed. On February 24 a UGOCM meeting of 2,000 farm workers, led by Lázaro Rubio Felix, threatened to renew the invasion of all lands held by foreigners along the frontier. Farm owners in the three states appealed to President Ruiz Cortines and to the Department of Defense for Army protection against future incursions.[46]

To remove some of the pressure for land in Sinaloa, the Department of Agrarian Affairs parceled out 4,840 hectares to four hundred eighty-four families in March and announced another grant of 14,000 to one thousand four hundred families in April, while the government financing agency, Nacional Financiera, proceeded under presidential order with the division of some of its holdings in the

[46] *El Universal*, February 6, 1958, pp. 1 and 12; February 14, 1958, pp. 1, 8, and 23.

state into 20-hectare plots. At the same time the government reiterated its policy of protecting private land not subject to seizure from squatter invasions.[47] By July the government had completed its negotiations for the purchase of the Cananea Cattle Company and in August it took possession. Just three days after the announcement of the expropriation in July, Jacinto López and several associates, ironically enough, were seized by the police for their invasions of the Company's lands. Serving five months of a six-month sentence on the charge of "social dissolution," López and his companions were released in early December by the new López Mateos Administration. The UGOCM leader announced that he was returning immediately to Cananea to resume direction of his union and to work for the division of the expropriated land. Following that, he said, he planned to investigate the land problems in southern Sonora and, if necessary, to continue with the land invasions. Asked by press correspondents if he feared being imprisoned again, he replied that he had got over that fear long ago.[48]

True to his word, López returned to Sonora where his agitation was renewed. Early in January 1959 he led 3,000 squatters in the seizure of lands just outside Ciudad Obregón in the southern part of the state. They remained in peaceful possession for about a week, when city and state police intervened. The squatters, organized in groups of 50, wrapped themselves in Mexican flags as the police approached, but evacuated the land without violence. The state government provided trucks to carry the squatters to their homes, and the chief of the Department of Agrarian Affairs promised a solution of the land problem within the law. He received López and Lázaro Rubio Felix the following day, requested them to cease their agitation and invasions, and assured them it was the strict policy of the Administration to obey the Constitution and the agrarian laws. They promised to cease their activities. In February the government began parceling the lands of the Cananea Cattle Company, the former Greene estate, and it appears that, following the expropriation, the National Peasant Confederation (Confederación Nacional Campe-

---

[47] *Ibid.*, March 17, 1958, pp. 1 and 11.
[48] *El Popular*, July 17, 1958, and December 3, 1958.

sina), with its government connections, seriously undercut the UGOCM in organizing the new peasant landholders. In an attempt to hold their followers, local UGOCM leaders in Baja California in July 1959, probably at the instigation of López, invaded several farms in the Valle de Guadalupe. UGOCM agitators appeared to be involved too in the pressures applied to some White Russian colonists to visit the Soviet Union in April 1960. When the colonists rebuffed these efforts, leftists in the area began a campaign to have them ousted from their lands.[49] Sporadic seizures of land have continued down to mid-1962. In March López threatened more land invasions, and 120 squatters or parachutists (*paracaidistas*), as the Mexicans call them, marched on a ranch in Puebla. Federal troops evicted them. In June, López and Braulio Maldonado, former governor of Baja California, Norte, led a hunger caravan from Sonora toward Mexico City to protest against government failure to solve agrarian problems. Other caravans and other land seizures that seemingly had no connection with the UGOCM or any other Communist organizations have occurred in 1961 and 1962. In March 1961 the Attorney General reported that his office had about two thousand complaints against squatters under study. The government in most instances has moved swiftly with a combination of force and concessions to head off these demonstrations before serious violence developed. The UGOCM may not be able to take credit for all agrarian agitation, but it has done more than any other organization in Mexico to point up the needs of the Mexican peasant and to do something about them.[50]

In 1956 the UGOCM and PPS showed considerable interest for a brief time in organizing and recruiting working women. In mid-March, with the approaching meeting of Presidents Eisenhower and Ruiz Cortines, a Women's Coordinating Committee for the Defense of the Country, apparently organized by the PPS for the occasion, declared itself opposed to any kind of a military pact with the United States which might endanger national independence or the lives of

[49] *El Universal*, January 8, 1959, p. 1; *El Popular*, January 9, 1959; *New York Times*, May 1, 1960, p. 32.
[50] *Excelsior*, May 23, 1962, pp. 1 and 11; May 26, 1962, pp. 1 and 11; June 8, 1962, p. 8; June 10, 1962, p. 1; June 12, 1962, p. 1; and June 15, 1962, p. 12.

Mexican troops.[51] The Committee has not been heard from since that time. In the following months the UGOCM announced a forthcoming world conference of working women to be held in Europe in June, sponsored by the WFTU. To prepare for that conference it was further announced that a National Conference of Working Women would be held beforehand to draw up discussion items to be presented by a Mexican delegation. The UGOCM report gave the impression that a great deal of activity was already being carried out in labor and government circles throughout the country.[52]

The National Conference of Working Women opened on Saturday, June 2, and closed Sunday, June 3. Attendance was poor. ORIT condemned the Conference and apparently Mexican government and labor leaders warned their members to boycott the affair. The directing board was dominated by women members of the PPS, notably Hortensia Rojas, a Lombardo follower of long standing, and Adriana Lombardo de Silva, daughter of the president of the PPS. Lombardo Toledano opened the proceedings with a call to those who would make up the delegation to the world conference to present an unvarnished view of conditions in Mexico. Marcel Brase, the secretary of the Metallurgical Workers of France, also spoke. Following the speeches three items of discussion were adopted for the conference: (1) discrimination against women, (2) problems of farm women, and (3) problems of women in public services. After consideration of these issues the assembled delegates concluded that the most pressing problems of women workers lay in the field of domestic service. Resolutions were thereupon passed to organize domestic servants, to extend social security to them, and to set up government inspection offices to protect them from exploitation. The Conference closed without naming a delegation to attend the world conference scheduled to meet in Budapest.[53] The delegation that finally left for Europe was apparently hand-picked by Lombardo Toledano. Nothing further seems to have been done to carry out the resolutions of the National Conference. For many months the group

[51] *El Popular*, March 16, 1956.
[52] *Ibid.*, April 18, 1956.
[53] *Excelsior*, June 3, 1956, p. 15; *El Popular*, June 3, 1956; June 4, 1956; and June 5, 1956.

apparently remained inactive except to announce that a series of National Seminars for working women was scheduled for November 1958. Since nothing further was reported on these meetings, presumably they were not held.[54] However, in November 1959, the UGOCM and the PPS sponsored the Second National Conference of Women Workers. It appears to have been no more successful in attracting an audience nor more vigorous in post-Conference activities than the first.

Other minor activities of the UGOCM in the past few years have included a protest to the President over the assassination of a teacher in Veracruz, attempts to establish farm credit societies in Sonora, and a protest to the governor of Michoacán over the detention of dissatisfied students in Morelia.[55]

THE CENTRAL UNION OF EJIDO SOCIETIES (UNIÓN CENTRAL DE SOCIEDADES EJIDALES—UCSE)

The Unión Central de Sociedades Ejidales (UCSE) was founded in 1940 by members of the PCM. It has constituted the labor wing of the Party but is not formally and officially affiliated. Actually, the UCSE is officially a branch of the UGOCM, the Mexican affiliate of the CTAL and WFTU, but because of the former's domination by Vicente Lombardo Toledano, with whom the PCM leaders are often at odds, the UCSE affiliation is only a formality. The two dominant officers of the UCSE, Arturo Orona and Alberto Loera, director and subdirector respectively, are both members of the PCM. Orona has long been a national Party leader, and probably because of his control over the vital segment of the Party in the Laguna region, survived the purges of the Thirteenth Party Congress in May 1960. He has long been a farmer in the area. Intelligent, shrewd, and well acquainted with local problems around Torreón, he has won the respect, however grudging it may be, of the bankers and businessmen of the area. His primary interest has been agitation for increased farm credits, but in this pursuit he has been careful not to present himself openly as a Communist and to keep his demonstrations peaceful.

[54] *El Popular*, September 22, 1958.

[55] *La Voz de México*, October 5, 1957; *El Popular*, February 4, 1956; and March 8, 1956.

The Communist nature of the organization has been known for many years by non-Communist farm organizations in the Laguna area, which is its headquarters and principal arena of activity. In 1948 the secretary general of the National Peasant Confederation (Confederación Nacional Campesina), an affiliate of the government party, demanded to know what the Communists were doing with various funds collected from the government, ostensibly for service to the *ejidatarios*. Presumably, the Party was pocketing at least some of the subsidy. There is no record that an investigation was made, and possibly the Party is still profiting from this source. In 1956 the Laguna Mutual Insurance Society also condemned the UCSE as Communist, but conceded that it controlled only a small fraction of the *ejidos* in the area.[56]

UCSE propaganda and agitation closely follow the lead of the Party, particularly with respect to issues affecting the farming population in northern Mexico. The official position of the organization was well summed up in an open letter to the President of the country early in 1960. Capitalizing on undeniable misery and considerable injustice in rural areas, the UCSE placed the blame on private individuals and private business enterprises as well as on *ejido* officials, local politicians, and agrarian leaders, whom they accused of serving the landholding bourgeoisie. Higher government officials were held responsible for permitting flagrant violation of the agrarian law. To remedy this situation the UCSE stressed the need of the government to cancel *ejido* debts for machinery, administration, interest charges, etc., to increase the amount of credit available from the Bank of Ejido Credit and to increase the guaranteed price of wheat. Neither the complaints nor the proposals were new except for a few specifics.[57] In 1956 cotton was a vital issue. Orona coupled criticism of U.S. "cotton dumping" with an insistent demand for the diversification of the Mexican cotton market. He named Poland, Czechoslovakia, and the

[56] *Excelsior*, June 14, 1956, p. 28. The advertisement stated that the UCSE had controlled the Mutual Society for some years and had used the funds it gained thereby to defray the cost of trips to the Soviet Bloc by Communist leaders. Officers of the Mutual Society claimed that the archives of their organization provided ample proof of the charges.

[57] *La Voz de México*, February 20, 1960.

USSR as likely purchasers, pointing out that they in turn could supply Mexico with machinery, paper, and manufactured articles now purchased with scarce dollars. At the same time the Society sent an urgent message to the Secretary of Agriculture demanding that the guaranteed price of wheat be raised because of increased costs and plague. In October 1957 a UCSE meeting passed a series of resolutions demanding aid from the federal government to relieve hardship caused by drought and scarcity of land. Specifically, the UCSE demanded more water for irrigation, increased federal subsidies, and higher guaranteed prices for farm products. Bands of *ejidatarios* were organized to demonstrate before the local Bank of Ejido Credit which sets minimum guaranteed prices, and a committee was named to interview the Secretary of Agriculture to induce him to carry out the demands.[58] In April 1958 Arturo Orona and Vidal Díaz Muñoz, formerly of the PPS, led a group of squatters in seizing land in the Laguna area. When the Secretary of Agriculture decreed that the lands were not subject to expropriation, the squatters abandoned the lands without protest.[59] The evidence seems to indicate that the UCSE does not carry out a sustained program of agitation and propaganda. It has no publication of its own, and has relied on the outlets normally available to the Communist Party: *La Voz de México* and occasionally *El Popular*, until its closing in November 1961.

THE WORKERS' FRONT (FRENTE OBRERO—FO)

The Workers' Front was founded in 1951 under the leadership of Juan Ortega Arenas. During its first three or four years it had the characteristics of a study circle and concentrated its efforts on preparing worker cadres for entry into the PCM. Its leaders considered it a temporary organization, and although occasionally they criticized the PCM, they looked to eventual full incorporation into the Party. From 1954 to 1957, however, the FO began to get politically involved in labor union activities, carrying out policies independently of the PCM and at times in opposition to it. Finally, in the years after 1957, the FO openly attacked the PCM and advocated the founding of a

[58] *El Popular*, April 8, 1956 and June 1, 1956; *La Voz de México*, September 17, 1957, and October 8, 1957.
[59] *El Popular*, April 13, 1958.

new political party. By 1960 the group reached its maximum strength of about seventy members, the majority of them workers. It regularly published a periodical, *La Verdad Obrera*, distributed propaganda material, and maintained contacts in labor and student circles. In 1961 the FO divided, with Juan Ortega leading off a minority faction that calls itself the Mexican Communist Workers' Front (Frente Obrero Comunista Mexicano). The majority faction kept the name Frente Obrero.[60]

THE WORKERS' UNIVERSITY (UNIVERSIDAD OBRERA—UO)

The Universidad Obrera (UO) was founded in February 1936 as a labor school.[61] Its creation was largely the work of Vicente Lombardo Toledano, the leading labor leader and organizer during the administration of reformer President Lázaro Cárdenas. Its purpose then was to establish a school geared to the educational desires and needs of the urban working classes.[62] While the school did not abandon this goal, it gradually began to emphasize the indoctrination of workers (and others who may wish to attend) in Marxian philosophy and economics, the Soviet interpretation of the Cold War, and the Marxian interpretation of Mexican history. This bent is indicated by some of the courses offered and their instructors. Lombardo himself, a self-declared Marxist and thoroughgoing and devoted supporter of Soviet views and attitudes, has taught Elements of Philosophy; Agustín Cué Cánovas, the History of Mexico; and Víctor Manuel Gutiérrez, an exiled member of the Guatemalan Communist Party, Imperialism and the Struggle in Colonial, Semicolonial, and Dependent Countries. Several teachers, such as Eulalia Guzmán, the archaeologist, and Javier Guerrero, the artist, have been drawn from the Mexican Communist Party. Other courses offered have included Political Economy, Dialectical Materialism and Historical Materialism, Trade Union Organization, and History of the Mexican and International Labor Movement.[63] No academic requirements are nec-

---

[60] Ricardo Flores, *Qué Es y Hacia Dónde Marcha el Frente Obrero*, pp. 3–5. Flores had been a member of the FO but joined the PCM in 1959.
[61] *El Popular*, February 15, 1956.
[62] *Ibid.*, January 27, 1956.
[63] *Ibid.*, January 27, 1956, and February 12, 1956.

essary for admission to any of the courses, and no degrees or diplomas are granted following a course of studies. Despite these academic weaknesses the government has long recognized the Universidad Obrera as a bona fide educational institution for purposes of government financial assistance, which was given, according to one account, through the government newsprint-control agency, PIPSA.[64]

To supplement its course offerings the UO conducts a series of conferences to which the public is invited, usually free of charge. It has an extension service, a research branch, and a publications office, though these seem to operate at low levels if at all. There is also a library, a theater group, and a student circle attached to the school.[65] Of greater importance are the Department of Cultural Relations, which has contact with cultural groups in the Soviet Bloc area, the Charles Chaplin Cinema Club, and the José Clemente Orozco Room, used for the exhibition of painting, photography, sculpture, and artistic productions. In December 1956 the Orozco Room exhibited a series of photographs on life in Rumania. The pictures were provided by a Rumanian delegate to the Conference of the International Association for Social Security held in Mexico in the fall of that year. From October 1 to 25, 1957, the UO sponsored, in honor of the anniversary of the founding of Communist China, an exposition on various aspects of life in "New China."[66] The Cinema Club has been active too. In January 1956 it presented the Soviet film *The Knight of the Golden Star* and a short feature, *The Zoological Park in Moscow*. In June it offered two "magnificent Soviet documentaries," and in September, *The Academician Pavlov*. The public was invited to these showings without cost or at a nominal price.[67]

Lombardo Toledano has maintained his interest in the UO, but he has turned over the immediate direction of its affairs to his daughter and son-in-law, Adriana and Federico de Silva, both of whom are active and influential members of the Partido Popular Socialista. In 1956 the cost of enrollment was 30 pesos and the monthly fee 40 pesos

[64] Jorge Prieto Laurens, "¿No Hay Communismo en México?" *El Universal*, May 9, 1956, p. 3.
[65] *El Popular*, February 12, 1956.
[66] *La Voz de México*, October 1, 1957.
[67] *El Popular*, January 1, 1956; June 16, 1956; and September 12, 1956.

(about U.S. $2.40 and $3.20 respectively). These fees are obviously insufficient to maintain the school. From its inception to 1946 it received a government subsidy, but this was discontinued with the inauguration of President Miguel Alemán. Currently, the school is supported by the contributions of friends of Lombardo, including ex-President Lázaro Cárdenas[68] who spoke at the twenty-fifth anniversary celebration of the school in 1961.

According to its own claims, the school enrolled some 15,000 students between 1936 and 1952, and in 1955 it enrolled 275. Most of the students now come from the PPS and the UGOCM although a few have come from other Latin American countries. Financial difficulties in 1959 forced serious curtailment of activities, although annually in October the school has sponsored well-publicized celebrations for the anniversary of the founding of the Chinese People's Republic. Former President Lázaro Cárdenas spoke at the 1959 celebration with extravagant praise for Red China, which he had visited earlier in the year.[69]

In November of 1959 General C. P. Cabell, deputy director of the U.S. Central Intelligence Agency, reported to a subcommittee of the Senate Judiciary Committee that "Marxist training centers, such as the Worker's University in Mexico City, are being expanded in an effort to broaden the appeal of Marxism, and to stimulate nationalism."[70] No specific activities were outlined at that time, but in May 1960 new personnel were added to both the teaching and administrative staffs.

The new members of the teaching staff and the courses offered were as follows: Luis Monter, Labor Union Journalism; José Enrique Gama, Elements of Law; Benjamín Vera, Products.

The new members of the administrative staff and their positions were: Primo Valdes, director of the Cinema Club; Bruno Guerrero, assistant at the Cinema Club; César Jiménez, in charge of periodicals

[68] *El Popular*, January 6, 1956 listed the fees. Lombardo reported on the former subsidy and present support at UO inaugural ceremonies March 11, 1959.

[69] *New York Times*, October 18, 1959, p. 24; *El Universal*, January 21, 1959, p. 1.

[70] Subcommittee To Investigate the Administration of the Internal Security Act, *Communist Threat*, p. 148.

at the UO Library; Fanny Elvira Perera, assigned to the scholastic department; Francisco Real, assistant librarian.

Obviously, Mexican labor is overwhelmingly non-Communist. Communist penetration in recognized unions is minimal and well controlled, and Communist-operated unions have had little impact on Mexican society, except for land distribution in the northwest.

V. The Mexican Government, the Mexican Communists, and International Communism

Introduction

For many years the Mexican government has appeared to be "soft on Communism" in the eyes of anti-Communists in Mexico and abroad. The popular-front activities of the Cárdenas Administration, the dominance of Lombardo Toledano over the labor movement until 1947, the continued usage by labor of Marxist terminology, the participation of Communist and crypto-Communist political organizations in national and state elections, Communist infiltration of Mexican public education, association of Mexican government officials with Communists, and the freedom permitted Communist exiles and the personnel of the Soviet Embassy, which is the largest diplomatic establishment in Mexico save that of the United States, constitute some of the more important factors which have influenced the "soft on Communism" opinion. Mexico's independent attitude toward the United States, its opposition to colonialism, and its refusal to sign military agreements of any kind with any Western power have seemed to reinforce the anti-Communists in their convictions. The charges against the government cannot be wholly denied, but they must be explained to understand fully Mexico's position in the Cold War and her attitude toward domestic Communists.

The Mexican Government and the Communists

The Revolutionary inheritance of a strong mixture of socialism with traditional liberalism resulted, of necessity, in the creation of a climate of broad political tolerance in Mexico. This meant that, once the destructive phase of the Revolution ended and the country began to return to constitutional government, political parties of all shades of belief from right to left were permitted to organize. When extremist parties threatened to use force to obtain their ends the government cracked down hard: the Communists were outlawed in the early 1930's, and the Sinarquistas in the early 1940's. Both have since been permitted to reorganize, though the Sinarquistas no longer have a political party in the usual sense. At no time, however, have the Communists, pro-Communists, or non-Communists, whether labor leaders, students, or politicians, been permitted to threaten the security of the government. Violence in strikes or political agitation has been consistently discouraged by the use of police and Army counterforce, but normally the demonstrators have been dispersed, or if arrested, released within at most a few hours. Only in those instances in which government authorities have been convinced that the leaders of these movements aimed as much at the serious disruption of order as at the achievement of specific benefits for themselves has the government resorted to imposing formal charges and lengthy imprisonments. In recent years, more and more frequently have such interpretations been given to the actions of Communist and pro-Communist leaders who have failed "to play the game" of Mexican politics. "Playing the game" in Mexico today means the acceptance of the basic power structure, with criticisms limited to specific persons, situations, and actions. The government on the whole is responsive to deep-seated and widespread dissatisfaction and will not only grant concession by way of material benefits to disgruntled groups but will also permit some personnel changes in government positions as well as in semigovernmental organizations such as labor unions. This expedient has frequently undercut Communist agitation in a most effective manner.[1]

[1] The vast lands of the Cananea Cattle Company (about 650,000 acres) were expropriated at a fair price in 1958. The area was settled with landless peasants by 1961, thus removing a major source of Communist propaganda. The ranch was owned by a U.S. family.

Until the mid-1950's the Mexican government refused to take seriously the dangers of Communist subversion in Mexico or in the Western Hemisphere; its position was in sharp contrast to that of the United States, particularly during the heyday of Senator Joseph McCarthy. The high point of Mexico's refusal to acknowledge the Communist threat was reached perhaps in the first six months of 1954 when the Mexican representation at the Tenth Inter-American Conference at Caracas refused to sign the so-called Caracas Declaration sponsored by U.S. Secretary of State John Foster Dulles. The Declaration called for joint action by the American nations in the face of international Communist subversion in one of the nations. It was obviously aimed at Guatemala, at that time heavily infiltrated by and in danger of complete control by Communists. Mexico refused to sign, not because she was pro-Communist but partly because of disbelief in the charges of Communist infiltration, and, more importantly, because of her longstanding, deeply ingrained revulsion to intervention in any form by one or more states in the internal affairs of another.[2] Furthermore, powerful political figures expressed disapproval of U.S. aid to the Guatemalan rebels led by Carlos Castillo Armas, who overthrew the government and exiled or jailed the Communist leaders. The Mexican attitude with regard to Guatemala under Arbenz may be contrasted with its attitude to Cuba under Castro. Still determined to maintain its basic foreign policy of nonintervention, the Mexican government extended all the formal courtesies to visiting Cuban President Dorticós in the spring of 1960, but restrained local Communists in their attempts to capitalize on the visit. The Mexican press, often responsive to government policies, has repeatedly indicated concern with Communist influence on the island, while the government itself has continued to follow a policy of correct diplomatic conduct toward, and to oppose any form of intervention in, Castro's Cuba.

The summer of 1954 proved to be a turning point of sorts in the attitude of the Mexican government toward Communists and Communism within Mexico. Political toleration of the left was by no means abandoned, nor were Mexico's doors closed to Red-hued exiles

[2] Cf. the policy statement of Ambassador Luis Quintanilla in "Controls and Foreign Policies in Latin American Countries," in Philip W. Buck and Martin B. Travis (eds.), *Control of Foreign Relations in Modern Nations*, pp. 226–227.

seeking asylum from neighboring countries. Neither did Mexico sign the Caracas Declaration (nor has she to the present), nor did she outlaw the Communist Party. But it has been reported that the Mexican government was rather deeply disturbed by the revelations that came to light concerning Communist subversion and infiltration in Guatemala during the summer of 1954 and that the resignation, as foreign affairs adviser, of Narciso Bassols, a Marxist and a founder of the PPS, constituted a rejection by President Ruiz Cortines of Communist influences in the Mexican government.[3] In October 1954, moreover, the police of Mexico City picked up and held for four days Valentín Campa of the POCM, Dionisio Encina of the PCM, and other Party members on charges of intent to disturb public order and good government.[4] For another two years, however, the government was cautious in dealing with Communist agitation and propaganda and up to 1956, the most notable anti-Communist accomplishment of the government was the quiet elimination of Communist leadership in the labor unions. This action was prompted in the beginning not so much by an anti-Communist attitude on the part of political leaders but by the unwillingness of the Communists and the crypto-Communists, such as Lombardo Toledano, to accept the more moderate social and economic reform programs adopted after 1940. Such a view appears to be borne out by the fact that Lombardo's followers have not been eliminated from leadership posts in the National Teachers' Union; in this organization a *modus vivendi* has been established between the two groups, probably based on some sort of equitable sharing of the spoils. The PPS group in the teachers' union still has considerable influence despite its temporary flirting with the rebellious Salazar group in Section IX. On the other hand, the Salazar group, unwilling to compromise with the government and the na-

[3] *New York Times*, July 26, 1959, p. 68; *Noviembre*, October 23, 1954 reported that Bassols' resignation was attributed to his disagreements with the government on economic policies and Mexican-United States relations. One more indication of government toleration of dissent and lack of concern with Communism was the fact that Bassols remained in government service until late 1954 despite his co-founding of the PPS and his presidency of the Campa Defense Committee in 1952. See *Noviembre*, April 2, 1952.

[4] *Noviembre*, October 30, 1954.

tional leadership of the teachers' union, has been subjected, as we have seen, to severe attack.[5]

During 1956 a sterner official attitude toward Communist agitation became discernible. In the May Day parade of that year the police quietly arrested a group of Communist railroad workers who were attempting to disrupt the marchers. At least eight were taken into custody but all were released shortly after the parade. Furthermore, it was due in large part to the anti-Communist, inter-American labor organization ORIT and its Mexican affiliates that the Communist-sponsored women's conference in the spring of 1956 met with such a poor reception from working women in Mexico City. Late in the year the government refused visas to members of the Peking Opera Company which had been touring Latin America.[6] The most spectacular government operation of the year, however, occurred with respect to the months-long student violence and rioting, extending from April to October 1956, centering around the National Polytechnic Institute (IPN). Cautious and compromising at first, the government first showed some determination in June when it refused entry into Mexico of Jacques Denis, secretary general of the World Federation of Democratic Youth, an international Communist front. Denis had come to Mexico apparently to confer with strike leaders. Through the summer, however, the government continued to vacillate in its relations with the students, to the disgust of the citizens of Mexico City. Finally, when public opinion was thoroughly aroused against the students, who normally enjoy wide popularity, the government moved with forcefulness.[7] José Ceniceros, the Secretary of Education, gave full support to the newly appointed director of the IPN who closed the boarding school. Ceniceros reported that the government intended to cleanse the IPN of corruption and disorder and to institute educational reforms to the benefit of all the students. The Department of

[5] See Chapter IV on organized labor.

[6] An "acrobatic and artistic team" touring Latin America in 1959 was also refused admittance. Five members of the team making preparations for exhibitions in Mexico were invited to leave the country. See *El Universal*, April 7, 1959, p. 1.

[7] Marion Wilhelm, "Mexico Curbs Rowdy Students," *Christian Science Monitor*, October 20, 1956.

Defense also alerted military commanders in other university centers to take prompt action against sympathy demonstrations for the IPN boarders. Nicandro Mendoza, a PPS member and close follower of Lombardo, and three other student boarders were arrested and committed to a federal penitentiary on charges of "social dissolution." Two were released after short imprisonments but Mendoza and Mariano Molina, leader of the student organization in the IPN, served more than twenty-six months. For weeks, troops patrolled the former boarding-school area of the IPN to prevent further disorder, and the government fired some public school teachers who had supported the student rowdyism. When the leftist youth organization, the CJM, attempted to stir up trouble the following spring by infiltrating the IPN with agitators from the provinces, the director issued credentials to all bona fide students, thereby making it virtually impossible for outsiders to gain entrance. Similar disturbances in the provinces were suppressed in 1956 and 1957, and since then, there have been no further serious student disorders.[8]

From late 1956 onward there can also be discerned for the first time a keen interest in Communists and their activities by the office of the Attorney General and by the Federal Judicial Police. Beginning in October of that year detailed police reports on Mexican Communism were made available to the capital city's police reporters. Eduardo Téllez of *El Universal*, for example, published a chart based on police reports of Communist propaganda distribution and outlet organs, indicating considerable prior investigation and analysis by police intelligence.[9] Subsequent reports have revealed that detailed dossiers, with information dating back many years, are maintained on rather obscure as well as on well-known Communists. The Attorney General's Office and the Federal Judicial Police have also in recent years been much freer in their accusation of Communist involvement in labor and student disturbances and much more zealous in confiscating Communist propaganda materials foreign and domestic, raiding Communist headquarters, and harassing Communist lead-

---

[8] See Chapter III on Communist youth fronts for details.
[9] *El Universal*, October 14, 1956, pp. 1 and 10.

ers.[10] At the same time the government appears much less concerned with respect for civil rights or with adverse reactions of public opinion.[11]

An intensification of government countermeasures against both Mexican and foreign Communists has been most evident when these have threatened internal order or Mexico's friendly relations with her neighbors. Early in 1957 the Mexican government for the first time began curbing activities of Guatemalan exiles (who numbered about 300, including some leading Communists) to the satisfaction of the Castillo Armas government.[12] The new Guatemalan government was seriously concerned about exile plottings in Mexico and their frequent crossings of the border in both directions, but for several years now Guatemalan exiles have not constituted a real problem. Despite this new approach to the Guatemalans, the Mexican government will not molest Communist or other exiles who are content to live quietly and apolitically in the country. In July 1956 *La Prensa*, reporting the views of the Department of Government, informed its readers that the government exercises strict surveillance and control over foreign Communists but that as long as they, or any other exiles, observe the laws and do not engage in subversive activities, they cannot be deported. Some foreign Communists, however, were never given the opportunity to demonstrate their intentions. René Charles Duhamel, president of the International Federation of Workers in Public Service and Allied Occupations, a trade department of the WFTU, arrived at the Mexico City airport in March 1957. Duhamel was scheduled to participate in a CTAL lecture series, but he never left the airport. Federal police put him back on the same plane on which he arrived. Several

[10] From 1956 on, the PCM and POCM complained bitterly that their newspapers were not delivered. See *Noviembre*, December 8, 1956.

[11] Prompt police and Army action in suppressing Communist-led landless campaigns in 1958 and 1959 might well be contrasted with the cautious attitude displayed for months toward rioting students in Mexico City in 1956. In the former disturbances, the police permitted gang wars in the streets of the city and General Miguel Molinar Sismondi, chief of police in the Federal District, when interviewed, reported that he had express orders to remain on the sidelines of the student conflict. See *El Universal*, June 1, 1956, p. 1.

[12] *New York Times*, January 20, 1957, p. 10.

months later a similar fate befell Efraín Alvarado Paredes, representative of the Ecuadoran Communist Party, and his companions. They
too were not permitted to leave the airport and were forced to depart
immediately.[13]

With Mexican Communists the same tough attitude has been taken.
In 1956 President Ruiz Cortines fired Alonso Aguilar, head of the
Circle of Mexican Studies (CEM), from a position in the National
Bank of Foreign Commerce, allegedly for Communist connections.[14]
In 1957 the director of the National Institute of Fine Arts (INBA), a
government agency, disavowed any official connection with Institute
members who attended the Moscow Youth Festival in the summer of
that year, and Vicente Lombardo Toledano, as director of the Workers' University was refused permission to use a room in the Palace of
Fine Arts for a series of conferences. In 1958 Narciso Bassols was
denied a diplomatic passport for which he had applied,[15] and in 1959,
a painting of Federico Silva, son-in-law of Lombardo Toledano, was
removed from an exhibit in the Palace of Fine Arts because of its attack on the office of the Attorney General.[16] On the other hand, the
government is by no means disposed to outlaw Communist parties or
Communist-front organizations. It takes the view that they are all so
small and weak as to constitute no serious danger to Mexico.

Despite increased government concern about Communism, accusations of Communist infiltration of government ordinarily cause little
public stir or investigation,[17] and known Communists and persons
with close Communist connections are invited to participate in official or semiofficial conferences. A few examples will suffice. Enrique

[13] Unión Cívica Internacional de México, "Comunismo en México," *Estudios sobre el Comunismo*, Año V, No. 17 (July–September 1957), p. 124. In
1961 the Foreign Office warned the Sino-Soviet Bloc members, including
Cuba, that propaganda was not to be imported through the diplomatic pouch.
When this admonition was ignored the police seized Bloc diplomatic pouches at
the end of 1961, collecting about four tons of Cuban, Soviet, and Chinese materials. See *New York Times*, July 9, 1961, p. 24.

[14] Ing. Manuel Arcos Fenal, "Paparouv, el Titiritero de Nuestros Comunistoides," *El Universal*, July 13, 1957, p. 2.

[15] *El Popular*, April 12, 1958.

[16] *Ibid.*, September 29, 1959.

[17] Manuel M. Reynoso, "¿Que Quiere el Comunismo en el Departamento
Agrario?" *El Universal*, July 9, 1956, p. 3.

Marcué Pardiñas, brother and publishing associate of Manuel Marcué Pardiñas, a PPS member, for years has been an official of the National Bank of Ejido Credit.[18] Manuel O. Padrés, former director and general manager of *El Popular*, accompanied President López Mateos to the United States as a member of the Press Information Committee.[19] Heriberto Jara, president of the CMP and a Stalin Peace Prize winner was received by and dined with President Ruiz Cortines at an official function, and in October 1959 received the Belisario Domínguez Medal, the Senate's highest decoration for civic merit.[20] In that same month Lombardo Toledano formally addressed the National Agrarian Congress of Toluca, a conference organized by the state of Mexico and inaugurated by President López Mateos himself.[21] President López Mateos declared the works of Communist Painter Diego Rivera to be historical monuments and the Minister of Education in the previous Administration named a public school in Veracruz after José Mancisidor (now deceased) onetime president of the IICMR and member of other Communist-front organizations.[22] Mancisidor is remembered not for his Communist affiliations but for his contributions to Mexican literature and his robust nationalism. And, finally, the Mexican Chamber of Deputies in December 1959 formally received a delegation of Czech legislators in reciprocation of an earlier reception of Mexican deputies in Czechoslovakia.

Within the labor movement, however, with its close political ties to the government through its virtual incorporation within the official party (the PRI), anti-Communist attitudes and activities have become much more direct and forceful. Not only were Communists forced out of leadership posts in the 1940's but a growing animosity could be detected in the 1950's. For example, in 1949 the railroad workers' union ousted Valentín Campa, former leader of the Communist-splinter party, the POCM, and denied him pension and other privileges. Appeals by Campa for restoration of these rights have been repeatedly denied, the final turndown being in 1957. (His

---

[18] *El Universal*, March 3, 1957, pp. 1 and 6; *El Popular*, September 29, 1959.
[19] *El Popular*, September 10, 1959.
[20] *Ibid.*, September 8, 1959; *El Universal*, January 1, 1958, p. 1.
[21] *El Popular*, September 29, 1959.
[22] *El Universal*, January 1, 1958, p. 1; December 15, 1959, p. 1.

re-entry into the union in 1958 was terminated by the union in April 1959.)[23] Moreover, late in 1956 the union quashed Communist agitation during negotiation for contract renewal and the union's electoral campaign for new officers. On the occasion of the swearing in of officers in February 1957, one of the union's principal leaders called for the prosecution of Communism in Mexico and all Latin America. He denounced Communists as "agents of evil" and "destroyers of freedom and human dignity," and branded the Soviet Union as a "monstrous dictatorship."[24] Unfortunately the failure of the government and the union leadership to keep wages in line with rising prices led to agitation and a successful bid for power by Demetrio Vallejo in the summer of 1958. A series of strikes for increased wages finally led to a government crackdown in late March and early April 1959. Vallejo and five other union leaders were arrested. An estimated 250 members were arrested and many more fired by the government from the nationalized railways. The government ruled the strike illegal, declared Vallejo a Communist, and accused two members of the Soviet Embassy of involvement in the plotting. The diplomats were officially requested to leave the country. Several leftist but non-Communist-led unions that had supported Vallejo disavowed him following these revelations. In June the Federal Security Police arrested Gilberto Robles, described as the link between the union leaders and the Mexican Communist Party.[25] Despite this recent Communist offensive, the bulk of the Mexican trade unions are led not only by non-Communists but by anti-Communists. The government-sponsored Labor Unity Bloc (Bloque de Unidad Obrera—BUO), designed as a loose confederation of Mexican unions to give greater unity to labor, requires an anti-Communist pledge from its affiliates and has established an anti-Communist committee to investigate and expose Communist subversion within labor ranks.

Direct government action against Mexican Communists has not been confined to labor chiefs. It has also been directed against Party

[23] For details see *supra*, Chapter IV, on organized labor.
[24] Statement of Fidel Tavares on February 1, 1957 at the inauguration of new officers of the railroad workers' union, Palace of Fine Arts, Mexico City.
[25] *New York Times*, June 21, 1959, p. 10.

leaders and Party headquarters, although PPS members have suffered less than their counterparts in the PCM and POCM. The one exception in the PPS has been Jacinto López, but his arrests may be attributed to his leadership of the squatters' movement in northwest Mexico, i.e., to his activities as a labor agitator rather than as a political leader. In July 1958, the Army, the Attorney General's Office, and the state police of Sonora cooperated in seizing López and five other PPS members in Cananea while other Army units dislodged thousands of squatters from the lands of the Cananea Cattle Company. Following their release from prison five months later, López and his lieutenants began attempts to organize the new *ejidatarios* who gained possession of the Cananea Cattle Company lands, which the government had acquired in the meantime.[26] However, the UGOCM lost out to the government-affiliated National Peasant Confederation in its bid for peasant support, and since 1958 the government has used force against López and his organization whenever squattings have occurred.[27] Apart from the harassment of López, the PPS has been left in peace for the most part. The Party has counseled moderation in labor and student disputes since its disastrous defeat in the 1956 student upheavals. The PPS faction in the teachers' union has given little aid or encouragement to the dissidents, and in the railroad troubles of 1959, Lombardo counseled caution. The only major government attack within the last few years has been the raid of April 1959 following the railroad strike on the offices of the Party's Federal District Committee. The Committee leaders accused the Federal Judicial Police of breaking into their headquarters, carrying off Party banners and archives, seizing thousands of copies of its newssheet, and destroying its property. An official Party protest was made to President López Mateos. An interview was held with the assistant attorney gen-

[26] Although the secretaries general of both the PCM and the POCM were arrested following the March 1959 railway strike, no prominent PPS leader was picked up despite the deep involvement of Lombardo Toledano himself. Lombardo, significantly, disapproved the extreme demands of the PCM and POCM, and condemned the violence attending the strike. For a list of the principal leaders arrested see H. Lara, "México," *Problemas de la Paz y del Socialismo*, Año III, No. 3 (March 1960), 131–132.

[27] *La Voz de México*, July 26, 1958; *El Universal*, July 16, 1958, pp. 1 and 6.

eral, who denied that the Judicial Police were responsible for the attack. The PPS leaders claimed to have proof to the contrary, but the matter was then quietly dropped.[28]

The PCM has not fared so well. In March 1958 local police in Ciudad Victoria broke up a campaign meeting of the Communist presidential candidate and detained several Party members for passing out Party propaganda.[29] Later that same year the police also raided the PCM print shop and Party headquarters in Mexico City and carried on a campaign of harassment against Camilo Chávez, a member of the PCM Political Committee.[30] In the last week of November, Mexico City police seized a hand press and about 100,000 leaflets denouncing the visit of U.S. Secretary of State John Foster Dulles to attend the inauguration of President Adolfo López Mateos. The police also arrested about six persons for agitation, including several well-known Communists. Among them was Miguel Aroche Parra, then an officer of the Communist-splinter POCM.[31]

During 1959 the pace of the attacks was stepped up, primarily because of direct PCM involvement in the railroad troubles. A Party storehouse was raided the first week of April and a large quantity of literature, allegedly designed to incite the railroad workers to agitation, was seized by the police. Several Party members were arrested and held for questioning. The Department of Government said that it was investigating possible connections between the strikers, the Communist Party, and the Soviet Embassy.[32] The most serious blows to the Communist Party, however, were struck in late 1959 and early 1960. On September 2, 1959, Dionisio Encina, Party secretary general, was arrested with three companions in his home town of Torreón in the offices of Lombardo Toledano's People's Party. Accused of civil disturbance for possessing subversive propaganda, he was held without benefit of counsel and without formal charges beyond the seventy-two hours permitted by the Constitution. On September 6 he was formally remanded to prison, without bail, by a

[28] *El Popular*, April 6, 1959.
[29] *El Universal*, March 23, 1958, p. 1.
[30] *La Voz de México*, January 3, 1959.
[31] *New York Times*, November 30, 1958, p. 4.
[32] *Ibid.*, April 7, 1959, p. 17; *El Universal*, April 5, 1959, pp. 1 and 7.

federal judge to await trial on charges of subversion and inciting to violence. The judge indicted him for direct involvement in the railway strike and the Attorney General's Office accused him of plotting a series of disturbances to begin in mid-September in northwest Mexico.[33] In June 1962 he was still being held. Further to demoralize the Party, the Federal Judicial Police in the spring of 1960 held for several weeks[34] Party leaders Fernando Cortés and Hilario Moreno, and in August arrested David Alfaro Siqueiros, who, with his companion Filomena Mata, was finally sentenced in March 1962 to eight years in prison and a fine of 2,000 pesos for the crime of social dissolution. The charge grew out of agitation he led in the streets of Mexico in the summer of 1960.

Harassings such as these have continued to the present. Arnoldo Martínez and Edelmiro Maldonado were held by the police for several days in August 1960, and PCM student leader Luis Monter Valenzuela, together with Manuel Marcué Pardiñas, PPS member and director of *Política*, were arrested and fined for attempting to demonstrate in behalf of Castro and the Cuban Revolution outside the lodgings of the visiting President Manuel Prado of Peru in January 1961. In September the police seized and inspected a huge quantity of propaganda being brought into the country by a delegation of PPS and PCM youths from Cuba and the Soviet Union. The group had been visiting the Bloc for the World Youth Forum in Moscow.[35] By mid-1962 the government had shown no disposition to ease up on its efforts to curb Mexico's Communists.

International Communism and the Mexican Movement

The long-term goal of the Soviet Union with respect to Latin America is, as it is everywhere, the establishment of Communist states through the successive stages of "people's democracies" and "socialist regimes." The immediate objectives, however, are to undermine the prestige and the influence of the United States and to enhance those of the Soviet Union. To these ends the Soviet Union brands U.S.

[33] *New York Times*, September 6, 1959, p. 3; September 8, 1959, p. 7.
[34] *El Popular*, March 20, 1960; *Visión*, October 21, 1960, p. 76.
[35] *Excelsior*, January 20, 1961, pp. 33–37 and September 5, 1961, pp. 1 and 11.

activities in Latin America as imperialistic and accuses the United
States of holding the area in bondage for the interests of U.S. capitalists and militarists; the terms "Wall Street" and "the Pentagon" are
often employed. The immediate weapons at hand for these purposes
are not armed strength but propaganda, political organization, and
alliance with extreme nationalists. Soviet propaganda and local Communist propaganda calls for the creation of an anti-imperialist front
composed of all "anti-feudal" forces, including some business groups,
under the leadership of a Communist-controlled party, with mass
support from the workers and peasants. Local enemies are those large
landowners and business interests allied with the United States. In
this campaign the Soviet Union has utilized the services of her East
European satellites to assist her in making cultural, political, and
economic contacts with the area. In 1952 Red China began to show
some interest in Latin America and stepped up her activities in 1956
with the founding of a training school for Latin American Communists and the beginning shortly thereafter of the publication of Spanish language materials. Chinese interests lag behind those of the
Soviet Union and East Europe, and while her over-all propaganda is
similar, she makes particular efforts to win votes for admission to the
United Nations.[36]

To escape criticism and possible prosecution for violation of the
Mexican electoral law, which forbids Mexican political parties to
maintain official relations with foreign political parties, all three Communist parties in Mexico carefully avoid any statement that would
link them formally to the international Communist movement. The
PCM statutes frankly admit the acceptance of Marxist-Leninist doctrine and the object of establishing "fraternal relations with workers
of all countries," but tempers this goal with an additional one of
creating in the Mexican working class "the purest and most authentic
patriotism."[37] The POCM, more circumspect in its statutes, limits the
statement of its goal to "socialism." On the other hand, the statutes
adopt the crossed hammer and sickle as part of the Party's official
emblem, and its declaration of principles points to the doctrines of

[36] Joseph Kalvoda, "Communist Strategy in Latin America," *Yale Review*,
(Autumn 1960), pp. 32–33.
[37] *Estatutos del Partido Comunista Mexicano*, p. 3.

Marx and Lenin as guideposts and to the experiences of the Soviet Union for leadership in Mexico's march to socialism.[38]

PPS leader Lombardo Toledano has always defined his political and economic position as Marxist, but prior to 1960 official Party statements seldom referred to Marx, Lenin, or other Communist theorists for source references. Furthermore, the PPS statutes specifically state that "in no case and under no circumstances will the Party subordinate itself in its activity to any international organization, nor will it maintain ties of dependency with foreign parties." Continuing this official nationalist line, the statutes state further that the Party works within the limits of the Mexican Constitution and the institutions established by it, for the complete independence of the nation, economic development, higher standards of living, attainment of a democratic regime, and "the friendship of Mexico with all the peoples of the earth, in a world of peace and justice."[39] Party statutes and programs have said nothing about the eventual establishment of a socialist or communist society. On the occasion of the Second National Assembly of the Party in November 1955, Vicente Lombardo Toledano proposed to the members that the Party publicly announce its intention to work for a "socialist" Mexico and draw up a "socialist" indoctrination program for the rank and file. The proposal was met with alarm and consternation on the part of many of the delegates, with the result that the project was abandoned for the time being.[40] At the Third National Assembly in October 1960, the Party changed its name to include the term "Socialist" and openly adopted Marxist-Leninist materialism and democratic centralism as Party doctrine. It appears, nonetheless, that the majority of PPS members are still "nationalist" rather than "socialist," much less "communist"; furthermore Party leaders have long been careful to refrain from activities that might be construed as linking the Party as such with the

[38] *Declaracion de Principios, Programma, Estatutos* (del POCM), pp. 4–7 and 45.

[39] *Razon Historica, Principios, Programa y Estatutos del Partido Popular*, p. 43.

[40] In the fall of 1960 Lombardo Toledano revived this idea with an announcement that his Party proposed to establish in Mexico a "people's democracy." Thus far the only practical effect has been the change in name of his party from People's Party to Socialist People's Party. Cf. *Visión*, November 4, 1960, p. 24.

international Communist movement. PPS relations and ties with international Communism must be sought in the tenor of its propaganda program and through the actions of its leaders and some of its members in national and international front groups.

All three parties, like their counterparts throughout the non-Communist world, promote Soviet goals without question and follow unswervingly the Soviet propaganda line. There have been no traces of "Titoism" within the parties, nor any hesitation in following the tortuous path of Soviet reasoning. There was no breaking of ranks within the parties over the revelations of the Twentieth Congress of the Communist Party of the Soviet Union or over the Soviet suppression of the Hungarian revolt in 1956.

Lombardo Toledano is the major link between the PPS and international Communism. Not only is he the founder and longtime leader of the CTAL,[41] but he has also been a vice president of the Executive Bureau of the Soviet-sponsored WFTU; he was appointed at its founding in 1945. In the latter capacity he has journeyed to Europe for Executive Bureau sessions two or three times a year. He made one such trip in February of 1956, attending first a congress of the Communist-dominated General Confederation of Italian Labor. He was also the leading Mexican at the Paris "peace" conference in 1949, and sponsored and dominated the American Continental Peace Congress in September of that same year. Lombardo and other PPS members were active in the national peace movement until it fell under PCM domination in the early 1950's. Despite their slackening of interests in the official peace movement they have staunchly supported Soviet "peace" efforts and have condemned the United States and its Western allies as warmongers.

Direct and open contacts between Mexican Communists and the Soviet Bloc have been maintained by the travel abroad of the Mexicans. Prior to World War II, delegates of the Mexican Communist Party were present at every Soviet Communist Party Congress except the first. Since the War they have broadened their contacts by attending international meetings of Soviet-sponsored organizations such as the World Peace Council (WPC), the World Federation of Demo-

---

[41] He announced his resignation in October 1960.

cratic Youth (WFDY), and the World Federation of Trade Unions (WFTU). Increasing numbers have also traveled abroad on programs of cultural interchange between Mexico and the Bloc. Since its founding in 1947 the PPS has increasingly participated in both types of programs, especially since Lombardo is an officer of the WFTU and the Party's youth wing is an affiliate of the WFDY.[42] With the rise of Castro in Cuba, the Mexican Communists have made frequent trips to the island. Lombardo, two of his associates in the PPS, and the artist D. A. Siqueiros of the PCM attended May Day celebrations in Cuba in 1960.

One of the most enlightening illustrations in recent years of Soviet contact with, and indoctrination of, Mexican Communists was the sequence of events in Mexico with respect to the Twentieth Congress of the CPSU in February 1956. At this Congress the Stalinist regime was attacked vigorously, Stalin himself was downgraded, the cult of the personality was condemned, and peaceful coexistence with the non-Communist world was proclaimed as doctrine. Communist delegates from all over the world, including some from Mexico, listened in shocked silence to the new leaders of the Soviet Union. Leading the Mexican delegation was Dionisio Encina, then secretary general of the PCM. Encina had long been known for his adulation of Stalin and his use of Stalinist methods in running his Party.[43] Speculation ran rife in the non-Communist Mexican press as to the possible impact of the Soviet Congress upon the PCM.

The Mexican Communists, meantime, gave no indication of their reactions. Doubtless, the Soviet Congress was widely discussed in Party circles, but no official Party statement was forthcoming. For almost two months the PCM and *La Voz de México* ignored the whole proceedings and refused to respond when questioned. Then on April 5 *La Voz* broke its silence by publishing "Why the Cult of the Personality Is Foreign to the Spirit of Marxism-Leninism," an article

[42] In 1958 about 30 out of 200 nontourist visitors from Mexico to the Bloc traveled for purposes of conducting Communist Party or Communist-front business. Cf. *Corporation for Economic and Industrial Research, Soviet Bloc-Latin American Activities*, pp. 92–93.

[43] Encina and several others also attended the Twenty-first Congress of the CPSU in 1959, but, significantly, no Mexicans were present at the Twenty-second Congress in 1961.

which had originally appeared in *Pravda* on March 28. No comment
was attached to the article except to explain that it was published because of its "transcendence and value." The same issue of *La Voz* also
carried certain remarks by Party member Diego Rivera which were
faithful to the new line. A fellow artist and PCM member, David Alfaro Siqueiros, in an interview with *La Prensa* admitted that Stalin
had committed errors but added that there were some extenuating
circumstances. In May a spate of articles on the Soviet Congress appeared, five on the "cult of the personality" and five more on peaceful
coexistence. Several were translations from articles which had previously appeared in Soviet Bloc publications and several were reports
or parts of reports Khrushchev and Malenkov gave at the Congress.[44]
For the most part, however, PCM members themselves were silent,
and the Party officially continued absolute silence.

Encina, in the meantime, remained abroad, presumably for further
instructions. Upon his return in June, the PCM Central Committee
went into session to draw up a formal Party resolution on the Twentieth Soviet Congress. The Resolution, although dated June 1956, was
not published in *La Voz de México* until the following month. The
gist of this lengthy document, covering four full newspaper pages,
was that both Stalin and the PCM had committed errors in propagat-
ing the cult of the personality and that changes would be carried out
to correct this error with the PCM. In an interview Encina said: "The
Twentieth Congress . . . boldly and energetically criticized . . . the cult
of the personality as something far removed from Marxist-Leninist
practices . . ."; he added that the decisions of the CPSU "will be carefully studied and assimilated in a creative manner, and in the light of
the specific concrete conditions in our country."[45]

The PPS reacted in a strikingly similar manner. For several
months its leaders remained silent on the Soviet meeting. Lombardo
was in Europe that spring, ostensibly to attend a meeting of WFTU
officials. Unquestionably he was briefed by Soviet officials on the
Twentieth Congress resolutions. Upon his return to Mexico he called
a conference of Party leaders for the night of June 5 and in an hour-

[44] See *La Voz de México*, May 10, 11, 12 15, 16, 1956.
[45] *Ibid.*, July 12, 1956.

long discourse gave his interpretation of the Congress. He remarked that these views were personal and did not represent the collective opinion of the National Directorate of the Party. A report on the PPS conference and the complete text of Lombardo's speech were reproduced in *El Popular* intermittently from June 6 to June 20.

Lombardo followed a summary of the events of the Soviet Congress with the observation that the "capitalist press," particularly that under U.S. influence, had been insisting that the Congress had denigrated Stalin. Lombardo emphasized that he himself had no such intention. He said:

> Joseph Stalin, in my opinion, is one of the great men of universal history. An eminent revolutionary thinker and one of the principal builders of the first socialist state. His work must be judged, to be objective and valid, by taking into account his accomplishments and his errors. To point out the latter—as the Twentieth Congress did—is useful and necessary, because the experience will serve to avoid them in the future.[46]

Commenting further on the Congress, Lombardo spoke of the need of collective leadership in government, the necessity of averting war, and the possibility of achieving socialism by various methods. On the last issue he referred to a PPS report of April 1955: "A year before the Twentieth Congress we reached conclusions which coincide with the opinions given by the Twentieth Congress of the CPSU with respect to the different roads to arrive at socialism."[47] Following the conference, various PPS members who commented on the Soviet Congress and Lombardo's speech accepted the major theses of both.

Several observations must be made in conclusion. First, although the PPS officially took no part in the Twentieth Congress and sent no delegates, Party leader Lombardo Toledano was in Europe during and after the Congress. Second, PPS members, like PCM members, made no comments on the Congress until the leader returned and interpreted the Congress. Third, Party members accepted without question or opposition the findings of the Congress and the interpretation of them by their Party leaders. And, finally and most significantly, Lombardo and the Party leaders felt the necessity not only of inter-

[46] *El Popular*, June 17, 1956.
[47] *Ibid.*, June 17, 1956.

preting the Congress but also of identifying their ideas and actions
with those of the CPSU.

For its part, the Soviet Bloc during the past decade has, by means
of increased economic, political, and cultural contacts, stepped up
its drive to gain influence in Latin America. Its immediate goal is
not primarily to gain power but to neutralize the area politically in
the East-West conflict. As a result the Soviet Union has not encouraged its satellite parties to rebellion and seizure of power in their respective countries. On the other hand, it does encourage them to
grasp every opportunity to infiltrate economic and political organizations, especially in periods of confusion and turmoil, as witness
Guatemala (1944–1954) and Cuba from 1959 to the present.[48] To the
Latin American Communists the common enemy, as defined by Moscow, is "United States imperialism."[49]

In cultural affairs the Soviet and satellite missions in Latin America have attempted to cultivate and convert to their viewpoint selected
non-Communists and through them to develop official contacts. In this
they have had at least some limited success in Mexico. They also have
striven to increase trade between Latin American countries and the
Sino-Soviet Bloc, but except for the recent trade agreements with
Cuba, these efforts have had relatively little impact on trade patterns
in the area. Negatively, they try to avoid involvement in situations
that could lead to, or be interpreted as, interference in domestic politics, labor relations, or interest groups, but their agents in Mexico
have suffered some notable failures in recent years. Nevertheless,
their principal role is to complement rather than to exercise direct
control over local Communist authorities.[50] One major exception,
perhaps, to this latter policy is the reported use of Czech diplomatic
personnel, operating largely out of the Mexico mission, to discipline
and direct local Communist labor leaders.[51]

Mexico has diplomatic relations at the ambassadorial level with

[48] Corporation for Economic and Industrial Research, *Soviet Bloc-Latin
American Activities*, pp. 3 and 57.

[49] Subcommittee To Investigate Administration of Internal Security Act,
Communist Threat, p. 141.

[50] *Ibid.*, p. 145.

[51] Corporation for Economic and Industrial Research, *Soviet Bloc-Latin
American Activities*, pp. 48–49.

the Soviet Union, Czechoslovakia, and Poland. Only the staff of the United States Embassy in Mexico is larger than that of the Soviet Union, which numbers over 100 members. It expanded approximately to its present size in 1946 when the Soviet spy ring in Canada was exposed. Most of its members are housed in one large area. Few non-Russians are employed although some Spanish-exile Communists have been utilized at times as translators, telephone operators, or for other such tasks.[52] Espionage activities are of course pursued, but there also have been repeated charges that the Soviet Embassy assists local Communist activities and supports them with Soviet funds. The charges have been difficult to substantiate, but a recent U.S. Central Intelligence Agency report asserted that certain officials in every Soviet diplomatic mission who are members of the Communist Party of the Soviet Union, monitor the activities of national Communist parties and leaders and report to Moscow. These officials work closely with the national leaders to clarify the Party line, advise on its application, and approve local people for travel and training in the USSR. They also attend to financial transactions between the Soviet Union and the local parties. Large direct subsidies are somewhat rare, but considerable support comes through indirect channels, and to front organizations rather than to the parties. The origin of funds is generally concealed. The more frequent methods used include payments for book translations, subsidies to the Communist press, lucrative contracts to Party members or sympathizers, gifts from international fronts, scholarships and tours with all or part expenses paid, and purchases of services by the Bloc missions. At present there is no evidence of military aid except to Fidel Castro in Cuba.[53]

Circumstantial evidence supports the CIA analysis, as specifically applied to Mexico. First of all, the Communist movement in Mexico is always so chronically short of money that obviously there are not unlimited resources available from the Soviet Embassy. The CTAL seems to receive some small assistance, and various organizations receive some free literature. Second, the ineptitude of Communist Party

[52] Demaree Bess, "Mexico Doesn't Want the Cold War," *Saturday Evening Post*, July 18, 1959, p. 54.
[53] Subcommittee To Investigate Administration of Internal Security Act, *Communist Threat*, pp. 146, 162, 172.

leaders and the greater competence of PPS leaders has resulted in greater success for the latter, indicating little if any direct intervention of outside forces in day-to-day internal Party affairs. Third, the frequent quarreling among the parties and their bitter struggle to control the various fronts also indicates a lack of superior controls to direct the whole movement. All Party leaders follow the international Communist line, but this does not come solely through the Soviet Embassy. It also comes through wire services, radio broadcasts, and authoritative periodicals imported from the Soviet Union and Red China.[54] Other contacts are also maintained besides those between Embassy officials and Party leaders. Some occur by means of public social affairs, such as the annual celebration of the October Revolution.[55] For example, on the seventieth birthday of Diego Rivera in 1956, a luncheon in his honor was attended by the Soviet ambassador, the Czech minister, and the Polish chargé d'affaires. Frequent contacts are made between the leaders of the binational centers (the IICMR and IICMC) and the respective diplomatic personnel. Very likely there were also contacts with Narciso Bassols (until his death in July 1959) as a leader of the peace movement,[56] and with Lombardo Toledano as head of the CTAL and a vice president of WFTU. The involvement of Soviet diplomats in Mexican domestic strife is unusual, but several members were accused of participating in the student riots of 1956 and 1957.[57] Then in the spring of 1959 the naval attaché and

[54] *La Voz de México* frequently reprints news reports and speeches from the Soviet Bloc and from Red China. In late 1956 and early 1957 considerable space was devoted to Chinese Communism. In November 1956 some ninety column inches were devoted to the proposals of the Eighth Congress of the Chinese Communist Party on the Second Five Year Plan, 1958–1962. In January 1957 *La Voz* ran a series of articles from a Peiping daily, on a meeting of the Politburo of the Chinese Communist Party. See also Subcommittee To Investigate Administration of Internal Security Act, *Communist Threat*, p. 148.

[55] *Noviembre*, November 20, 1954.

[56] Unión Cívica Internacional de México, "Comunismo en Mexico," *Estudios sobre el Comunismo*, Año V, No. 17 (July–September 1957), 126.

[57] *Ibid.*, p. 126. Accusations were leveled particularly at the Soviet cultural attaché, Yuri Paparov, who reportedly worked through Jaime Rozzoto, ex-private secretary of former President Jacobo Arbenz of Guatemala. Rozzoto, in turn, was reportedly in contact with leading student agitators in Morelia. As a result of these alleged machinations of Soviet personnel, the Nationalist Party of Mexico demanded severe travel restrictions on Soviet officials in Mexico.

a second secretary were accused of intervening in labor agitation among the railroad workers. The Mexican police charged that they had evidence that the two diplomats supplied money as well as propaganda to Communist labor leaders as part of a master plan to gain control of Mexican organized labor. The police accusations may well have been overdrawn, but the Mexican government was sufficiently satisfied with the diplomats' involvement to request their departure. Rumors were circulating at the time that others, including a Pole and a Czech, were to be declared *persona non grata*. No further official action was taken, but a few days later four other members of the Soviet Embassy left for Moscow amid press reports that their connection with the recent Communist agitation had destroyed their diplomatic usefulness.[58]

The Soviet Embassy, with assists from the satellite missions, has also made itself a center for the dissemination of propaganda throughout Middle America particularly for the purpose of increasing trade between those areas and the Soviet Bloc. The first Bloc bid for economic penetration of Latin America came in the form of an interview published in the Spanish-language magazine *Visión* in January 1956 between a Mexican journalist and then Soviet Premier Nikolai Bulganin. In a series of questions and answers on Soviet trade interests in Latin America, Bulganin made clear the Soviet Union's intent to expand its commercial activities there. Since that time Soviet and satellite personnel have frequently toured the area. In May 1959 a Bloc contingent spent two weeks in Panama. Officially the group came as observers to the biennial sessions of the United Nations Economic Commission for Latin America (ECLA). Russian and Polish delegates, in open discussions on the floor, and the Soviet Ambassador to Mexico, Vladimir I. Bazykin, in private conversations, spoke alluringly of the prospect of increased trade between the Bloc and Latin America, and of Soviet aid "without strings" through the UN technical assistance program. In an interview with the Panamanian Minister of Economy, Ambassador Bazykin urged an exchange of Panamanian meat and coffee for Soviet capital goods. Despite then current disputes between Panama and the United States

[58] *New York Times*, April 17, 1959, p. 7; April 9, 1959, p. 14.

over the Canal, the Panamanian Minister firmly rejected the Soviet offer; Panama newspapers, however, gave Mr. Bazykin considerable attention.

The Soviet drive to increase trade in the Caribbean bore little fruit until the early months of 1960. Although, beginning in 1955, Cuba had become an important exporter to the Bloc, the percentage of her total trade remained small.[59] No Central American or Caribbean country except Mexico had concluded a formal trade agreement with any Bloc country by the end of 1959. Mexico's agreement with Czechoslovakia was apparently defunct, and Cuba dealt with the Bloc on a contract basis only.[60] In November of 1959, however, the Soviet Union launched a new and powerful trade offensive in the area. On November 18 Anastas I. Mikoyan, Soviet First Deputy Premier, and a party of over twenty persons arrived in Mexico for a ten-day visit to open a Soviet Trade Exposition and to review the Mexican steel and petroleum industries. Mikoyan was the first high Soviet official to visit Mexico. The press reported that the crowd of about 1,000 who greeted the visitors was on the whole unenthusiastic, although a group of about 200 led by the Communist Party member and famous artist David Alfaro Siqueiros shouted "Long live Russia" and "Long live the Soviet Union." On the following day Mikoyan made the expected calls on the President, the Secretary of Foreign Affairs, and the Soviet ambassador. He opened the fair on November 22, and within a day or two the Exposition had become a battleground between Communists and anti-Communists. Mexican police had to move in to prevent violence over arguments on slave labor and illiteracy in the Soviet Union. Meanwhile Mikoyan had begun his tour of the country. Despite some initial popular hostility, and continued press hostility toward Mikoyan, the Soviet trade fair drew large crowds daily. Although it has had no visible impact on Soviet-Mexican economic relations, it apparently contributed to increased cultural contacts. In the last week of November, while the fair was still open, Dmitri Shostakovich visited the country and Soviet film festivals

[59] Robert L. Allen, *Soviet Influence in Latin America: The Role of Economic Relations*, p. 9.
[60] *Ibid.*, pp. 22–23.

opened in Mexico City and Acapulco. In December the Bolshoi Ballet arrived.[61]

As events have developed, the Mexican fair was but the prelude to a deeper and more persistent Soviet penetration in the Caribbean by way of Cuba. Already in 1959 the assistant commercial attaché of the Soviet Embassy in Mexico was stationed indefinitely on the island, and by 1960 other Embassy officials were handling various aspects of Cuban-Soviet relations. Furthermore, Castro's campaign of vituperation against the United States and his friendly overtures to the Soviet Union had well prepared the way for the reception of a Soviet trade fair in Havana in February 1960. As in Mexico the fair was opened by Mikoyan, but unlike Mexico it bore fruit in trade and credit agreements not only with the Soviet Union but also with several satellite countries. In addition, diplomatic relations were renewed between Cuba and the USSR. Recently Communist China has shown increased interest in Latin America, but Cuba has been the only country to grant her diplomatic recognition. The only official body of Chinese Communists in the Western Hemisphere is the New China News Agency set up in Havana in 1959.[62]

Currently Mexico is still one of the principal centers for the dissemination of international Communist publications in Latin America, although it has by now been surpassed by Cuba. About 100 periodicals and numerous special studies on the Sino-Soviet Bloc are distributed in Latin America. Cooperating in this venture are some thirty bookstores and publishing houses in Mexico, of which half or less are Communist controlled; the remainder are involved for purely business reasons.[63] The Soviet Embassy in Mexico reportedly sends the material throughout Middle America using the distribution facilities of the IICMR and other organizations. Among the better-known

[61] *New York Times*, November 19, 1959, p. 21; November 20, 1959, p. 16; November 21, 1959, p. 3; November 24, 1959, p. 15; November 29, 1959, p. 27. See also X.X. "Actividades comunistas en América Latina," *Estudios sobre el Comunismo*, Año VIII, No. 24 (July–September 1960), 87–88.

[62] "Nuevos horizontes para Mao," *Visión*, XIX, No. 2 (March 20, 1960), 32.

[63] Subcommittee To Investigate Administration of Internal Security Act, *Communist Threat*, pp. 168–170; Corporation for Economic and Industrial Research, *Soviet Bloc-Latin American Activities*, pp. 54–55.

periodicals are the monthlies *Unión Soviética, Cultura y Vida, La Mujer Soviética,* and *Literatura Soviética,* and the weekly *Tiempos Nuevos. La Polonia de Hoy,* an attractive 152-page paperback with slick paper and good photography, appeared in 1954, and *La Salud en la USSR,* smaller, cheaper, and printed in Mexico, came out in 1955. Finally, the Soviet Embassy publishes a weekly *Boletín de Información de la Embajada de la URSS* and (five times a week) the *Servicio de Noticias de la Oficina de Prensa de la Embajada de la URSS;* the Czechoslovak Embassy publishes the monthly *La Nueva Polonia.* Poland also published in 1957 the *Visita de una Delegación Oficial Polaca a siete países de Asia,* and China began distributing its monthly *China Reconstruye* early in 1960. A flood of Chinese literature has poured into Mexico and other parts of Latin America since José Venturelli of the Communist Party of Chile went to China to translate Chinese materials into Spanish. Some fifteen to twenty titles have been picked up in Mexico during the past few years. The World Peace Council, an international Communist-front organization, publishes a Mexico City edition of its periodical, *Horizontes.*[64]

During 1959 Bloc radio broadcasting to Latin America averaged something over 100 hours weekly. About 70 hours were beamed in Spanish, of which 28 hours originated in the Soviet Union, 28 in the satellite countries, and 14 in Communist China. The USSR and Czechoslovakia also broadcast about 14 hours weekly in Portuguese, while Poland, Hungary, and Bulgaria directed another 20 hours in their own languages.[65] Bloc countries have also encouraged exchange of persons and cultural exhibits. In 1957 and 1958 almost 200 nontourist Mexicans visited behind the Iron Curtain while between 30 and 50 Bloc visitors came to Mexico. In 1958 nine Bloc exhibits were shown in Mexico, but only one in the USSR.[66] The Soviet Union and Red China have also encouraged the sending of local Communists for training in Communist battle and agitation techniques as well as

[64] Corporation for Economic and Industrial Research, *Soviet Bloc-Latin American Activities,* pp. 89–91.

[65] *Ibid.,* pp. 87–88; *New York Times,* March 27, 1960, Section 4, p. 3; March 4, 1962, Section E, p. 3, reported that Radio Moscow alone was broadcasting sixty-three hours weekly to Latin America.

[66] Corporation for Economic and Industrial Research, *Soviet Bloc-Latin American Activities,* pp. 87 and 92–93.

in doctrine and theory. The usual curriculum is a two- or three-year course, but there are no figures as to the number of Mexicans currently participating.[67] In the mid-1950's a group of about eight or ten members of the PCM were sent for such training.

A leading principle of Mexican foreign policy, the right of asylum, coupled with the country's broad political tolerance has made Mexico one of the leading centers of Latin American Communist exiles. It has also led to some low-voltage disputes with several of her Caribbean neighbors who have been fearful of subversive plots hatched on Mexican soil. As a result of revolutions and changes of political climate in several Latin American countries in recent years which permitted them to return home, Communist exile activities in Mexico have declined in importance. For the most part Communist exiles in Mexico have refrained from participation in Mexican politics and have limited their contacts with Mexican Communists to a minimum. As a result they have met little opposition from Mexican authorities. The Mexican newspaper *Ovaciones* has long charged that much of the Communist agitation in the mid-to-late-1950's was inspired by various exile groups, but there has been little evidence to support the charges. However, suspicions of exile involvement in agitation in 1958 led to the brief arrest of about fifty foreigners.[68]

U.S. Communists in Mexico attained their greatest numbers in the early 1950's at the height of Senator Joseph McCarthy's anti-Communist campaign. With the Geneva thaw in the Cold War in 1954, many returned to the United States. At present there are probably less than 100 in Mexico. Well-known U.S. Communists who have recently resided in Mexico include Alfred and Martha Dodd Stern, Jack and Myrna Sobel, and Gus Hall. Hall was extradited to the United States in late 1958, but such proceedings are not common. The others left for Europe before the end of 1957.[69]

[67] Subcommittee To Investigate Administration of Internal Security Act, *Communist Threat*, pp. 146–148.

[68] *New York Times*, September 11, 1958, p. 16; September 14, 1958, p. 32.

[69] Luis Alfonso Galán, "Cuartel General Soviético en Tacubaya," *El Universal*, September 7, 1957, p. 2. See also Richard English, "Mexico Clamps Down on Stalin," *Saturday Evening Post*, August 30, 1952. The Federal Security Police whom the author interviewed revealed that their files indicated that at the time there were about 150 U.S. Communists in Mexico. Most of them

For many years one of the most important groups of Communist exiles in Mexico has been the Spanish. Thousands of Spanish Republicans sought refuge in Mexico with the victory of the Franco forces in Spain in 1939. Among these refugees were hundreds, perhaps several thousand, of Communists and pro-Communists. Over the years many of the latter have abandoned the cause and settled down into a quiet and obscure existence in their new homeland. Several hundred, however, have remained militant, retaining their ties with the Central Committee of the Spanish Communist Party in Europe. The Spanish Communists in Mexico are also the most highly organized of the exile groups. They have edited at least three periodicals: *Nuestro Tiempo, Revista Española de Cultura,* directed by Juan Vicens; *España Popular,* a weekly newspaper, their principal propaganda organ, directed by Santiago Gilabert, Wenceslao Roces, and Juan José Manso; and *Alkartu,* the organ of the Basque Communist Party. In addition to the Basque and Spanish parties, there is also the Unified Socialist Party of Catalonia. The Spanish Peace Council, an affiliate of the international-front World Peace Council, is directed by Wenceslao Roces, a member of the Central Committee of the Spanish Communist Party. Santiago Gilabert and José Castellote direct the Eugenio Mesón Club, the Spanish Atheneum, and the Federation of Organizations for Aid to European Refugees (FOARE). The latter two are organized into a loose federation called the Groups of Spaniards and are reportedly in contact with Bloc diplomatic missions in Mexico.[70]

Other important Communist exile groups in the past few years have included several hundred Guatemalans, over one hundred Venezuelans, and a few Cubans. The Guatemalans constituted the most serious threat of disturbing Mexico's relations with her neighbors. Many Guatemalan Communists settled in Tapachula on the Guatemalan-Mexican border, and with relative ease crossed back and forth

were settled around Cuernavaca and San Miguel de Allende, attracted to the latter by that city's School of Fine Arts. The Mexican authorities reported that U.S. Communists did not mix in Mexican politics.

[70] Pierre Faure, "El Partido Comunista Español," *Estudios sobre el Comunismo,* Año V, No. 15 (January–March 1957), 81; Año V, No. 16, p. 77; *El Universal,* October 14, 1956, p. 10, and July 11, 1957, p. 22.

over the frontier. With the return to constitutional government in Guatemala in 1958, many exiles returned home, with only the top Communist leaders being barred from that country.[71] Even many of these were permitted to return during 1961.[72] Because of geographical barriers, the Venezuelan Communists caused little concern to the dictatorial regime of Marcos Pérez Jiménez. With the dictator's overthrow early in 1958, the Venezuelans, including Party leader, Gustavo Machado, returned home. Cuban Communist exiles were unable to organize seriously against the Batista regime, but a few joined the Castro movement in 1956. Lázaro Peña, the leading Cuban Communist in Mexico, appears to have remained aloof from exile activities, devoting himself to the CTAL, of which he is an officer. Peña, a top Cuban labor leader in the 1940's, returned home with the overthrow of Batista in 1959. Events of the past few years have thus reduced exile activity to near an all-time low.

[71] The Guatemalan government continued to be apprehensive over the activities of former Communist leaders. See *El Popular*, March 15, 1959, and *El Universal*, January 21, 1958, pp. 1 and 24.

[72] *Miami Herald*, May 12, 1961, p. 7, reported that two of Arbenz' leading aides, Carlos Manuel Pellecer and Víctor Manuel Gutiérrez, recently returned to Guatemala after seven years of exile in Mexico.

VI. The Failure of Mexican Communism

After more than forty years of struggle in Mexico, the Communist movement appears to be not just stalemated but in decline. Certainly it is at its lowest ebb since the Mexican Communist Party and its suborganizations were outlawed and their leaders persecuted for having attempted armed rebellion some thirty years ago. The movement is split into three political parties, all of which are ridden with factionalism and dissension; its so-called front groups are for the most part well-known and shunned by most active and knowledgeable non-Communists, even by some of radical and Marxist views. Its attempts in recent years to lead or participate in labor, political, or student agitations have ended in disaster. Furthermore, the Mexican government, at various times friendly, tolerant, or at least apathetic, has in the past few years demonstrated an increasing concern over subversive activities. The authorities have not hesitated to use police and troops to scatter demonstrators, harass Party members, and arrest their leaders. Only in certain phases of its propaganda campaign can the movement take comfort, but it is obvious to friend and foe alike that Communist "success" in attracting support has been achieved only on those issues that would strike a responsive chord in Mexicans even though there were no Communists. The Communists have not been able to capitalize on their propaganda victories to the extent of seizing and holding the leadership in any important political, social, or economic movements in the country. Today, for the most part, the Communists are talking to themselves, quarreling among themselves, and sometimes voting for themselves.

What accounts for the debility of Communism in Mexico? In many respects the country appears ripe for a new round of revolutionary activity to diminish evergrowing U.S. influence and to correct grave social and economic disparities that still exist there. Despite much criticism of the "turn to the right" that the Revolution has experienced since 1940, the Communists have not been able to place themselves at the head of an effective politico-economic reform movement. Vicente Lombardo Toledano, though still respected in official and unofficial circles, exercises little real political influence, while writers and artists who belong to the movement no longer seem able to sway the masses. Even public school teachers, many of whom have been infected with Communism for over twenty years, seemingly make little lasting impression on their charges. While it is true that Mexican students have exhibited a high degree of radicalism, few are directly influenced by Communists and still fewer appear to carry that radicalism beyond their student days. Why?

The primary reason for the past ineffectiveness of Communism in Mexico lies in the fact that Mexico had already experienced a thoroughgoing political, economic, and social Revolution that undercut the original blandishments the early Bolsheviks dangled before the people. Despite the "turn to the right" in 1940, the Communists have experienced continued frustration because succeeding governments during the past twenty years have practiced a "carrot and stick" policy toward powerful but dissatisfied elements of society. The government, with its ear to the ground to catch the swells of popular discontent that arise from time to time, has frequently offered concessions by removing an unpopular governor or labor leader, by granting wage increases or greater fringe benefits, by extending Social Security or the public housing program, or by opening new farm lands through irrigation or an occasional expropriation. Although this policy has not "solved" any of the major problems facing the country it has eased some of the most dangerous pressures threatening the political stability and the balanced economic growth that have characterized Mexico for two decades and more. When such concessions have emboldened the leaders of the discontented to reach for political power outside the existing political framework, the government has not hesitated to use force to subdue or eject this new leadership, as witness action taken in the railroad strike in the spring of 1959.

What is the framework of power in Mexico today? Since 1929 political control has been exercised through an official government party, today called the Institutional Revolutionary Party (Partido Revolucionario Institucional—PRI). Dominated for its first six years as a political holding company by General and former President Plutarco Elías Calles, this party later became the vehicle for the institutionalization of power in Mexico. This process was begun by Calles' protégé, and later opponent, President General Lázaro Cárdenas (1934–1940). The spectacular social, economic, and educational reforms of Cárdenas have usually overshadowed his more cautious political reforms, but the latter in the long run have proved to be no less important for the currently peaceful, stable, and prosperous condition of the nation. It was Cárdenas, for example, who forced the Army, first, to exercise its political influence within the Party framework, and later to share power 'with the labor unions and the bureaucracy, when the two civilian elements were incorporated into the PRI. Cárdenas also strengthened the precedents of a one-term presidency and abstention from behind-the-throne political control.

The political patterns developed by Cárdenas have been in part continued or expanded, and in part modified by his successors. The Army has been virtually removed from politics until its present political influence is largely indirect. *Campesino* influence has remained at a low level while that of labor has declined relative to that of bureaucracy, which has grown enormously. A new political element, under heavy attack during the 1930's, has emerged as a major contender for power—the business community. Commercial and industrial leaders and their trade organizations have not gained the corporate status within the official party that is enjoyed by labor, farm groups, and the bureaucracy, but through their various "chambers" of industry and commerce that have direct personal contacts as well as formal economic relations with government and party leaders, they exercise at times preponderant influence in policy. Although Mexi-

can leaders have not entirely abandoned the revolutionary ideal of
dividing and redividing the economic cake, emphasis today is more
strongly placed on the goal of producing a bigger cake to divide.
Politically, the majority of the "revolutionary left," including the
still powerful Lázaro Cárdenas, has remained within the official party.
The left, however unhappy with the more moderate pace of social
and economic reform (some lament the death of the Revolution),
still feels that its goals are best obtained within the PRI. For the past
two decades the moderates who have governed the country and the
party have so successfully maintained a balance of interests that no
major bloc within the party feels itself forgotten or isolated and
therefore frustrated in improving its lot. This environment, that at
its highest level seeks to combine the socialist dream of universal
economic well-being with the capitalist ideal of ever-increasing production, has not boded well for Communism.

The traditional Communist sources of strength among students,
intellectuals, and labor and farm groups are present in Mexico, as in
other countries of similar development in America, Asia, and Africa.
But they are of much less importance. There can be no denial of the
grinding poverty of the Mexican countryside; rural people have
benefited least from the Revolution with respect to a higher standard of living. But there has been an agrarian reform that still continues on a reduced scale, education has been extended in part at
least to rural districts, and a national farm organization has been
established with official ties to the government and party to present
the most pressing needs of the *campesino*. Poor and isolated though
he may be, the Mexican *campesino* is not for the most part a rural
proletarian adrift in an alien society. In some sense he belongs, either
to his native village with its customs and lands or, if aware of something beyond his *patria chica*, to the Revolution, to Mexico, or to
his farm organization. For the *campesino* without land or with insufficient land, two courses are open. He may seek part-time work as a
bracero in the United States, under the terms of a treaty with wages
and benefits that are good by Mexican rural standards, or he may
abandon farm life entirely and swell the ranks of the immigrants moving to the large industrial centers. As a bracero he is processed (and
perhaps cheated) by minor government officials, but once in the

United States, his status and treatment are carefully watched by the Mexican government and public for treaty violations—at times he has become a national hero and martyr. If he breaks entirely with his old way of life to try his fortune in the city he may be assisted in the process of transition by one or another of the new, revolutionary institutions such as labor unions or social welfare agencies. Most rural migrants, however, are not so fortunate as to be absorbed in this manner, and many try, for a while at least, to recreate some of their village patterns, particularly in regard to family and spiritual relations. Despite the fact that the extended family and paternal authority, customary in the village, cannot be maintained in the city, and that a high degree of social disorganization afflicts the poor, the urban lower classes of Mexico have not been attracted into revolutionary or Communist movements. This situation results in part, of course, from the lack of sustained Communist organizational efforts at the grass-roots level, but it may also result in part from an unconscious absorption by the migrants of the Revolutionary mystique, so pervasive in the Mexican urban atmosphere, that conditions not only improved for the lower classes under Cárdenas but that they have continued to improve, though more slowly, in the years since 1940. The fact remains that the Mexican lower classes show few signs of revolutionary inclinations. Nowhere is this better illustrated than in the recent studies on the "culture of poverty" by Oscar Lewis in his *Five Families* and *Children of Sánchez.*

The Mexican student body in secondary, technical, and higher education has a streak of radicalism that sometimes manifests itself in sporadic violence. However, armed revolt such as the students of Caracas perpetrated in the fall of 1960 would be almost unthinkable in Mexico. Educational opportunities at these levels are moderately good, and prospects for a career in Mexico's expanding industrial, cultural, and professional society appear bright. Mexican students, like their fellows elsewhere in Latin America, are sensitive to the inequities and injustices in their society, but lack the others' sense of despair in their country and in their government to drive them to the extremes of rebellion or even of radical solutions.

Once graduated into the business, intellectual, or professional ranks, these onetime students seemingly become more conservative.

While this trend is not surprising in the business community or among certain professional groups, such as doctors and lawyers, it is surprising that it is true to some extent among writers, teachers, and artists. Only a minority of Mexico's journalists are Marxist, fewer still Communists. Teachers are less given to agitation than are students, and largely for economic or educational improvements, not for political goals. Only among the artists is there still some Communist influence, but this has been declining. Rivera is dead, but even before his passing his political influence had waned, and Siqueiros, the last of the great triumvirate (Rivera, Siqueiros, Orozco), although still revered, is honored more for past than for present performance. A new generation of artists, though still loyal to the Revolution, is freeing itself from earlier Marxist dogmatism. A dissatisfied, intellectual left certainly exists among these groups, but it seeks solutions for Mexico's ills not in an alien ideology but in the Mexican Revolution itself.

The Army in Mexico, as in most Latin American countries, is almost entirely free of Communist influence and is a supporter of the status quo. Communist attacks on the military of Mexico attract little support in Mexico, not only because the status quo is so different from that of countries that have not yet experienced their revolution, but because the Mexican military itself was a creation of the Revolution. Traditionally the Army has supported revolutionary regimes and accepted with good grace its removal from active political life. Furthermore, it is known widely that budget allotments for the military have been modest for many years and that the military has not objected to the performance of nonmilitary tasks.

Another vital factor that explains the greater resistance to Communism of Mexico and Latin America over that of the newly emerging nations of Asia and Africa lies in its basically Western-oriented culture. This is not to say that every human being in this continent and a half speaks a European language, understands and practices European political activities, and adheres to the Christian religion or one of its ideological offshoots. Millions live in primitive isolation, wedded to a folk culture, and speaking languages that antedate the Discovery. Other millions have adopted only the rudiments of Western practices, which they have somehow harmonized with vital features of their native culture. Mexico ranks among the top five countries of Latin America that suffer from this problem of partial and/or nonassimilation of important sectors of its population in economic, cultural, and political life. Nonetheless, as these folk cultures break down, as they have been doing slowly for centuries, the peasant or the villager adopts Western ways. If he by chance becomes politically active, or economically influential, or culturally productive, it is as a Westerner. Benito Juárez, a full-blooded Zapotec from a village in Oaxaca, made his mark on Mexican society not as an Indian, but as a Western-educated lawyer, politician, and statesman. No other culture in the Americas can successfully challenge Western civilization, as can a Chinese culture in the East, nor is its base so narrow that it could be repudiated, as is possible in some of the newly emerging states of Africa. Latin Americans, including Mexicans, consider themselves an integral part of Western civilization.

Concomitantly, the Latin Americans are not subject in the same way as are Africans and Asians to the Communist denunciation of Western colonialism. For most, the Spanish yoke was thrown off well over a hundred years ago. At times the Latins have regarded their own independence movements as part of the same historical trend that encompassed the U.S. Revolutionary War. Once independence was achieved their political independence was never again seriously threatened by the mother countries, Spain and Portugal. Despite the French invasion of Mexico in the 1860's, Latin Americans, including Mexicans, demonstrate little or no hostility to Europe; on the contrary, Latin American intellectuals have long taken pride in their affinity to European, particularly French, culture. Their attitude toward the present Western leader, the United States, is another matter. In many respects, the Latin Americans are ambivalent toward their powerful northern neighbor. They have long admired (and envied) her tremendous economic, technological, and industrial strides, and some have copied in their constitutions her political structure, seeking thereby to achieve the degree of political stability and individual freedom that U.S. citizens enjoy. On the other hand they have long been fearful of and hostile to the U.S. political and military overlordship in the Americas and more recently of U.S. economic penetration. Communist cries of "economic colonialism" and "Monroe Doctrine imperialism" touch sensitive nerves in Latin America and on occasion have been able to incite, stimulate, or intensify anti-U.S. demonstrations. Mexico, however, has been among the Latin nations least responsive to Communist propaganda in this area, although non-Communist Mexicans of both the right and the left have not hesitated to take the United States severely to task for past and present attitudes and policies. Mexicans may condemn imperialism and colonialism, Mexicans may socialize important parts of their economy, Mexicans may criticize the United States and its people, but they will do so on their own terms, in light of their own historical experience, and in the language of their own Revolution. They have not accepted the Soviet way, the Soviet philosophy, or the Soviet interpretation of history. They condemned U.S. intervention in Guatemala in 1954, but they also condemned, and more vigorously, the Soviet suppression of Hungary in 1956.

Beyond these general internal conditions which present obstacles to the success of Communism in Mexico, there exist at least two major features within the Communist movement itself that contribute to its failure. One is the inflexible nature of Communist propaganda, and the other is the weaknesses apparent among Mexican Communist leaders. Mexicans, and for that matter, most Latin Americans, are too sophisticated (and perhaps too cynical) to accept a doctrine or thesis which, first, puts all issues in terms of black and white, and, second, frequently changes its interpretations of men and events. Few Mexicans hold that the United States and its people are all bad and that the Soviet Union and its citizens are all noble. The very inflexibility of the Communist propaganda line is self-defeating in a country that is relatively stable and that lacks widespread revolutionary discontent. With its mass communications well developed and its great freedom of expression in both the written and spoken word, blatant propaganda, whether from the U.S. or the USSR, has little chance of success. Two cases in point are the failure of the "peace" offensive in 1950–1951 after its exposure as a Communist maneuver and the failure of the United States to convince Mexico of the need of a bilateral military alliance for Hemisphere defense. Both propositions were defeated as foreign campaigns not in the interest of Mexico but in the interest of their foreign promoters.

If the rigidity of Communist dogma were not sufficient to weaken

the movement, the flaws and divisiveness of its leadership would perform the same function. Communism does not present a united front
to its opposition in Mexico. Unseemly quarreling, at times hidden,
but all too frequently exposed to public amusement and ridicule, has
made the movement an object of derision and suspicion. The leaders of both the Communist Party and the splinter party, respectively, have been much too narrow, doctrinaire, and violent. Of lower-
class origin and with little education, they cannot command respect.
Lombardo has been too egotistical and, although more clever than
his colleagues in hiding his direction from abroad, has aped them
in his distrust of new leaders and in the monolithic control that he
exercises over his party. Although all leaders have paid lip service
to collective leadership, none fully practices it. The results have been
purges or rebellions within the parties, leading to weakness and further division. Such conditions are not those to inspire trust in the
ability of these parties to unify, lead, and govern Mexico in search
of solutions for its pressing problems. If the Communists cannot put
their own house in order, how can they direct the nation? The smooth
functioning and the practical accomplishments of the PRI, despite
its many faults, are much more attractive.

One final condition of Mexico and Latin America must be at least
mentioned as a possible obstacle to Communism: the Catholic Church
and the Catholic faith of the people. Although often treated as a
single factor, in reality two distinct, but related and interdependent,
situations are involved. In many parts of Latin America, the Catholic
Church as an organization, meaning primarily the hierarchy, exercises a powerful influence on political life by mobilizing influential
sectors of society for or against specific persons, parties, and issues.
Colombia is perhaps the best example of this influence. Elsewhere
the Church's political position varies from moderate to weak or
nonexistent. The Church in Mexico, having recovered from the worst
days of the 1920's and 1930's, has by no means regained its pre-1910
status, much less that of the early nineteenth century. It owns no
property, although it has *de facto* control over its churches, schools,
and some residences. Economically, it has no strength. There is no
"Catholic" political party, although the National Action Party
(PAN) proclaims its adherence to Catholic social principles. The

clergy, the bishops and most priests, carefully refrain from open participation in politics, and insist that they have no connection, official or unofficial, with any political party. They do on occasion publicly support some of the welfare measures of the government, such as the eradication of disease, irrigation projects, or the fight against illiteracy. A large segment of the politically active public in Mexico reacts strongly against any move on the part of the clergy that smacks of political involvement. In the mid-1950's an episcopal pastoral letter, outlining the broad principles of a Catholic's political obligations, e.g., the duty to vote, drew sharp fire from private and official sources. As a result of these conditions that have now prevailed for many years, most Mexicans who are politically conscious not only do not look to their clergy for political leadership but in fact reject the very notion that political leadership is a proper clerical function.

Just as the political influence of the Church in Latin America varies, so does the breadth and depth of religiosity among the people. Estimates by U.S. Catholics, lay and clerical, on the extent of religion in Latin America uniformly indicates a weakness of practice and belief. For Chile and Argentina, estimates on practicing Catholics run as low as 5 or 10 per cent, and of these most are women and/or children. Faith is strongest, according to these observers, in Colombia, where political influence of the Church is probably the highest, and in Mexico, where political influence is almost the weakest. One of the firmest indicators of the strength of religious faith in Mexico is the fact that in the mid-1950's one third of all seminarians and one third of all newly ordained priests in Latin America were Mexicans. Those choosing the priesthood as a vocation come primarily from families with firm religious roots, spiritual and intellectual. Despite Mexico's high standing in absolute figures as compared with the rest of Latin America, practicing Catholics are not a majority; they are probably a third or less. Of these many are illiterate, understanding only the rudiments of the faith and virtually nothing of its philosophical or theological positions. Specific promises by Communists could easily be reconciled with their simple faith.

Several conclusions may be drawn from this brief survey on religion. First, the official census figures on religion in Latin America are meaningless, and, second, while the degree of political influence and of the religiosity of the people may coincide, they do not necessarily do so, as witness Mexico. Third, even in a highly religious Latin American country, such as Mexico, the role of Catholicism as an anti-Communist force is less important than is that of several secular institutions, for the very reason that the group intellectually and spiritually armed to resist the doctrine is in fact a small minority of the population, even a minority of the politically active. France and Italy offer two excellent examples of so-called Catholic countries in which large portions of their populations support the Communist Party. Most Latin American countries, including Mexico, are their parallels in the matter of popular religiosity.

What then is the future of Communism in Mexico?

First, there is no evidence that vital internal changes are taking place within the movement. Except for occasional weak efforts by the PPS, Mexican Communists will continue to show little interest in building real political parties to gain power by constitutional means; neither do they indicate any intention of seizing power by force under present conditions. They have never had a true espionage or sabotage apparatus and give no indication of building one. They could inflict some damage on particularly vulnerable installations such as oil pipelines, but it is highly unlikely that they would do so except in the most extreme circumstance. Popular reaction against such attempts would cause greater harm to their cause than any temporary damage might profit it.

Second, the movement will continue to emphasize support for and distribution of its various propaganda organs to enhance the prestige of the Sino-Soviet Bloc and to disparage the West. Some effort may also be expended on strengthening Party cadres to keep intact a militant core of Communists to take advantage of any disruption of the presently stable political and economic conditions.

Third, the Communists will continue to enjoy considerable freedom of action for their principal preoccupation, propaganda, but not for accompanying agitation. Despite this tolerance on the government's part, appreciable strengthening of the movement is not foreseen. Factionalism will continue to plague it.

Fourth, the Mexican masses will continue to ignore the blandishments of the Communists as long as government leaders can and do adhere sufficiently, with concrete performance, to the Revolutionary goals of economic and social justice. Thus far, Mexican officialdom not only has been responsive to grass-roots demands for immediate improvements, but has also formulated long-term plans for raising general standards of living. As long as the masses retain this minimum confidence in their present leaders they will not be tempted by foreign radical and exotic solutions.

Fifth, two conditions, both beyond national control, could disrupt the present balance and bring to the fore a Castro-type regime in which Communist influence, particularly that of Lombardo Toledano, could be preponderant. The first condition is that a world-wide economic depression would seriously affect the Mexican economy. Mexico has considerable internal strength and vitality, owing to her recently achieved economic improvements. Her resistance to the U.S. recession of 1957–1958 is a case in point. She no longer has a one-crop economy, but a prolonged crisis in world trade and finance would have disastrous consequences economically and politically. The other condition is the danger that her continuing high birth rate (about 3.5 per cent per year), may outrun the rate of increase of her GNP, thus frustrating the expectations of her people of a rising standard of living. But stability could yet be maintained with a program of aid from the United States, to continue until the imbalance should be resolved.

The latter event is more likely than the former, and U.S. policy makers, it is to be hoped, are planning for this eventuality. Such aid would have to be forthcoming quickly enough to prevent an upheaval, and be granted without strings or grudges, lest it embitter U.S.-Mexican relations and give opportunity to extremists to capture control of the populace.

We can help to prevent in Mexico today what we could not prevent in Cuba yesterday.

Postscript

Introduction

The primary research for this work was completed in the summer of 1962. Since then the basic patterns of the Mexican Communist movement have not altered appreciably. None of the Communist political parties or front groups has been able to stir up broad popular support. The MLN, still the most important Communist organization, recognized this weakness by not transforming itself into a political party and by refusing to support an opposition candidate for President in 1964. The PPS again supported the candidate of the official party, and the PCM, although not offering a candidate as it did in 1958, sponsored a new party, the Electoral Front of the People (Frente Electoral del Pueblo—FEP) to oppose the PRI. Neither the PPS nor the PCM have offered any new or fresh approaches to Mexico's political and social problems. Propaganda themes for the election were in principle identical with those of six years ago. The government for its part has continued to punish agitators swiftly and severely. Furthermore, the PRI nominated for its 1964 presidential candidate one of its most anti-Communist leaders, Gustavo Díaz Ordaz, Secretary of Government in the cabinet of President López Mateos.

Despite the persistence of these basic patterns, several new developments have occurred in the past two years. Perhaps the most surprising event was the merger of the remains of the POCM with the

PPS, and not with the PCM. This strengthening of the PPS was counterbalanced, however, by the defection of several of its leaders and by the final demise of the CTAL. The PCM during this period held its Fourteenth Party Congress, which ratified the changes in leadership effected in 1960 at the Thirteenth Party Congress. Furthermore, early in 1963 the PCM sponsored a new peasant organization to compete with the CNC and a new political party to compete with the PRI in the 1964 general elections. Since mid-1962 the PCM has been plagued, though in minor degree, by the Sino-Soviet split. In this conflict the Moscow line has predominated. Finally, independent Marxists and far leftists have succeeded in increasing their influence within the movement through two notable publications: *Política* and *El Día*, both operated by groups split off from the PPS. *Política*, a biweekly begun in 1960, has become one of the most attractive news magazines in the country, and *El Día*, a daily newspaper inaugurated in June 1962, appears to be the successor to *El Popular*, that succumbed in November 1961.

The Political Parties

THE PCM

For the past two years the Mexican Communist Party has witnessed no major changes within its leadership, although internal dissension has continued and even intensified. Neither has there been any significant change in the social composition of the rank-and-file membership. After some experimentation with structural changes in the organization of the Party between 1960 and 1963, the leadership apparently returned to the older forms by the time of the Fourteenth Party Congress in December 1963.[1] However a degree of collective leadership continues, in contrast to the dictatorial control exercised by Dionisio Encina prior to his imprisonment in 1959. The Party press has continued to publish Party documents, the bookstore has continued to function, and *La Voz de México* has been appear-

[1] *Política*, January 15, 1964, p. 21. Arnoldo Martínez Verdugo replaced Manuel Terrazas as first secretary of the three-member secretariat of the Central Committee. Terrazas was relieved of his post probably because of his assumption of major duties within the FEP and CCI. He and Fernando Cortés are the other two members of the secretariat.

ing regularly about once a month. No important advances have occurred in Party finances, recruitment techniques, or training programs. In 1963, however, the PCM sponsored two new organizations:
the Electoral Front of the People (Frente Electoral del Pueblo—
FEP), a political party, and the Independent Peasant Central (Central Campesina Independiente—CCI), a rural labor organization.
Both of these aroused considerable political stir at the time of their
founding, but during 1964 they were losing much of their momentum
and limiting their activities largely to formal protests of government
policies. In its own propaganda program the PCM continued with
its denunciation of the Alliance for Progress, U.S. imperialism, and
those Mexicans who cooperate with the United States. It has also
continued to call for leftist unity against imperialism, support for
Castro's Cuba, and the release of political prisoners, among whom
are former PCM leaders.[2] One new note has been added: involvement in the Moscow-Peking conflict.

The PCM has long been noted for its subservience to Moscow and
the overthrow of the old leadership at the Thirteenth Party Congress
in 1960 did not alter this basic policy. Without naming its opponents,
the Ninth Plenum of the Central Committee, meeting in February
1963, condemned "dogmatic and sectarian" attacks on the Moscow
line as it was enunciated in 1957 and again in 1960.[3] The Twelfth
Plenum the following July not only reaffirmed its adherence to Moscow but stated specifically that the Party did not agree with the
Chinese Communist Party because of its divisive attitudes. Furthermore, the PCM said, Chinese propaganda materials varying from
the Moscow line would not be distributed by the PCM. The Central
Committee ended its statement with a note urging unity. In August
La Voz de México supported the nuclear test ban treaty and expressed
the hope that an agreement on general and complete disarmament
would be reached eventually.[4]

Despite the PCM claim that the Party "unanimously" condemned
the international policy of the Chinese Communist Party,[5] support

<hr>

[2] *La Voz de México*, August 5, 1963.
[3] *Ibid.*, April 8, 1963.
[4] *Ibid.*, August 5, 1963.
[5] *Política*, January 15, 1964, p. 19.

for the Soviet Union was not unanimous, and has led to serious quarreling within the Party. One source stated that the resolution of the Twelfth Plenum was reached only after heated debate and by a vote of 6 to 4. It was also reported that two pro-Chinese members of the Central Committee were excluded before the proceedings began.[6] A "Declaration" of the Central Committee at the time of the Twelfth Plenum condemned "adventurers" who impeded united action such as the Frente Obrero, a small labor organization, against imperialism and the "ultras" who were expelled early in 1962.[7] Just prior to the Fourteenth Party Congress in December, the majority in the Central Committee expelled three members from their midst: Samuel López for supporting the Albanian Workers' Party, an ally of the Chinese, and Camilo Chávez and Edelmiro Maldonado for slandering the Communist Party of the Soviet Union.[8] In addition to this conflict over ideologies, strategy, and tactics, personalistic quarrels have continued between the leaders of the Federal District Committee and the national Central Committee. Much of the strength of the opposition that overthrew the Encina group in 1960 was centered in the Federal District organization. When several of its members moved up into the Central Committee, new members were chosen to replace them. New conflicts arose as early as 1961, and by 1963 they had become exceedingly bitter.[9] These struggles do not appear to have been resolved.

THE PPS AND THE POCM

The principal event involving the People's Socialist Party and the Mexican Worker-Peasant Party was their merger in June 1963. With the loss of several of its leaders to the PCM, declining membership,

[6] Branko Lazitch, "El Comunismo Latino-Americano y el Conflicto Moscú-Pekín," *Este & Oeste*, November 15–30, 1963, p. 10.

[7] *La Voz de México*, August 5, 1963.

[8] "La Confesión del Partido Comunista Mexicano," *Este & Oeste*, January 1–15, 1964, p. 9.

[9] Edelmiro Maldonado L., *Informe al V Pleno del Comité Central sobre el Tercer Punto del Orden del Día (7–13 Dic.—61)*, pp. 4, 16, 36, and 46. See also Manuel Castillo, "Sinsabores Comunistas en México," *Este & Oeste*, Año I, No. 20 (May 1–15, 1963), 3. I doubt the accuracy of Castillo's details, but he does point up the intra-Party conflict.

and the apparent intransigence of the PCM in refusing to absorb its total membership, POCM leader Carlos Sánchez Cárdenas quietly opened talks with Lombardo Toledano in mid-1962. The talks continued off and on for almost a year, the formal merger resulting at the end of a series of meetings held between May 31 and June 2. The total POCM membership, then numbering perhaps no more than 300, joined the PPS. Several POCM leaders, including Sánchez Cárdenas, were placed on PPS governing boards. Imprisoned POCM leaders Alberto Lumbreras and Miguel Aroche gave their blessings to the union, and the POCM ceased to exist.[10] Six months earlier the POCM official publication, *Noviembre,* expired on orders of a federal court. The Publications Qualifying Commission, a government agency, had brought suit to forbid its publication on the grounds that it was violating the press law by slandering the government.[11]

The quarrel between Lombardo Toledano and the MLN continues. Several leading PPS members, however, disregarded Lombardo's orders to disassociate with the MLN, and have gradually become estranged from the PPS. Several Socialist People's Youth (JPS) members severely criticized Lombardo Toledano in late 1962 and early 1963, and tried to persuade JPS members to join the MLN. A more damaging blow to the PPS occurred with the disaffection of Jorge Carrión, a PPS leader for many years, and of Manuel Marcué Pardiñas, editor of *Política* and other notable publications. Both men continued to support the MLN, and in January 1964 the PPS announced their resignations from the Party.[12]

No major changes have occurred with respect to PPS top leadership, Party structure, activities, or propaganda themes. A new set of Party statutes, issued at the Third Extraordinary National Assembly on December 1, 1963, simplified the old statutes, but introduced no new significant changes. In practice, Lombardo Toledano continues to dominate the Party and Jacinto López, as number-two man, continues to lead *"paracaidistas"* to squat on lands of large estates, par-

[10] *Política*, June 1, 1963, pp. 8–9; *El Día*, May 12, 1963, p. 3; June 2, 1963, p. 9; and June 3, 1963, p. 1.

[11] *Hispanic American Report*, XVI, No. 1 (March 1963), 19.

[12] *Ibid.*, XVII, No. 1 (March 1964), 15.

ticularly in the northwest.[13] In international affairs the PPS supports the Moscow line against that of Peking, and on the home front it has continued its limited support of the PRI and its policies. The PPS protested state elections in Veracruz in 1962 to the point of establishing a rump legislature,[14] but in that same year Lombardo supported the PRI candidate for governor of Michoacán even though the PRI leaders passed over two pre-candidates favored by Cárdenas.[15] By mid-1963 Lombardo Toledano strongly suggested that he would support the PRI presidential candidate for the 1964 elections, tacking on the proviso, "if acceptable." He did not spell out acceptability, but at the PPS National Assembly in November 1963, the Party officially endorsed Gustavo Díaz Ordaz, whom most of the leftists vehemently denounced as a strident anti-Communist and rightist.[16] In an interview with *Visión* in that same month Lombardo explained that the PPS electoral platform was substantially that of 1948 and that his Party supported the positive work of the López Mateos Administration, including the admission of foreign capital as long as it remained subject to Mexican law and complemented other sectors of the economy.[17] Later he defended his support of the PRI by calling it a "democratic and popular party," and likened what he called the PPS-PRI alliance on the national scene to peaceful coexistence between capitalist and socialist states in the international arena.[18] The Mexican daily *Excelsior* claimed that with the expense of running a presidential campaign and a state of near bankruptcy, the PPS had no choice but to support Díaz Ordaz.

Despite the so-called alliance with the PRI, the PPS ran a large slate of congressional candidates.[19] Only one PPS deputy served in the 1961–1964 congressional term, but with the changes in the electoral law which provide for a degree of proportional representation,

[13] *New York Times*, November 10, 1963, p. 32; *El Día*, January 6, 1964, p. 13.
[14] *Hispanic American Report*, XV, No. 10 (December 1962), 885.
[15] *New York Times*, June 10, 1962, p. 27.
[16] *El Día*, December 1, 1963, p. 3.
[17] *Visión*, November 1, 1963, p. vi. These remarks were made in an interview with a *Visión* reporter.
[18] *Excelsior*, December 1, 1964, p. 1.
[19] *Política*, April 1, 1964, p. 17.

the PPS could obtain up to twenty seats in the lower house. With this prospect, Lombardo himself announced his candidacy from his birthplace, Tezuitlan, Puebla. The PPS was awarded ten seats in the Chamber of Deputies.[20]

THE ELECTORAL FRONT OF THE PEOPLE (FRENTE ELECTORAL DEL PUEBLO—FEP)

The PCM and other Marxist groups were planning the creation of another party of the left to participate in the 1964 general elections at the very time that talks were proceeding for the merger of the POCM and PPS. The idea of organizing a new leftist party was conceived in 1961 when the National Liberation Movement (MLN) was being formed. Some of the MLN members suggested that "the democratization of the internal regime of Mexico" required a new political party.[21] Although the total leadership of the MLN looked to the eventual creation of such a party to break the PRI power monopoly, the dominant group believed in 1963 that the proper conditions had not yet arisen. Repeatedly MLN spokesmen declared that their movement was not a political party, that its members could affiliate with any party they wished provided they continued to fight for the MLN program.

In March 1963 rumors began to circulate through leftist circles in Mexico City that a call for a new party was imminent. Next, the leaders of the PCM circulated a letter to other leftist groups proposing a political alliance of the left.[22] Finally the PCM leaders and several Communist sympathizers released a press bulletin on April 10 and held a press conference on April 22 officially launching the new party, Frente Electoral del Pueblo, the FEP.[23]

For the next two months, the leaders of the new Party organized a series of state assemblies to rally support and register members to meet the requirements of the Federal Electoral Law for obtaining a place on the ballot. The first such assembly was held on Sunday May 18 at Torreón, Coahuila, the one important center of PCM strength

---

[20] *Excelsior*, August 31, 1964, pp. 1 and 12.
[21] *Política*, May 1, 1963, pp. 27–29.
[22] *Ibid.*, April 1, 1963, p. 14.
[23] *Ibid.*, May 1, 1963, pp. 24–27.

outside the Federal District. A notary public certified that 3,200 citizens participated and declared themselves members of the new Party. *Política* described the majority as peasants from the villages in the Laguna district, with the remainder coming from the mining and manufacturing centers of Monclova and Nueva Rosita to the north.[24] The constituent assembly for the Federal District was called for June 16, but a poor turnout forced a week's postponement. The second meeting resulted in still fewer delegates (200–300), but the assembly was held regardless. By early July the FEP claimed over 3,200 members in the capital. Twenty-two other state assemblies also met during this period, with Baja California, Norte claiming the largest enrollment, 9,370, and San Luis Potosí the smallest, 1,252. Then on June 26–27 the FEP held its National Constituent and Registration Assembly in Mexico City. The official PCM organ, *La Voz de México*, claimed that 800 delegates attended the session and represented almost 84,000 registered members. The Assembly elected permanent officers and adopted a program, statutes, and a declaration of principles.[25]

The governing bodies of the FEP consist of a five-member collective National Presidency and a 10-member Central Executive Commission, chosen from a 60-member National Committee which the National Assembly of June 26–27 selected. The center of power resides in the National Presidency, composed of Manuel Terrazas, one of the two top leaders of the PCM; Ramón Danzós Palomino, a PCM peasant leader of the northwest; Renato Leduc, a journalist long active in Communist fronts; Braulio Maldonado, former PRI member and governor of Baja California, Norte, for some years closely associated with PCM leaders; and Raul Ugalde, a lawyer.[26] It appears too that at least one member of the Central Executive Committee, Alfonso Garzón, has an important voice in Party affairs. Garzón, a peasant leader in Baja California, Norte, and expelled PRI member, probably accounted for a sizable portion of the large enrollment from his state. Like Maldonado he has worked closely with PCM leaders for the past two years.

[24] *Ibid.*, June 1, 1963, p. 9.
[25] *La Voz de México*, August 5, 1963.
[26] *Ibid.*

Party leaders began the process of registration between July 5 and 7 when they submitted to the Department of Government various documents on the holding of state assemblies and the registration of members. The government accepted the documents and investigated their authenticity. Having completed its study, the Department announced in October that it had denied registration to the FEP because of fraud and other irregularities. In the state of Chiapas, for example, 2,675 signatures were declared fictitious and 30 other signatures were of residents in the state who denied membership in the FEP.[27] Despite this setback, the Party held its national convention in November as scheduled, and nominated PCM leader Ramón Danzós Palomino as its candidate for President.[28] During December Danzós made his first campaign tour, speaking in the northwestern states of Baja California, Norte, and Sonora. He spoke without harassment in Mexicali, Tijuana, and Ensenada, but at San Luis Río Colorado in Sonora, the police broke up the rally.

The program adopted by the National Assembly repeated long-popular nationalist, leftist, and Communist themes. It opposed imperialism, inter-American organizations and treaties, foreign capital, the Mexican-U.S. Joint Defense Commission, the entry of Mexico into any sort of military pact, and the Guaymas tracking station agreement. It supported "freedom for the working class," dissolution of remaining *latifundia*, nationalization of banking, educational reform, aid for Cuba, support for "liberation movements" in other countries, participation in the "fight for peace," Mexican relations with all countries, and nonintervention and self-determination of nations. Several of these planks were repeated in the campaign platform drawn up at the November convention, and a few others added. The platform denounced the law of "social dissolution" and demanded the freeing of political prisoners and the nationalization of foreign holdings. In his campaign tour through the northwest Danzós bitterly attacked Lombardo Toledano and the PPS as turncoats, but directed most of his barbs at the official candidate, Díaz Ordaz, whom

[27] "México: Contratiempos del Frente Electoral del Pueblo," *Les Informations Politiques et Sociales*, February 10, 1964.
[28] *Política*, November 15, 1963, p. 9.

he accused of association with the rightist, Alemán wing of the PRI.[29] Without registration and a place on the ballot, however, the FEP could expect but a few thousand votes from its hard-core membership who would write in the names of the FEP candidates. As a result, it won less than 20,000 votes in the July elections.[30]

Communist-Front Organizations in Mexico

Since 1962 most Communist-front activity has continued in low key except for that of the National Liberation Movement. The MLN seemingly has absorbed most of the energy and interest of virtually all important members of fronts. While the affiliated groups have continued to carry on sufficient activities to maintain their organizations, many have conducted their major propaganda programs through MLN auspices. In October 1963 the MLN National Committee increased its membership by about 75 per cent and further broadened its base to include members of additional leftist factions.

Three significant developments have affected the MLN since mid-1962.[31] First of all, Cárdenas cooled in his support of the Movement as the PRI increased its pressures on him. Between October 1962 and January 1963 a bitter polemic broke out between him and former President Emilio Portes Gil over Cárdenas' participation in the MLN and in the new Independent Peasant Central (CCI). Portes Gil denounced the MLN for its Communist orientation, and condemned Cárdenas for his association with it.[32] Cárdenas angrily denied that the MLN was Communist. At the same time he disclaimed any direction of the movement or any proselytizing in its behalf.[33] Apparently realizing that continued antagonism of the ruling hierarchy in the government and PRI would only further diminish his political in-

[29] *La Voz de México*, August 5, 1963; *Política*, February 15, 1964, pp. 19–20; April 1, 1964, p. 10; May 1, 1964, pp. 5–6.

[30] *Excelsior*, September 9, 1964, p. 10.

[31] David T. Garza, "Factionalism in the Mexican Left: The Frustration of the MLN," *Western Political Quarterly*, XVII, No. 3 (September 1964), 447–460. My interpretation of the MLN relies heavily on Mr. Garza's article.

[32] *Ibid.*

[33] "Declaraciones del C. Gral. Lázaro Cárdenas," *La Central Campesina Independiente*, p. 6.

fluence, Cárdenas began to withdraw from active support of both these organizations. He never withdrew his membership, but by the spring of 1964 he had made his peace with the López Mateos Administration and was supporting the PRI presidential candidate, Gustavo Díaz Ordaz.[34] Second, PCM influence that appeared to be increasing in mid-1962 was arrested by early 1963. Control solidified in the hands of flexible front group leaders such as Alonso Aguilar, Guillermo Montaño, and Manuel Mesa Andraca, who are closely identified not with political parties but with front groups such as the Circle of Mexican Studies (CEM). The PCM and its affiliates have continued to support the MLN as a matter of basic policy, but the PCM Fourteenth Party Congress in December 1963 complained of the "exclusive measures" adopted by the MLN directors.[35] PCM leaders continued to occupy posts on the National Committee, but they were excluded from the Executive Commission, the ruling organ, when that body was reorganized in October 1963. Third, the MLN leaders, following policies adopted by the CEM, have refused to become involved in a head-on clash with the PRI and the government. While it is obvious that some MLN leaders and members sponsored both the FEP and the CCI to challenge the PRI on the political and labor fronts respectively, the dominant group within the MLN denied any affiliation of their organization with these new bodies. Alonso Aguilar, top MLN spokesman, vehemently repudiated any association with the FEP. He insisted that the MLN would not support any political party or group, because such action would violate the fundamental bases on which the organization was founded, and would provoke grave internal divisions. He added that its purpose was to " 'group together large sectors of the people to fight united, above political and ideological differences.' "[36] This policy has been maintained despite PCM pressure for open support of its protégé, the FEP. As the 1964 elections drew near, MLN limited its activities to reiteration of its principles and mild criticism of the PRI and its presidential candidate, Gustavo Díaz Ordaz.

[34] *Política*, May 15, 1964, p. 7; *El Día*, May 8, 1964, pp. 1–2.
[35] *Política*, January 15, 1964, p. 21.
[36] *Visión*, May 3, 1963, p. 28.

Organized Labor and the Communists

Following government suppression of Communist attempts to take over the railroad and petroleum workers' unions in 1958 and 1959, PRI-affiliated leaders have maintained firm control over these organizations. Some Communist cells continue to function but constitute little danger to old-guard control. In the teachers' union the PPS faction continues to cooperate with the established leadership. A convention of Section IX of the teachers' union removed the last of the followers of Othón Salazar from office in the summer of 1962 and elected a slate that represented all factions but Salazar's. Salazar had been supported by the PCM, and his defeat decisively closed positions of influence to the Communist Party in the teachers' union.

Among Communist-controlled labor organizations, old policies have continued and several new developments have occurred. The General Union of Workers and Peasants of Mexico (UGOCM) has successfully maintained its pressure for land distribution without provoking the government to use severe repressive tactics. Jacinto López, its leader, has promoted numerous raids by *paracaidistas* on large landed estates forcing promises of expropriations, and in several instances actual expropriations of land. López and other UGOCM-PPS leaders were particularly active in the fall of 1963 in their chosen area, the northwest. Several large cotton farms in the Yaqui and Mayo valleys were invaded by UGOCM-led squatters. As usual, federal troops and state police evicted them without violence, but the seriousness of the situation led federal and state officials to confer with López. After further agitation several hundred UGOCM peasants were granted land.[37]

Two other Communist-controlled organizations have been virtually inactive. The Confederation of Latin American Workers (CTAL) under the direction of Vicente Lombardo Toledano officially ceased to exist on February 21, 1964,[38] while the PCM-dominated Central Union of Ejido Societies (UCSE) had apparently merged its activities with the Independent Peasant Central. Because of the in-

[37] *New York Times*, November 10, 1963, p. 32.
[38] *Visión*, February 21, 1964, p. 18.

effectiveness of the CTAL, the suggestion for the creation of a new
Latin American trade union central was made at a WFTU meeting in
Leipzig in 1957. The question was raised at the Havana Conference
of Peoples in 1959, and again at the Fifth Congress of the WFTU in
Moscow in December 1961. A conference of Latin American labor
leaders in Santiago, Chile, in February 1962 appointed a committee
to prepare for an inter-American labor congress. The conference was
duly held but so few delegations attended that no permanent body
could be formed. Two other congresses convened, one in La Paz July
1963, and one in Brasilia January 1964, but on both occasions too
few labor leaders attended to create a new inter-American labor
union. It has been frequently reported that a new organization was
needed because Fidel Castro has so far outpaced Lombardo Toledano
as a leftist political and labor leader in Latin America. In 1962, probably under Soviet orders, the Cuban labor leader Lázaro Peña replaced Lombardo on the directive board of the WFTU. It must be
noted, however, that except for the years 1959 and 1960 Cuba has
played a secondary role in promoting a new Hemisphere-wide labor
union. The main thrust appears to originate in Chile, and plans for a
permanent council to promote such an organization call for headquarters to be established in that country at Santiago.[39]

The most significant event among Communist-controlled labor
groups was the creation of the Independent Peasant Central (Central
Campesina Independiente—CCI) in January 1963. For many years
PCM programs had called for the founding of labor organizations
free of government control. Normally such statements passed without
implementing action. In October 1962, however, an organizing committee issued a "Convocation to the National Peasantry" that resulted in a congress of peasant leaders in January 1963. Foremost
among the organizers were PCM leaders such as Arturo Orona and
Ramón Danzós Palomino, later to be chosen presidential candidate
of the Electoral Front of the People (FEP). Associated with Orona

[39] Manuel Castillo, *¿Hacia una Central Comunista de Trabajadores de
América Latina?*, pp. 4–10; *Visión*, February 21, 1964, p. 18; October 5, 1962,
p. 14.

and Danzós were peasant leaders who were cooperating with the PCM such as Alfonso Garzón and Domingo Esquivel.[40]

The constituent congress of the CCI, held January 6–8, 1963, named three secretaries as a collective governing board: Arturo Orona, Ramón Danzós, and Alfonso Garzón. It also appointed a twelve-member board in charge of various Party activities, a National Vigilance Committee, a Judicial Affairs Committee, and a General Advisory Board. Clearly, PCM members dominated the new organization, but the participating non-PCM peasant leaders gave the impression that the CCI represented a broad spectrum of rural labor.[41] Furthermore, the presence of Lázaro Cárdenas at the opening session provided an aura of respectability. His brief remarks could in no way be interpreted as pro-Communist, but he defended the new organization on the grounds that the course of the Revolution had been marked by the existence of a multiplicity of labor organizations. Later in a press interview he denied that the CCI was divisive, arguing that it was mobilizing *campesinos* who were presently not active in any organization.[42] The general reaction, however, to the founding of the CCI was critical. Even some leftists who ordinarily supported Cárdenas, such as Lombardo Toledano and Heriberto Jara, condemned the new Central and Cárdenas' support of it.[43] By April, as noted above, Cárdenas showed increasing reticence in supporting the CCI openly, and public interest and attention began to wane. Broad popular support did not materialize and the CCI appears destined to follow the path of frustration and ineffectiveness that has been the lot of the Central Union of Ejido Societies, the old labor wing of the PCM.

In its Declaration of Principles and Program, issued at the founding Congress in January 1963, the CCI repeated most of the slogans

[40] "Convocatoria al Campesinado Nacional," *La Central Campesina Independiente*, pp. 15–21.

[41] Rodrigo García Treviño, "Crisis del comunismo mexicano," *Este & Oeste*, Año I, No. 20 (May 1–15, 1963), 5–6; *Política*, January 15, 1964, p. 3.

[42] "Discurso del C. Gral. Lázaro Cárdenas" and "Declaraciones del C. Gral. Lázaro Cárdenas," *La Central Campesina Independiente*, pp. 5–7.

[43] García Treviño, "Crisis del comunismo mexicano," *Este & Oeste*, Año I, No. 20 (May 1–15, 1963), 7.

and themes long current among Communists and those of the far left. Many dealt with rural needs such as land, water, credit, education, and health. Others, more broadly political in scope, criticized the government by attacking the law of "social dissolution," demanding the freedom of political prisoners, and condemning Yankee imperialism in Mexico. Still others supported various Communist and leftist programs such as general disarmament, "peace," the Cuban revolution, the MLN, and "progressive" labor forces in Mexico and abroad.[44] Efforts to carry out this program have resulted in little more than propaganda campaigns and support for the FEP presidential candidate, Ramón Danzós, who is one of the directors of the CCI. Various complaints have been directed toward the state and national governments concerning abuses suffered by CCI members. Late in 1963 CCI leaders also conducted a march on Mexico City of peasants from Morelos demanding land, and demonstrations in Chihuahua were carried out in the spring of 1964. These efforts have been to no avail since the Department of Agrarian Affairs and Colonization have ignored complaints.[45] Thus, neither in activities, propaganda, or recruitment has the CCI succeeded in building an effective organization.

The Mexican Government and the Communists

Government policy toward political opposition has remained basically unchanged. Those groups and individuals who criticize the administration, pressure for reforms and benefits, and exercise restraint in public demonstrations can expect a high degree of toleration and some concessions if they do not press their demands to the point of violence and are willing to accept limited accommodations. Among the Communist groups, the PPS and to a lesser extent the CEM and the MLN have played this game successfully. Their leaders have enjoyed a relative freedom from harassment, their propaganda programs operate with few barriers, and in the case of the PPS some of

[44] "Declaraciones de Principios y Programa de la Central Campesina Independiente," *La Central Campesina Independiente*, pp. 23–43.
[45] *Política*, March 15, 1964, p. 9; *El Día*, May 23, 1964, p. 3; May 26, 1964, p. 2.

their demands (e.g., in land distribution) have been at least partially satisfied. Furthermore, when government harassment takes place, it can be quickly rectified, as demonstrated by the arrest and rapid release in June 1962 of the editor and the chief printer of *Política*, the semiofficial organ of the MLN.

On the other hand, intransigent groups such as the PCM and its affiliates, the CCI and FEP, receive little consideration from the government. The Communist leaders of the violent railroad strike of 1959 are serving prison sentences ranging up to sixteen years. Even the well-known artist, David Alfaro Siqueiros, remained in prison for over four years because of the violent demonstrations that he led in the streets of Mexico City during the summer of 1960. Later, in August 1963, a general brawl ensued when police attempted to disperse a large group, representing the PCM, PPS, CCI, FEP, and MLN, that protested the sentencing of the leaders of the railroad strike. The mob threw to the ground and disarmed several policemen; some of the agitators suffered fractured skulls and ribs.[46] The Mexican government has also restricted the distribution of propaganda materials from Cuba, and photographs all travelers to that country that pass through Mexico. Furthermore, the authorities frequently incarcerate known agitators when foreign dignitaries visit Mexico. About 400 leftists, including Othón Salazar, were picked up in February 1963 in anticipation of President Betancourt's visit.[47]

As the 1964 general elections drew near, the authorities inaugurated a systematic campaign of harassment against the FEP and its leaders. Presidential candidate Ramón Danzós was briefly held under arrest, political rallies were routed, and other FEP candidates and members were threatened.[48] Finally Braulio Maldonado, former PRI member and now a leader of the FEP, was arrested in March and interrogated. In April he suddenly departed Mexico under rumors that the government had advised him to go into exile. Even his family would not comment on his departure.[49] The government has obviously toughened in its attitude toward the left in the past two years.

[46] *Política*, September 1, 1963, pp. 16–20.
[47] *Ibid.*, March 1, 1963, pp. 1 and 15.
[48] *Ibid.*, April 1, 1964, pp. 19–20; April 15, 1964, p. 24; May 1, 1964, p. 20.
[49] *Ibid.*, May 1, 1964, p. 14.

The Mexican Communists and the International Communists

No major new developments have occurred recently with respect to international Communist activities in Mexico. The USSR, Poland, and Czechoslovakia still maintain embassies in Mexico City and Czechoslovakia has a consulate at Monterrey.[50] A flurry of speculation that Mexico was considering recognition of Red China occurred at the time of French President De Gaulle's visit early in 1964. It died quickly when President López Mateos announced that during his administration Mexico would maintain relations solely with the Chinese Nationalists.[51] President López Mateos, however, stopped in Poland and Yugoslavia in the spring of 1963 as he traveled through Western Europe attempting to broaden Mexico's trade relations. The Mexican government concluded no new trade or credit agreements with Communist countries, but it did sign a commercial protocol with Poland that encouraged increased trade and agreed to the exchange of economic experts.

Although the vast majority of Mexican Communists have lined up with the Soviet Union in its conflict with Red China, the latter has continued its attempts to increase its influence in Mexico. Exchange of personnel has been somewhat limited, but publication and radio broadcasts have increased year by year. By late 1962 Red China was broadcasting about thirty-five hours weekly to Latin America, with presumably half of this reaching Mexico. The propaganda portions of the broadcasts stressed the similarity of China's struggles to those of Latin America: the fight against imperialism, the need for agrarian reform, and the drive for economic development.[52] In late 1963 the Chinese opened an industrial and trade exhibit in Mexico City, their first in the Western Hemisphere. The exhibit had the effect of emphasizing China's economic underdevelopment, and probably harmed rather than benefited Chinese interests in Mexico.[53]

[50] U.S. Department of State, Bureau of Intelligence and Research, *Sino Soviet Bloc Missions in Latin America*, p. 4.

[51] *New York Times*, March 15, 1964, p. 26.

[52] "La Acción de China Comunista en América Latina," *Este & Oeste*, Año I, No. 14 (January 15–30, 1963), 3–9; *Les Informations Politiques et Sociales*, September 11, 1962; "La ofensiva radiofónica de los Países Comunistas en América Latina," *Este & Oeste*, Año I, No. 9 (November 1–15, 1962), 4.

[53] *New York Times*, February 16, 1964, p. 26.

Soviet and East European Communist propaganda activities directed toward Latin America have also increased steadily. Russian and satellite radio programs during 1962 totaled over 100 hours weekly, of which about 50 reached Mexico. In 1963 the Soviet Union alone tripled its program to 120 hours weekly to Latin America.[54] All of these countries continued to flood the area with publications as well.

Cuba, too, has become a major source of Communist propaganda flowing into Mexico. The Mexican authorities have confiscated large caches of printed materials on the grounds that they constitute outside interference in domestic politics. Broadcasting cannot be stopped, but Cuba appears to direct her radio propaganda mostly to the Central American countries.[55] Neither the publications nor the broadcasts have been particularly successful in winning Mexican converts to Communism.

Despite the founding of a new political party and a new peasant organization, despite the attractiveness of the news magazine *Política*, despite the activities of the MLN leaders, despite the merger of the PPS and the POCM, the Communist movement in Mexico has failed during the past two years to increase significantly its popular appeal. Neither in whole nor in its many parts can it offer substantial and meaningful opposition to the government party and the basic power structure of Mexico. The whole movement, even the MLN, remains too deeply committed to Communist ideology to prove attractive to Mexican political leaders, and its inability to offer hope of real benefits to the lower classes negates its potential mass appeal. Neither disillusionment nor frustration have become so serious in Mexico as to erode support from the PRI or to swing important political sectors to radical organizations.

[54] *Ibid.*, September 8, 1963, Section E, p. 3.
[55] "La ofensiva radiofónica de los Países Comunistas en América Latina," *Este & Oeste*, Año I, No. 9 (November 1–5, 1962), 5.

BIBLIOGRAPHY

Principal Newspapers and News Magazines Consulted—Communist and Non-Communist

El Día. Appeared June 1962; published by former PPS members Enrique Ramírez and Rodolfo Dorantes; seems to be a revival of *El Popular* under a new name.

Diario de los Debates de la Cámara de Diputados. The official record of the Mexican national legislature.

Excelsior. Mexico City daily; moderately conservative.

Hispanic American Report. The only monthly periodical in English that describes major events in every Latin American country.

New York Times.

Noviembre. Official organ of the Communist-splinter Mexican Worker-Peasant Party (POCM) ; ceased publication January 1963.

Política. Communist-oriented; edited by former PPS members; published semimonthly.

El Popular. Originally the official organ of the Mexican Confederation of Labor (CTM) ; the unofficial mouthpiece of the Socialist People's Party (PPS) from 1948 to the late 1950's, when it reverted to an independent Marxist journal until its demise in November 1961.

El Universal. Mexico City daily; moderately conservative.

Visión. Spanish-language biweekly published in the United States; special section on Mexico in almost every issue.

La Voz de México. Official organ of the Mexican Communist Party (PCM).

Other Communist Party Periodicals

OF THE MEXICAN COMMUNIST PARTY (PCM)

Boletín Nacional de la Campaña Económica. Published by the National Directorate in early 1958; short-lived.

Boletín Nacional del Secretariado del C.C. Published irregularly by the Central Committee during 1961 and 1962.

Cultura Popular. Bibliography bulletin of the PCM publishing house, Fondo de Cultura Popular.

Liberación. Organ of the PCM Central Committee; founded early in 1957; now defunct.

El Machete. Organ of the PCM from mid-1920's to late 1930's; famous for its revolutionary sketches by Rivera, Siqueiros, and others.

Nueva Epoca. Organ of the PCM Central Committee; founded 1962 to replace *Revista Teórica.*

Nueva Vida. Short-lived organ of the Mexican Communist Youth (JCM) of the late 1950's.

El Proletario. Published irregularly by a local group in the Federal District during 1961.

Revista Teórica. Organ of the PCM Central Committee; founded c. 1960 to replace *Liberación*; now defunct.

Teória. PCM theoretical journal; replaced by *Liberación.*

Vida del Partido. Short-lived organ of the PCM Federal District Committee; founded early 1958.

Vida Nueva. First official organ of the PCM; founded January 1920.

OF THE SOCIALIST PEOPLE'S PARTY (PPS)

Avante. Organ of the PPS Central Committee; founded late 1960.

Boletín Informativo del Partido Popular en el Distrito Federal. Organ of the PPS Federal District Committee; appeared irregularly 1956–1959.

Correo del Partido Popular en el Distrito Federal. Short-lived replacement of the *Boletín Informativo.*

Juventud Popular. Organ of the People's Youth (JP) ; founded late 1957; now defunct.

El Mexicano. Short-lived organ of the PPS; founded late 1957.

El Popular Socialista. Organ of the PPS; founded late 1960 after the Party added "Socialist" to its title.

Communist-oriented Periodicals Circulated in Mexico

OF MEXICAN ORIGIN

Agronómica. Edited by Manuel Marcué Pardiñas, member of the PPS.

Ahí Va El Golpe. Edited by Alberto Beltrán, PPS member until about 1957; defunct since 1959.

Ciencia y Técnica. Short-lived publication of the Mexican-Russian Institute of Cultural Exchange (IICMR) ; founded in 1955.

Cuadernos del Círculo de Estudios Mexicanos. Organ of the Circle of Mexican Studies (CEM).

Cultura Soviética. Organ of the IICMR from 1944 to 1955.

Frente. Organ of the Socialist Front of Lawyers of Mexico; now apparently defunct.

Guión de Acontecimientos Nacionales e Internacionales. Founded 1956 by Narciso Bassols Batalla, close friend and associate of Vicente Lombardo Toledano, president of the PPS.

Intercambio Cultural. Founded early 1955 as replacement for *Cultura Soviética,* organ of the IICMR.

Liberación. Organ of the National Committee for the Liberty of Political Prisoners and the Defense of Constitutional Liberties.

Paralelo 20. Edited by Jesús Alejandro Martínez, onetime PPS member and intimate friend of Lombardo Toledano; now defunct.

Paz. Organ of the Mexican peace movement; now defunct.

Polémica Sobre el Arte y la Cultura. Founded 1954 by Federico Silva, PPS member and son-in-law of Lombardo Toledano; now defunct.

Política. Edited by Manuel Marcué Pardiñas and Jorge Carrión Villa, a former officer of the PPS. Founded in May 1960, *Política* has become one of the most important periodicals in Mexico for political news and commentary.

Problemas Agrícolas e Industriales de México. Edited by Marcué Pardiñas.

Problemas de Latinoamérica. Edited by Marcué Pardiñas.

Problemas de México. Edited by Marcué Pardiñas.

Siglo Veinte: Reseña Mundial de la Política y la Cultura. Published monthly in Mexico City; pro-Castro; anti-U.S.; with several Cubans among its principal contributors.

UO Revista de Cultura Moderna. Organ of the Universidad Obrera; now apparently defunct.

OF INTERNATIONAL COMMUNIST SPONSORSHIP

Horizontes. Spanish edition of the organ of the World Peace Council.

El Movimiento Sindical Mundial. Spanish edition of the organ of the World Federation of Trade Unions (WFTU).

Noticiero de la CTAL. Organ of the Confederation of Latin American Workers (CTAL).

Problemas de la Paz y del Socialismo. Spanish edition of the *World Marxist Review: Problems of Peace and Socialism.*

OF THE SOVIET-BLOC EMBASSIES IN MEXICO

Boletín de Información de la Embajada de la USSR. A weekly of the Soviet Embassy.
Checoeslovaquia de Hoy. A monthly of the Czech Embassy.
La Nueva Polonia. A monthly of the Polish Embassy.
Servico de Noticias de la Oficina de Prensa de la Embajada de la URSS. Monday through Friday from the Soviet Embassy.

OF THE SPANISH COMMUNIST EXILES

Alkartu. Organ of the Basque Communist Party.
España Popular. Weekly organ of the Spanish Communist Party.
Nuestro Tiempo: Revista Española de Cultura. Edited by Juan Vicens.

OF SOVIET BLOC ORIGIN

China Reconstruye, Red China.
Cultura y Vida, USSR.
Literatura Soviética, USSR.
La Mujer Soviética, USSR.
Tiempos Nuevos, USSR.
Unión Soviética, USSR.

Chinese Publications Circulated in Mexico since 1958

China Sobrepasa a Los Estados Unidos en la Producción de Trigo. Pekín: Ediciones en Lenguas Extranjeras, 1958. Photo album.
Contra la Ocupación de Taiwan por los Estados Unidos y la Conspiración de los Dos Chinas. Pekín: Ediciones en Lenguas Extranjeras, 1958.
Estatutos del Partido Comunista de China—Informe sobre Modificaciones en los Estatutos del Partido Comunista de China. Pekín: Ediciones en Lenguas Extranjeras, 1958.
Ju Chiao-Mu. *Treinta Años del Partido Comunista de China.* Pekín: Ediciones en Lenguas Extranjeras, 1957.
Lu Ding-Yi. *Es Necesario Combinar la Enseñanza con el Trabajo Productivo.* Pekín: Ediciones en Lenguas Extranjeras, 1958.
———. *Que Cien Flores Se Abran: Que Compitan Cien Escuelas Ideológicas.* Pekín: Ediciones en Lenguas Extranjeras, 1958.
Mao Tse-Tung. *Acerca de la Aparación de la Revista "El Comunista."* Pekín: Ediciones en Lenguas Extranjeras, 1957.
———. *Informe sobre Investigación Verificado en Junan acerca del*

Movimiento Campesino. Pekín: Ediciones en Lenguas Extranjeras, 1957.

———. *Mayor Preocupación por la Vida del Pueblo: Mayor Atención a los Métodos de Trabajo.* Pekín: Ediciones en Lenguas Extranjeras, 1959.

———. *Nuestro Estudio y la Situación Actual.* Pekín: Ediciones en Lenguas Extranjeras, 1958.

———. *Sobre la Acertada Manera de Resolver las Contradicciones en el Seno del Pueblo.* Pekín: Ediciones en Lenguas Extranjeras, 1958.

La Oposición a los Provocaciones Militares de los EE. UU. en la Region del Estrecho de Taiwan. Pekín: Ediciones en Lenguas Extranjeras, 1958.

El Pueblo Chino Construye la Industria Impetuosamente. Pekín: Ediciones en Lenguas Extranjeras, 1959.

Refutación al Revisionismo Moderno. Pekín:Ediciones en Lenguas Extranjeras, 1958.

Sobre la Actual Situación Internacional. Pekín: Ediciones en Lenguas Extranjeras, 1958.

Tung Da-Lin. *El Camino de la Cooperación Agrícola en China.* Pekín: Ediciones en Lenguas Extranjeras, 1958.

Documents of the Communist Parties in Mexico

OF THE MEXICAN COMMUNIST PARTY (PCM)

La Central Campesina Independiente. México, D.F.: Fondo de Cultura Popular, 1963.

Chávez, Camilo. *Urge un Cambio Radical en la Situación Económica del Partido.* México, D.F.: Ediciones del Comité Central, 1962.

IV Pleno (ampliado) del Comité Central del PCM: Resolución. México, D.F.: Ediciones del Comité Central, 1961.

XIII Congreso. Resolución General: Encauzar á la Nación por el Camino Democrático e Independiente. [México, D.F.]: Ediciones Julius Fucik, [1960?].

Encina, Dionisio. *Liberemos a México del Yugo Imperialista.* México, D.F.: Fondo de Cultura Popular [1954?].

———. *Posición del Partido Comunista Mexicano Frente á la Sucesión Presidencial* in *Problemas de México,* I, No. 4 (July 15, 1958).

Estatutos del Partido Comunista Mexicano. Aprobados por el XII Congreso Nacional Ordinario del PCM, Celebrado en la Ciudad de México del 20 al 25 de Septiembre de 1954. México, D.F.: Fondo de Cultura Popular, 1954.

Flores, Ricardo. *Qué Es y Hacia Dónde Marcha el Frente Obrero.* México, D.F.: Ediciones del Comité Central, 1962.

González, Tereso, and Lozada, Eduardo. *Nuestro Lugar Está en el Partido Comunista.* México, D.F.: Ediciones del Comité Central, 1961.

Hacia una Educación al Servicio del Pueblo: Resoluciones y Principales Estudios Presentados en la Conferencia Pedagógica del Partido Comunista. Mexico, 1938.

Maldonado L., Edelmiro. *Informe al V Pleno del Comité Central sobre el Tercer Punto del Orden del Día (7–13 Dic.—61).* México, D.F.: Ediciones del Comité Central, 1962.

Materiales del Comité del D.F. para su Discusión en el XIII Congreso del Partido Comunista Mexicano. México, 1959.

El Partido Comunista y la Devaluación del Peso. México, D.F., 1954.

Pérez, J. Encarnación. *Sobre las Modificaciones a los Estatutos.* México, D.F.: Fondo de Cultura Popular [1954?].

Plataforma Electoral del Partido Comunista Mexicano in *Problemas de México,* I, No. 4 (July 15, 1958).

¡Una Política y Un Candidato Que Sí Responden a Los Intereses del Pueblo! in *Problemas de México,* I, No. 4 (July 15, 1958).

Resolución de la Conferencia del Partido Comunista en el Distrito Federal 11–23 de Agosto 2–19 de Septiembre. México, D.F.: [Ediciones del Comité del D.F. del Partido Comunista Mexicano], 1957.

III Congreso Estatal Extraordinario. Partido Comunista Mexicano en N.L. Resolución. [Monterrey?]: Ediciones Román Guerra Montemayor [1962?].

Terrazas, Manuel. *Hacia un Nuevo Programa del Partido Comunista Mexicano.* México, D. F.: Fondo de Cultura Popular [1954?].

Tesis sobre el Trabajo Feminil del Partido Comunista. [México, D.F.: Ediciones del Comité Central, 1962?].

OF THE MEXICAN WORKER-PEASANT PARTY (POCM)

Carta del Partido Obrero—Campesino Mexicano al Partido Comunista: Proposiciones para la Unidad Orgánica o la Realización del Frente Unico. México, D.F.: Ediciones Noviembre, 1957.

Declaración de Principios, Programa, Estatutos. México, D.F.: Ediciones Noviembre, 1955.

El PO-CM da Respuesta a las Proposiciones Unitarios del P.C.M. México, D.F.: Ediciones Noviembre, 1958.

Sánchez Cárdenas, Carlos. *La Crisis del Movimiento Comunista Mexicano.* México, D.F.: Ediciones Noviembre, 1957.

OF THE SOCIALIST PEOPLE'S PARTY (PPS)

IV Asamblea General Ordinario del Partido Popular en el Distrito Federal que Se Celebrará en la Ciudad de México, los Días 30, 31 de Octubre y 1° de Noviembre de 1959. México, D.F.

Dictamen del Partido Popular sobre el Informe de la Dirección Nacional y la Participación del Partido en las Elecciones Federales de 1958 in *Problemas de México,* I, No. 4 (July 15, 1958).

Estatutos del Partido Popular Socialista in *Política,* December 15, 1963, pp. XVI–XXI.

Lombardo Toledano, Vicente. *Ante la Crisis de Hungria.* México, D.F.: Ediciones del PP, 1956.

———. *En Torno al XX Congreso del Partido Comunista de La Unión Soviética.* México, D.F.: Ediciones del PP, 1957.

———. *La Perspectiva de México: Una Democracia del Pueblo.* México, D.F.: Ediciones del PP, 1957.

———. *La Situación Política de México con Motivo del Conflicto Ferrocarrilero.* México, D.F.: Ediciones del PP, 1959.

———. *La Sucesión Presidencial de 1958.* México, D.F.: 1957.

Razón Histórica, Principios, Programa y Estatutos del Partido Popular. México, D.F., 1948.

La Situación Política de México: El Partido Popular Frente a la Sucesión Presidencial in *Problemas de México,* I, No. 4 (July 15, 1958).

Tesis sobre México: Programa del Partido Popular in *Problemas de México,* I, No. 4 (July 15, 1958).

Books

Alba, Víctor. *Historia del Comunismo en América Latina.* México, D.F.: Ediciones Occidentales, 1954.

Alexander, Robert J. *Communism in Latin America.* New Brunswick, N.J.: Rutgers University Press, 1957.

Allen, Robert Loring. *Soviet Influence in Latin America: The Role of Economic Relations.* Washington, D.C.: Public Affairs Press, 1959.

Beals, Carleton. *Glass Houses: Ten Years of Free-Lancing.* New York: J. B. Lippincott Company, 1938.

British Society for International Understanding. *The Trojan Horse: Communist Front Organizations* in *The British Survey,* Main Series N.S. No. 129. London: Benjamin Franklin House, December 1959.

Buck, Philip W., and Martin B. Travis (eds.). *Control of Foreign Relations in Modern Nations.* New York: W. W. Norton, 1957.

Clark, Marjorie Ruth. *Organized Labor in Mexico.* Chapel Hill: University of North Carolina Press, 1934.

Communism in Latin America. New York: Visión, Inc., 1958. A *Visión* report.

La Confederación de Trabajadores de América Latina (CTAL) y la Federación Sindical Mundial: Estudio sobre la Explotación Comunista. 2d ed. México, D.F.: Ediciones Occidentales [1953?].

Corporation for Economic and Industrial Research. *United States-Latin American Relations; Soviet Bloc-Latin American Activities and Their Implications for United States Foreign Policy.* A study prepared at the request of the Subcommittee on American Republics Affairs of the Committee on Foreign Relations, United States Senate, Eighty-sixth Congress, second session. Washington, D.C.: Government Printing Office, 1960.

Facts about International Communist-front Organizations. April 1957. A pamphlet.

Fuentes Díaz, Vicente. *Los Partidos Políticos en México.* 2 vols. Vol. II: *From Carranza to Ruiz Cortines.* México, D.F., 1956.

García Treviño, Rodrigo. *La Ingerencia Rusa en México.* México, D.F.: Editorial América, 1959.

Industrial Research and Information Services, Ltd. *The Communist Solar System.* London: Hollis & Carter [1957].

Katayama, Sen. *The Labor Movement in Japan.* Chicago: C. H. Ken & Company [1918].

Kirkpatrick, Evron M. (ed.). *Year of Crisis: Communist Propaganda Activities in 1956.* New York: Macmillan Company, 1957.

Lombardo Toledano, Vicente. *Diario de un Viaje a la China Nueva.* México, D.F.: Editorial Futuro, 1950.

————. *Lo que Vive y Lo que Ha Muerto de la Constitución de 1857.* México, D.F.: Imprenta Ramírez, 1958.

————. *Una Ojeada a la Crisis de la Educación en México.* México, D.F.: Publicaciones de la Universidad Obrera de México, 1958.

————, and Víctor Manuel Villaseñor. *Un Viaje al Mundo del Porvenir.* [México, D.F.]: Universidad Obrera, 1936.

López Zamora, Emilio. *El Problema del Abastecimiento de Aguas para los Servicios Públicos de la Ciudad de Tijuana, B.C.* [Tijuana, 1957?]. Publication of the Circle of Mexican Studies, Tijuana branch.

Overstreet, Gene D., and Marshall Windmiller. *Communism in India.* Berkeley: 1959.

Perche, Maurice. *El Vaticano: Gran Potencia Capitalista.* México, D.F.: Editora y Distribuidora Nacional de Publicaciones, 1958.

Pérez Leiros, F. *El movimiento sindical de América Latina.* Buenos Aires: Imprenta "La Vanguardia", 1941.

Revueltas, José. *El Realismo En El Arte.* México, D.F.: Talleres de Impresiones Modernas [1956].

Rienffer, Karl. *Comunistas Españoles en América.* Madrid: Editora Nacional, 1953.

Rubottom, Roy R. *Communism in the Americas.* Department of State Publication 6601, Inter-American Series 53. Washington, D.C.: Government Printing Office, 1958.

Salazar, Rosendo, and José G. Escobedo. *Las Pugnas de la Gleba, 1907–1922.* 2 vols. in one. México, D.F.: Editorial Avante, 1923.

El Saldo de White Sulphur Springs, México, D.F., 1956. Publication of the Circle of Mexican Studies (CEM).

Sánchez Cárdenas, Carlos. *Defensa de México: O derechos Democráticos Constitucionales O Ley Fascista sobre "Disolución Social."* [México, D.F.?], Ediciones Nueva Democracia [1953].

Subcommittee To Investigate the Administration of the Internal Security Act and Other Internal Security Laws, Committee of the Judiciary, United States Senate, Eighty-sixth Congress, First session. Hearings, November 5, 1959. Published as *Communist Threat to the United States through the Caribbean.* Washington, D.C.: Government Printing Office, 1960.

Tamayo, Jorge L. *Oaxaca en el Siglo XX.* México, D.F., 1956. Publication of the Circle of Mexican Studies.

Treviño, Ricardo. *El Espionaje Comunista y la Evolución Doctrinaria del Movimiento Obrero en México.* México, D.F.: [A. del Bosque], 1952.

United States Department of Labor, Office of International Labor Affairs. *Directory of Labor Organizations, Western Hemisphere.* Washington, D.C., 1957. Mimeographed.

———. *Directory of World Federation of Trade Unions.* Washington, D.C., 1958. Mimeographed.

United States Department of State, Bureau of Intelligence and Research. *Sino/Soviet Bloc-Latin American Relations.* Intelligence Report No. 8372, summary data. Washington, D.C., November 1, 1960. Mimeographed.

————. *Sino-Soviet Bloc Missions in Latin America*. Research Memorandum RAR-33. Washington, D.C., July 16, 1963. Mimeographed.

————. *World Strength of the Communist Party Organizations*. Washington, D.C., 1957–1964. An annual report. Mimeographed.

Zendejas, Adelina. *La Crisis de la Educación en México*. México, D.F., September 1958.

Articles

"La Acción de China Comunista en América Latina," *Este & Oeste*, Año I, No. 14 (January 15–30, 1963), 1–9.

"Actividades Comunistas en Iberoamérica," *Estudios sobre el Comunismo*, Año IX, No. 32 (April–June 1961), 86–114.

Alba, Victor. "Communism and Nationalism in Latin America," *Problems of Communism*. VIII, No. 5 (September–October 1958), 24–31.

Arcos Fenal, Ing. Manuel. "Paparouv, el Titiritero de Nuestros Comunistoides," *El Universal*, July 13, 1957, p. 2.

Bess, Demaree. "Mexico Doesn't Want the Cold War," *Saturday Evening Post*, July 18, 1959.

Cabrera, Enrique. "Paz y Liberación Nacional," *Política*, Año I, No. 1 (May 1, 1960), 32–33.

Castillo, Manuel. "¿Hacia una Central Comunista de Trabajadores de América Latina?," *Este & Oeste*, Año I, No. 10 (November 15–30, 1962), 1–10.

————. "Sinsabores Comunistas en México," *Este & Oeste*, Año I, No. 20 (May 1–15, 1963), 3.

"El Círculo de Estudios Mexicanos y la Política," *Excelsior*, October 13, 1958.

"Comunismo en América: Más Rico, Más Fuerte . . . Mejor Dirigido," *Visión*, November 7, 1958, pp. 20–32.

"Comunismo en México," *Razón y Fe*, Vol. 158, No. 731 (Madrid, December 1958), 449–462.

"Los comunistas defienden los intereses de los trabajadores del campo," *Problemas de la Paz y del Socialismo*, Año III, No. 3 (March 1960).

"La Confesión del Partido Comunista Mexicano," *Este & Oeste*, Año II, No. 36 (January 1–15, 1964), 9.

"Crisis del Comunismo en México," *Les Informations Politiques et Sociales*, Año III, No. 19 (May 10, 1963).

English, Richard. "Mexico Clamps Down on Stalin," *Saturday Evening Post*, August 30, 1952.

Faure, Pierre. "El Partido Comunista Español" Part II, *Estudios sobre el Comunismo*, Año V, No. 15 (January–March 1957), 78–83; Part III, Año V, No. 16 (April–June 1957), 71–78.

Fiorini, Mario. "El Comunismo en México," *Estudios sobre el Comunismo*, Año V, No. 15 (January–March 1957), 71–77.

Frey, John P. "Trade Unions and the Civil War in Mexico," *American Federationist*, XXXI, No. 4 (April 1924), 303–308.

Galán, Luis Alfonso. "Cuartel General Soviético en Tacubaya," *El Universal*, September 7, 1957, p. 2.

Garciá Treviño, Abelardo. "Próximas Purgas Rojas en México," *El Universal*, January 22, 1958, p. 2.

García Treviño, Rodrigo. "Crisis del comunismo mexicano," *Este & Oeste*, Año I, No. 20 (May 1–15, 1963), 4–8.

Garza, David T. "Factionalism in the Mexican Left: The Frustration of the MLN," *Western Political Quarterly*, XVII, No. 3 (September 1964), 447–460.

"Influye, no decide: La izquierda mexicana," *Visión*, July 13, 1962, p. 14.

Kalvoda, Joseph. "Communist Strategy in Latin America," *Yale Review* (Autumn 1960), pp. 32–40.

Lara, H. "México," *Problemas de la Paz y del Socialismo*, Año III, No. 3 (March 1960), 131–133.

———. "México: El anticomunismo conduce al fascismo," *Problemas de la Paz y del Socialismo*, Año III, No. 12 (December 1960), 96–97.

Lazitch, Branko. "El Comunismo Latino-Americano y el conflicto Moscú-Pekín," *Este & Oeste*, Año II, No. 33 (November 15–30, 1963), 4–10.

Lumbreras, Alberto. "Lo Positivo y Negativo en la Campaña," *Guión*, III, No. 25 (June 1958), 31–35.

MacKaye, Milton. "Will Mexico Go Castro?" *Saturday Evening Post*, October 29, 1960.

Mendoza, Samuel. "La Reunión del Comité Ejecutivo de la Federación Mundial de la Juventud Democrática (FMJD)," *Estudios sobre el Comunismo*, Año IX, No. 33 (July–September 1961), 71–95.

"México: Contratiempos del Frente Electoral del Pueblo," *Les Informations Politiques et Sociales*, Año IV, No. 28 (February 10, 1964).

Múzquiz, Eugenio. "Un Arte del Pueblo," *Intercambio Cultural*, II, No. 9 (November 1955), 28–32.

"Nuevos horizontes para Mao," *Visión*, XIX, No. 2 (May 20, 1960), 32–34.

"La ofensiva radiofónica de los Países Comunistas en América Latina," *Este & Oeste*, Año I, No. 9 (November 1–15, 1962), 3–5.

Orozco, Lino León. ¡"El Camino Está a la Izquierda!" Pero ¿Donde Está la Izquierda?" *El Popular*, April 16, 1960.

"The Party Enters upon a New Stage," *World Marxist Review: Problems of Peace and Socialism*. III, No. 9 (September 1960).

Prieto Laurens, Jorge. "¿No Hay Comunismo en México?" *El Universal*, May 9, 1956, p. 3.

Reynoso, Manuel M. "¿Que Quiere el Comunismo en el Departamento Agrario?" *El Universal*, July 9, 1956, p. 3.

Sudorov, A. A. "El Taller Gráfica Popular en Moscú," *Intercambio Cultural*, I, No. 5 (July 1955).

Unión Cívica Internacional de México. "Comunismo en México," *Estudios sobre el Comunismo*, Año V, No. 17 (July-September 1957), 124–128.

"La Unión Internacional de Estudiantes," *Este & Oeste*, Año II, No. 30 (October 1–15, 1963), 1–24.

Washington, S. Walter. "Mexican Resistance to Communism," *Foreign Affairs*, Vol. 36, No. 3 (April 1958), 504–515.

Wolfe, Bertram D. "Art and Revolution in Mexico," *The Nation*, CXIX, No. 3086 (August 27, 1924), 204–208.

Wright, Chester M. "Mexico, the Hopeful: A Survey of Her Political and Industrial Situation As She Takes Her First Steps in Reconstruction," *American Federationist*, XXVII, No. 12 (December 1920), 1087–1094.

X.X. "Actividades Comunistas en América Latina," *Estudios sobre el Comunismo*, Año VIII, No. 29 (July–September 1960), 78–108.

———. "Actividades Comunistas en Iberoamérica," *Estudios sobre el Comunismo*, Año X, No. 35 (January–March 1962), 64–79.

INDEX

PCM members in, 129. SEE ALSO peace movement, Mexican
Comité Nacional de Defensa Proletaria: establishment of, 17
Comité Nacional Pro-Paz: 128. SEE ALSO peace movement, Mexican
Communism, international:
—, in Latin America and Mexico: propaganda of, 204, 213–214, 215–217, 248–249; efforts to promote trade in, 215; foreign Communists as exiles, 217–219; since 1962, 248–249
—, and Mexican Communists: Mexican parties link with, 103, 204–206, 210–212; means of contact between, 206–212, 207 n., 212 n. SEE ALSO labor; Sino-Soviet Bloc; Soviet Bloc; Soviet Union
Communism, Mexican: present state of, vi, 31, 220–221; reasons for ineffectiveness of, 31, 221–230, 249; future of, 230–231. SEE ALSO *campesinos*; Communism, international; fronts; government, Mexican; land reform; labor; Partido Comunista Mexicano (PCM); Partido Obrero-Campesino Mexicano (POCM); Partido Popular Socialista (PPS); propaganda and programs, Mexican Communist; students; youth
—, history of: antecendents of PCM in, 3–6; in labor, 3, 9–10, 12–14, 16–18, 20, 22–23, 24, 27; PCM in, 6–22; 1919–1929, 7–14; 1929–1934, 14–15; 1934–1940, 16–19; 1940–1962, 19–31; PPS in, 23–25; POCM in, 25; Cárdenas and unity in, 28–31; MLN in, 28–31; relation of parties in, 25–28; since 1962, 233–249
Communist Federation of the Mexican Proletariat. SEE Federación Comunista del Proletariado Mexicano
Communist Party of Mexico (Gale's): formation of, 6; activities of, 6–7, 9; disappearance of, 7
Communist Party of the Soviet Union: reaction to Twentieth Congress of, 106–107, 207–210; mentioned, 36, 206, 207 n., 235
Communist Party of the United States: 11, 18, 20, 217 and n.
Communist Peasant International: Mexican peasant organizations in, 14;

Galván expelled from, 15
Communist Union of Painters and Sculptors: 10
Communist Youth of Mexico. SEE Juventud Comunista de México (JCM)
Communists, foreign: in Mexican Communist movement, 4–7; exiles in Mexico, 217–219. SEE ALSO Communism, international
Communists, Mexican. SEE Communism, Mexican
Confederación de Jóvenes Mexicanos (CJM): connection of, with PPS, 85, 87, 151, 157; organization and purpose of, 150–151; Ramírez faction in, 151; affiliates of, 151 and n., 152; size and influence of, 152 and n., 158; activities of, since 1956, 152 and n.; denies political affiliation, 154; protests government treatment of Denis, 155; on replacement of Peralta, 158; student agitation by, 196; mentioned, 157 n., 171
—, and IPN student strike: strike reveals factions in, 85, 151, 154–155; effect of strike on, 152; support of strike by, 153, 154
Confederación de Trabajadores de América Latina (CTAL): CTM withdrawal from, 23, 113, 174; cooperation of, with POCM, 75–76; FNC withdrawal from, 85, 86 n.; Sánchez' attitude toward, 166; Latin American affiliates of, 174; founding and organization of, 174; demise of, 174, 233, 243; relations of, with non-Communist unions, 174, 176–177; affiliated with WFTU, 174, 177, 178; officers of, 174 and n.; Lombardo as leader of, 174–178 *passim*, 175 n.; purposes of, 175; propaganda of, 175, 177–178; activities of, 175–176; relations of, with Communist labor organizations, 177; newspaper of, 177–178; UGOCM as affiliate of, 178; Soviet Embassy aid to, 211; mentioned, 179, 184, 206, 212, 219
Confederación de Trabajadores Mexicanos (CTM): organized by Lombardo, 17, 82; Communists' withdrawal from, 17–18; Lombardo and followers purged from, 21, 23; splits from official party, 22–23; withdraws from CTAL,

canos (CTM); World Federation of Trade Unions (WFTU)

—, leaders of: desire single labor confederation, 9; trips of, to USSR, 11; imprisoned, 15, 27, 29; as anti-Communist, 160; Castro as, 244; mentioned, 11, 29, 183. SEE ALSO Lombardo Toledano, Vincente

— movement: as antecedent of PCM, 3–4; anarchist principle of, 3–4; anti-Communist attitude of, 199–200; mentioned, 118

—, organizations of: and PRI, 86 n; Communist-infiltrated, 161–172; protest government violence, 170–171; Communist-controlled, 172–190, 243–246; BROS, 169, 170. SEE ALSO *campesinos*; Universidad Obrera (UO); Frente Obrero (FO)

— unions: political action by, 3–4, 9; PCM infiltration of, 7, 12, 42; bakers', 8, 9; textile, 9, 12, 21; streetcar workers', 9, 21; brewers', 9; in Federación Comunista del Proletariado Mexicano, 9; affiliation of, with A. F. of L., 9; Communist, for artists and intellectuals, 10; Liga de Escritores y Artistas Revolucionarios (LEAR), 10; Communist Union of Painters and Sculptors, 10; Sindicato Revolucionario de Obreros Técnicos y Plásticos, 10; miners', 12, 17, 23, 113; as CSLA affiliate, 12–13; electrical workers', 17, 113, 162, 165; PCM recruiting in, 19; expulsion of Communists from, 21, 23, 194, 195; petroleum workers', 23, 113, 160, 162, 243; POCM infiltration of, 25; FNC, 85, 86 n., 178–179; control of, by political parties, 101 n.; PPS influence in, 113; Lombardo's influence in, 113; LEAR, 140; Sindicato de Pintores Revolucionarios, 140; Communist success in, 160–161; Communist failure in, 160, 161; telephone workers', 161, 162, 171; FNTICE, 166; SME, 166–167; STMMRM, 165; Mexican Teachers' Union, 168; MRM, 168–172; non-Communist, in WFTU, 173–174; non-Communist, in CTAL, 174, 176, 177; FO in activities of, 186; political influence of, 222; since 1962, 243–246. SEE ALSO Sindicato Nacional de Trabajadores de la Educación (SNTE); Sindicato de Trabajadores Ferrocarrileros de la República Mexicana (STFRM)

Laborde, Hernán: in railroad union, 12; in PCM, 20, 33; mentioned, 17, 18, 20, 33

Labor Unity Bloc. SEE Bloque de Unidad Obrera (BUO)

Laguna Mutual Insurance Society: charges of, against UCSE, 185 and n.

Laguna region: Communist strength in, 20; agitation for land in, 20, 86; PCM in, 35, 45, 184; JCM in, 40; UDMM in, 150; UCSE in, 185, 186; FEP in, 239; mentioned, 30

land reform: under López Mateos, 24, 104 n., 181; PCM on, 53, 54; POCM on, 72; PPS on, 98, 101, 104; MLN on, 123; Carrión on, 149; under Ruiz Cortines, 180–181; UGOCM pressure for, 243

— agitation for: in Laguna area, 20; encouraged by Cárdenas, 30; PPS in, 24, 113–114; led by López, 24, 179–182, 201, 236–237; in Sonora, 113–114, 162, 179–180, 181; CEM on, 148; UDMM in, 150; by UGOCM, 179–182; in Sinaloa, 180; in Baja California, 182; non-Communists in, 182; by UCSE, 186; by CCI, 246

Latin America: ties of, with Sino-Soviet Bloc, 49–50; propaganda on U.S. in, 105, 128; WIDF congresses in, 120 n.; trade of, with Sino-Soviet Bloc, 210, 213–215; Communists of, as exiles in Mexico, 217, 218–219; western orientation of, 225–226; feeling of, on Western colonialism, 226–227; influence of Catholic Church in, 228–229; religiousness in, 229–230; mentioned, 49, 127, 195 and n., 224, 227

— international Communism in: objectives of Soviet in, 203, 210; tactics encouraged by, 203–204, 210; Soviet and satellite missions in, 210; propaganda of, 205–206 and n., 227, 248, 249; reasons for ineffectiveness of, 225–230

— trade union confederations in: WFTU, 173, 174; CTAL, 174, 175–176, 177; proposal for new, 244

Latin American Peace Conference: 128

testing, 109; on Berlin, 109; on Tibet revolt, 109; on Sino-Indian conflict, 109; on disarmament, 109; on missile-tracking installation, 114–115; on Castro's entry into Mexico, 176; on Soviet de-Stalinization, 208–209
— as PPS leader: in party organization, 23, 83, 93–94; nature of, effect of, 23–24, 79, 82; declares party's socialist orientation, 23–24, 102–103, 205 and n.; and PPS in peace movement, 30–31, 125, 126–127, 129, 206; on merger with ASU, 64; demotes Ramírez, 82, 83–87, 118–119; on PPS committees, 88; power of, in PPS, 95 and n., 236; on PPS goals, 96 n.; on PPS in economic progress, 98 n.; in PPS recruitment, 111; in PPS training and indoctrination, 112 n., 113; and PPS in MLN, 123, 125, 129, 236; in POCM-PPS merger, 236
— in student groups: agitation of, 24, 40, 82, 158 n., 170; influence of, 24, 40, 82, 113, 158 n., 170; proposes JP program, 89; in CJM, 151; in FNET, 153, 157. SEE ALSO Partido Popular Socialista (PPS)
Lopéz, Jacinto: leads agitation for land reform, 24, 148, 179–182, 236–237, 243; in PPS, 82, 86, 88, 92 n., 95; in UGOCM, 179–182; arrest of, 148, 181, 201; release of, 162, 181; mentioned, 171
López Mateos, Adolfo: land distribution program of, 24; handling of Cárdenas by, 30 and n.; *La Voz de México* on Latin American tour of, 49; Eisenhower visit to, 60; rejects PPS *Tesis*, 102; refuses nomination by PPS, 116 and n.; releases student strike leaders, 157 n.; releases Salazar and followers, 171; handling of labor unrest by, 161; releases López and followers, 181; action of, in Sonora land agitation, 181, 182; honors Rivera's works, 199; Lombardo on work of, 237; on relations with China, 248; mentioned, 185, 201, 202, 232, 242
— support of: by PPS, 102 and n., 115–116; by POCM, 102, 116; by PCM, 102, 116; Carrión on, 149; by CJM, 152 n.
LPI. SEE Liga Popular Israelita

Lumbreras, Alberto: in POCM, 65, 66; and POCM-PPS merger, 236; mentioned, 77
Lux: on Hungarian revolt, 166

Machete, El: as PCM organ, 10; official suppression of, 15; engravings in, 140
Maestro Mexicano, El: 168
Maldonaldo, Braulio: in PRI and MLN, 31 n.; in protest march, 182; arrest of, 247; in FEP, 239; mentioned, 124
Maldonado, Edelmiro: expelled from PCM, 235
Mancisidor, José: in IICMR, 131–132, 133; in SAURSS, 134; mentioned, 133, 199
Marcué Pardiñas, Enrique: 198–199
Marcué Pardiñas, Manuel: in Lombardo-Ramírez dispute, 86–87; in PPS, 88, 236; publications of, 117, 118; breaks with Lombardo, 125; in CEM, 146, 147; mentioned, 199, 203
Márquez Rodiles, Ignacio: in IICMC, 136; founds SARPP, 137
Marshall Plan: opposition to, 64
Martínez Verdugo, Arnoldo: in PCM, 38, 233 n.
Marxism: in Mexican parties' political orientation, 79, 91, 204–205; in teachers' union, 113; in UO, 187
Mata, Filomeno: 203
Mayo valley: UGOCM squatters in, 243
Méndez Docurro, Eugenio: policy of, in student disturbances, 158
Méndez, Leopoldo: in TGP, 140–141; mentioned, 86
Mendoza, Nicandro: as IPN student strike leader, 40, 153–157; power of, in FNET, 153, 157; criticism of, 85, 154, 155; arrest of, 156–157 and n., 196; mentioned, 86, 155 n., 157 n.
Mendoza López, Miguel: as PCM presidential candidate, 28, 61–62
Mesa Andraca, Manuel: in IICMR, 133–134; in CEM, 146, 147; mentioned, 129, 134 n., 242
Mexicali, Baja California: agitation for land in, 180; mentioned, 31 n., 146, 240
Mexican-Bulgarian Friendship and Cultural Exchange Society. SEE Sociedad de Amistad y de Intercambio Cultural Mexicano-Bulgara (SAICMB)

Mexican Committee Impulse in the Struggle for Peace. SEE Comité Mexicano Impulso de la Lucha por la Paz

Mexican Committee for Peace. SEE Comité Mexicano por la Paz (CMP)

Mexican Communist Party. SEE Partido Comunista Mexicano (PCM)

Mexican Communist Workers' Front. SEE Frente Obrero Comunista Mexicano

Mexican Confederation of Electrical Workers, The. SEE Confederación Mexicana de Electricistas (CME)

Mexican-Cuban Institute of Cultural Relations "José Marti." SEE Instituto Mexicano-Cubano de Relaciones Culturales "José Marti"

Mexican-Czechoslovak Institute of Cultural Exchange, The. SEE Instituto de Intercambio Cultural Mexicano-Checoeslovaco (IICMC)

tural Exchange Institute, The. SEE In-Mexican-Hungarian Friendship and Cultural Exchange Institute, The. SEE Instituto de Amistad y Intercambio Cultural Mexicano-Hungaro (IAICMH)

Mexicano, El: PPS publication, 116–117

Mexican Peace Committee. SEE Comité Mexicano por la Paz (CMP)

Mexican Peace Movement. SEE Movimiento Mexicano por la Paz; peace movement, Mexican

Mexican Revolution: effect of, on Mexican Communism, v, 221; and effect of PCM, 3; political sections of, join Communists, 89; accomplishments of, and PPS goals, 96; PPS in context of, 103; Carrión's definition of, 148–149; effect of, on future political climate, 192; mentioned, 16, 71, 77, 114, 223, 245

Mexican-Rumanian Friendship and Cultural Exchange Society, The. SEE Sociedad de Amistad y de Intercambio Cultural Mexicano-Rumania (SAICMR)

Mexican-Russian Institute of Cultural Exchange, The. SEE Instituto de Intercambio Cultural Mexicano-Ruso (IICMR)

Mexican Socialist League: establishment of, 78

Mexican Socialist Party: Gale in, 4; of-

ficial organ of, 4; Roy in, 5–6

Mexican Society of Friends of Revolutionary Guatemala, The. SEE Sociedad Mexicana de Amigos de Guatemala Revolucionario (SMAGR)

Mexican Society of Friends with People's China. SEE Sociedad Mexicana de Amigos con China Popular (SMACP)

Mexican Union of Electrical Workers. SEE Sindicato Mexicano de Electricistas (SME)

Mexican Unitary Trade Union Confederation. SEE Confederación Sindical Unitaria Mexicana (CSUM)

Mexican Worker-Peasant Party. SEE Partido Obrero-Campesino Mexicano (POCM)

Mexico: army revolt in (1929), 15; Communists on U.S. influence in, 47, 48–49, 48 n., 52–53, 71–72, 105; military alliance of, with U.S., 50, 104, 147, 240; POCM goal for, 70–71; anti-U.S. sentiment in, 122; nature of politics in, 192; political tolerance in, 192; international Communist activities in, 203–219 *passim*, 248–249; international Communist propaganda in, 204, 215, 248, 249; exiles in politics of, 217 and n.; foreign Communists as exiles in, 217–219, 217 n., 218 nn.; right-of-asylum policy of, 217–219; U.S. aid to, in future, 231; mentioned, 47, 50, 56, 120 n., 173, 174 and n., 185, 224. SEE ALSO government, Mexican

— Communist influence in, affected by: Catholic Church in Mexico, 228–229; religiousness of Mexico, 229–230; Western orientation of Mexico, 225–226; political framework of Mexico, 222–223; future, and economic conditions, 231; future, and birth rate, 231

— economic and social problems of. SEE propaganda and programs, Mexican Communist, on domestic issues; labor; land reform; rural problems

— relations of, with other countries: with Sino-Soviet Bloc, 47, 49–50; with Cuba, MLN promotes, 123; cultural, with Soviet, 64, 133, 134; trade, with Poland and Yugoslavia, 248; with Czechoslovakia, IICM promotes, 136; with Communist China, SMACP pro-

Revolutionary Union of Technical and Plastic Workers. SEE Sindicato Revolucionario de Obreros Técnicos y Plásticos
Revueltas, José: 38, 78
RILU. SEE Red International of Labor Unions
Rivera, Diego: in PCM, 10, 15, 34; unions formed by, 10, 140; in CSUM, 10; on Hungarian revolt, 51; in IICMR, 132–133; in FNAP, 143–144; works of, honored, 199; on Soviet de-Stalinization, 208; mentioned, 14, 155 n., 212, 225
Rodríguez, Guadalupe: and PCM plan to seize power, 15
Rodríguez Triana, Pedro V.: 14
Rojas, Hortensia: 80–81, 183
Roy, Manabendra Nath: in Mexican socialism, 4–6; with Germans in World War I, 5
Rubio Felix, Lázaro: in agitation for land, 180, 181; mentioned, 112 n., 179, 180
Ruiz Cortines, Adolfo: Lombardo supports, 27; visit of, to U.S., 114; handling of strikes by, 155–157, 161, 162; handling of land agitation by, 180–181; meeting of, with Eisenhower, 182; removes Communists from government, 194 and n.; 198; mentioned, 104 n., 135
Rumania: relations of, with Mexico and SAICMR, 136; exhibit on, 188
Rural Normal Schools: strikes at, 154
rural problems: government policy on, 89, 104 n.; braceros as, 101–102, 104; PCM on, 53, 54; PPS on, 98, 101–102, 104; farm credits as, 184, 185; UCSE on, 185–186; CCI on, 246. See also *campesinos*; land reform
Russia. SEE Soviet Union

SAC. SEE Sociedad de Amigos de Cuba
SAG. SEE Sociedad de Amigos de Guatemala
SAICMB. SEE Sociedad de Amistad y de Intercambio Cultural Mexicano-Bulgaria
SAICMR. SEE Sociedad de Amistad y de Intercambio Cultural Mexicano-Rumania
Sainz, Juan Pablo: 152 n., 168, 169

Salazar, Othón: as leader of SNTE dissidents, 147, 168–172; ties of, with Communists, 168; government treatment of, 170, 171, 247
— dissident followers of: demonstrations of, 147, 168, 169–171, 172, 194–195; government action on, 147, 168, 170, 171, 172, 194–195; in dispute with SNTE, 168–169, 171–172; removal of, from SNTE, 172, 243
Salazar Mallén, Mario: in CEM, 145, 147
Salud en la USSR, La: 216
Sánchez Cárdenas, Carlos: in POCM, 65, 66; in PPS-POCM merger, 236; mentioned, 77
Sánchez, Enrique W.: 168, 170
Sánchez Delint, Agustín: as leader of SME, 166–167; supports labor agitation, 166; relations of, with Communists, 166–167
SARPP. SEE Sociedad de Amigos de la República Popular de Polonia
SAURSS. SEE Sociedad de Amigos de la URSS
Sáyago, Indalecio: 86, 88, 116–117, 170 n.
Servicio de Noticias de la Oficina de Prensa de la Embajada de la URSS: 216
Siempre: 118
Silva, Federico: in UO, 188; mentioned, 84, 106, 136, 198
Sinaloa: agitation for land reform in, 180; PPS in, 81, 111–112; UGOCM in, 179
Sindicato de Pintores Revolucionarios: 140
Sindicato de Trabajadores Ferrocarrileros de la República Mexicana (STFRM): Communist infiltration in, 160, 162–165; Vallejo rebellion in, 162–163; Vallejo as leader of, 162–164; Campa in, 163, 164, 199–200; anti-Communist actions in, 199–200; PRI control of, 243; mentioned, 12, 17, 21, 23, 113
—, strikes of: PCM in, 24, 75–76, 201 n., 202–203; PPS in, 24, 75–76, 201 and n.; government action in, 37, 200, 202–203; arrest of leaders of, 37, 41, 65, 114, 163; imprisonment of leaders protested, 41, 49, 74, 104 n., 121–122, 247; POCM internal conflict over, 66; CTAL in, 75–76; telegraphers', Com-

115; UGOCM in, 179; mentioned, 35, 61, 184, 240

Soviet Bloc: Mexican Communists' trips to, 56, 59, 185 n., 206–207; aids PCM financially, 57; exchange societies with, as fronts, 121, 129, 134, 136, 137, 139; front groups' exhibits in, 142, 144, 216; in WFTU, 173; UO in cultural relations with, 188; trade of, with Cuba, 215; exchange of persons of, with Mexico, 216; mentioned, 29, 103
— in Latin America: diplomatic and cultural relations of, 128; goal of, 210; efforts of, to gain influence, 210; propaganda of, 213, 216 and n., 249; trade of, 213–215; Soviet contacts through, 214
— missions of, in Mexico: relation of, to local Communists, 210–213; activities of, in Mexico, 210–213; propaganda of, 213; Spanish Communists' contact with, 218

Soviet Union: diplomatic relations of, with Mexico, 11, 15, 21; anti-Fascist line of, 21; Browderism as policy of, 21–22; Mexican Communist parties' attitude toward, 25; reactions to action of, in Hungary, 26–27, 108, 166, 227; Mexican Communists follow line of, 38, 50, 51, 55, 106–107, 120, 206, 207–210, 234, 237, 248; PCM propaganda on, 47, 49, 62; peace line of, and PCM, 50; response to Communist propaganda on, 55, 227; financing of PCM trips by, 56; financial aid of, to PCM, 56, 57; cultural contacts of, with Mexico, 64, 130–132, 214–215; policy of, to counter capitalism, 70; PPS propaganda on, 106–109; Ramírez on errors of, 108; nuclear testing by, 109, 128; book of congresses of, 113; as source of national liberation movement, 123; de-emphasis on, in peace movement, 127; IICMR as front to promote, 130–132; fronts for, 159; Sánchez and Galván on imperialism of, 166; involvement of, in railway strike, 167; control of WFTU by, 172, 173; CTAL disseminates propaganda of, 175 and n.; UCSE on, trade with, 185–186; UO promotion of, 187, 188; objectives of, in Latin America, 203, 210; tactics of, in Latin America, 203–204; propaganda of, in Latin America,

130, 198 n., 204, 213, 215–217, 216 n., 249; Mexican Communists' reaction to de-Stalinization in, 207–210; tactics encouraged by, in Latin America, 210; trade fairs of, in Latin America, 214–215; in training of Mexican Communists, 216–217; publications of, used by Mexican Communists, 212 and n.; split of, with China, 233, 234–235, 237, 248; mentioned, 11, 17, 28, 70, 131, 133, 135, 141, 143, 164, 177, 182, 200, 203, 205, 206, 213, 227. See also Communism, international; Sino-Soviet Bloc; Soviet Bloc
— Embassy of, in Mexico: financial aid of, to local Communists, 130, 211; influence of, on IICWR, 133; in railway strike, 164, 200, 202; in Mexican domestic affairs, 210, 212–213, 212 n.; activities of, in Mexico, 211–212; propaganda of, to increase trade, 213; distribution of publications by, 215–216; mentioned, 83, 134, 145, 248

Spain: Civil War in, 18; Mexican recognition of, 100 n.; Communists of, as Mexican exiles, 211, 218; mentioned, 6, 226

Stalin, Joseph: pact of, with Hitler, 17–18; Mexican Communists on denunciation of, 106–107, 207–210; mentioned, 20

Stalin Peace Prize: Cárdenas' acceptance of, 126 and n., 127–128; mentioned, 29, 132, 199

STFRM. See Sindicato de Trabajadores Ferrocarrileros de la República Mexicana

STMMRM. See Sindicato de Trabajadores Mineros y Metalúrgicos de la República Mexicana

strikes: Communist parties in, 27 and n.; of teachers' union, 27, 169–170; during Rúiz Cortines administration, 161; PCM propaganda urging, 162; government action in, 192, 195–196. See also Instituto Politécnico Nacional (IPN), student strike at; Sindicato de Trabajadores Ferrocarrileros de la República Mexicana (STFRM), strikes of

students: PPS influence among, 80, 113; influence of Communism on, 157–159,